ILTS 114 Social Science: History
Teacher Certification Exam

By: Sharon Wynne, M.S.

XAMonline, INC.
Boston

Copyright © 2013 XAMonline, Inc.
All rights reserved. No part of the material protected by this copyright notice may be reproduced or utilized in any form or by any means, electronic or mechanical, including photocopying, recording or by any information storage and retrievable system, without written permission from the copyright holder.

To obtain permission(s) to use the material from this work for any purpose including workshops or seminars, please submit a written request to:

XAMonline, Inc.
25 First Street, Suite 106
Cambridge, MA 02141
Toll Free 1-800-301-4647
Email: info@xamonline.com
Web www.xamonline.com

Library of Congress Cataloging-in-Publication Data

Wynne, Sharon A.
 Social Science: History 114: Teacher Certification / Sharon A. Wynne. -2nd ed.
 ISBN 978-1-58197-982-4
  1. Social Science: History 114.   2. Study Guides.   3. ILTS
  4. Teachers' Certification & Licensure.   5. Careers

Disclaimer:
The opinions expressed in this publication are the sole works of XAMonline and were created independently from the National Education Association, Educational Testing Service, or any State Department of Education, National Evaluation Systems or other testing affiliates.

Between the time of publication and printing, state specific standards as well as testing formats and website information may change that is not included in part or in whole within this product. Sample test questions are developed by XAMonline and reflect similar content as on real tests; however, they are not former tests. XAMonline assembles content that aligns with state standards but makes no claims nor guarantees teacher candidates a passing score. Numerical scores are determined by testing companies such as NES or ETS and then are compared with individual state standards. A passing score varies from state to state.

Printed in the United States of America

ILTS: Social Science: History 114
ISBN: 978-1-58197-982-4

TEACHER CERTFICATION STUDY GUIDE

TABLE OF CONTENTS

SUBAREA I: SOCIAL SCIENCE FOUNDATIONS 1

Competency 1.1 Understand basic sources, tools, and methods of social science inquiry and connections among the social sciences and other learning areas 1

Skill 1.1.a Be able to describe each of the social science disciplines and explain each one's methods of study and tools for research 1

Skill 1.1.b Be able to show knowledge and understanding of concepts, vocabulary, and the interrelationships of the disciplines 5

Competency 1.2 Understand the use of analysis, interpretation, and evaluation in social science inquiry 7

Competency 1.3 Understand basic political concepts, systems, and organizations and examine major features of national, state, and local government in the United States 10

Skill 1.3.a Explain the major concepts of the U.S. Constitution, separation of powers and Federal versus State authority 10

Skill 1.3.b Be familiar with the history of the American electoral process 13

Skill 1.3.c Be familiar with the history of political parties in the United States ... 14

Skill 1.3.d Define the rights and responsibilities of United States citizens 17

Competency 1.4 Understand economic concepts and systems and the operation of the U.S. and world economies 20

Skill 1.4.a Be able to apply the principles of consumer economics 20

Skill 1.4.b Show an understanding of the role of markets 20

Skill 1.4.c Be familiar with other economic systems 22

Skill 1.4.d Be able to understand and illustrate global economic concepts 29

HISTORY

TEACHER CERTFICATION STUDY GUIDE

Competency 1.5 Understand basic tools and methods of geographic inquiry and apply knowledge of cultural and physical geography 30

Skill 1.5.a Know the earth's physical features and be able to give examples and their locations 30

Skill 1.5.b Know the difference between climate and weather and the descriptions and locations of different types of climates 32

Skill 1.5.c Be able to explain how physical and political locations are determined and give examples 35

Skill 1.5.d Be able to show an understanding of the relationship of geography to culture 37

Competency 1.6 Understand concepts, terms, and theories related to human behavior and development 38

Skill 1.6.a Be able to explain basic psychological concepts 38

Competency 1.7 Understand concepts, terms, and theories related to the study of cultures, the structure and organization of human societies, and the process of social interaction 39

Skill 1.7.a Be able to explain basic sociological concepts 39

Skill 1.7.b Be able to explain basic anthropological concepts 39

Skill 1.7.c Be able to explain basic archaeological concepts 40

SUBAREA II: HISTORY COMMON CORE 41

Competency 2.1 Understand basic historical terms and concepts, comparative history, and the interpretive nature of history 41

Competency 2.2 Understand major trends, key turning points, and the roles of influential individuals and groups in U.S. history 44

Skill 2.2.a Understand the importance and results of the Age of Exploration 44

Skill 2.2.b Know the significance of the Colonial Period 46

Skill 2.2.c Explain the crucial effects of the period of the American Revolution 52

TEACHER CERTFICATION STUDY GUIDE

Skill 2.2.d Understand how the new nation developed from 1791 to 1860 63

Skill 2.2.e Know the effects of westward expansion 72

Skill 2.2.f Make comparisons of the political, economic, and social characteristics of both North and South from 1815 to 1860 74

Skill 2.2.g Be knowledgeable about the Civil War and Reconstruction from 1860 to 1877 81

Skill 2.2.h Understand the significance of post-Reconstruction industrialization and reform 87

Skill 2.2.i Understand the importance and impact of events, issues, and effects of the period of World War I 91

Skill 2.2.j Understand the importance and impact of events, issues, and effects of the period of World War II 94

Skill 2.2.k Know and understand the key events and issues pertaining to foreign affairs from post World War II to the present 99

Skill 2.2.l Recognize and be able to discuss the political, economic, and social issues of the 20th Century 104

Skill 2.2.m Recognize the significant accomplishments made by immigrants, racial, ethnic, and gender groups 106

Skill 2.2.n Be able to demonstrate knowledge of Illinois history 108

Competency 2.3 Understand major trends, key turning points, and the roles of influential individuals and groups in world history 108

SUBAREA III: HISTORICAL CONCEPTS AND WORLD HISTORY 114

Competency 3.1 Understand the prehistory of human civilization and the development of world civilizations from 1000 B.C.E. to 1500 C.E 114

Skill 3.1.a .Establish an understanding of prehistory and the ancient civilizations, including the non-Western world 114

Skill 3.1.b Understand the important contributions of classical civilizations, including the non-Western world 115

Skill 3.1.c Demonstrate an understanding of the period known as the Middle Ages 117

Skill 3.1.d Demonstrate an understanding of the importance and accomplishments of the Renaissance and Reformation periods 118

Competency 3.2 Understand major social, intellectual, economic, and geopolitical developments of the First Global Age, the Age of Revolution, and the Industrial Revolution, from 1450 to 1850 .... **120**

Skill 3.2.a Understand the importance and results of the Age of Exploration .. 120

Skill 3.2.b Understand the significance of revolutionary movements 121

Competency 3.3 Understand major political, geopolitical, social, cultural, and economic developments since 1850 .... **123**

Skill 3.3.a Understand the importance of the growth of nationalism 123

Skill 3.3.b Understand the causes and results of the wars of the 20th century 124

Skill 3.3.c Show an understanding of major contemporary world issues and trends 127

Skill 3.3.d Know the differences between the world's major religions 127

SUBAREA IV: U.S. AND ILLINOIS HISTORY **129**

Competency 4.1 Understand the development of colonial settlements in North America, the Revolutionary War, and the creation of the U.S. government **129**

Competency 4.2 Understand westward movement in U.S. history, major developments of the early national and Jacksonian periods, the Civil War, and Reconstruction **154**

Competency 4.3 Understand industrialization in the United States and the effects of industrialization on U.S. economic, social, and political life **170**

Competency 4.4 Understand political and diplomatic developments, economic trends, and social movements in the United States from World War I to the present **175**

Competency 4.5 Understand major developments in Illinois history **179**

TEACHER CERTFICATION STUDY GUIDE

Bibliography 182

Sample Test 184

Answer Key 209

Rationales for Sample Questions 210

THIS PAGE BLANK

TEACHER CERTFICATION STUDY GUIDE

SUBAREA I: SOCIAL SCIENCE FOUNDATIONS

Competency 1.1   Understand basic sources, tools, and methods of social science inquiry and connections among the social sciences and other learning areas.

Skill 1.1.a   Be able to describe each of the social science disciplines and explain each one's methods of study and tools for research.

The disciplines within the social sciences, sometimes referred to as social studies, include anthropology, geography, history, sociology, economics, and political science. Some programs include psychology, archaeology, philosophy, religion, law, and criminology. Also, the subjects of civics and government may be a part of an educational curriculum as separate from political science.

ANTHROPOLOGY is the scientific study of human culture and humanity, the relationship between man and his culture. Anthropologists study different groups, how they relate to other cultures, and patterns of behavior, similarities and differences. Their research is two-fold: cross-cultural and comparative. The major method of study is referred to as "participant observation." The anthropologist studies and learns about the people being studied by living among them and participating with them in their daily lives. Other methods may be used but this is the most characteristic method used.

ARCHAEOLOGY is the scientific study of past human cultures by studying the remains they left behind--objects such as pottery, bones, buildings, tools, and artwork. Archaeologists locate and examine any evidence to help explain the way people lived in past times. They use special equipment and techniques to gather the evidence and make special effort to keep detailed records of their findings because a lot of their research results in destruction of the remains being studied. The first step is to locate an archaeological site using various methods. Next, surveying the site takes place starting with a detailed description of the site with notes, maps, photographs, and collecting artifacts from the surface. Excavating follows either by digging for buried objects or by diving and working in submersible decompression chambers, when underwater. They record and preserve the evidence for eventual classification, dating, and evaluating their find.

CIVICS is the study of the responsibilities and rights of citizens with emphasis on such subjects as freedom, democracy, and individual rights. Students study local, state, national, and international government structures, functions, and problems. Related to this are other social, political, and economic institutions. As a method of study, students gain experience and understanding through direct participation in student government, school publications, and other organizations. They also participate in community activities such as conservation projects and voter registration drives.

ECONOMICS generally is the study of the ways goods and services are produced and the ways they are distributed. It also includes the ways people and nations choose what they buy from what they want. Some of the methods of study include research, case studies, analysis, statistics, and mathematics.

GEOGRAPHY involves studying location and how living things and earth's features are distributed throughout the earth. It includes where animals, people, and plants live and the effects of their relationship with earth's physical features. Geographers also explore the locations of earth's features, how they got there, and why it is so important.

What geographers study can be broken down into four areas:

(1) Location: Being able to find the exact site of anything on the earth;
(2) Spatial relations: The relationships of earth's features, places, and groups of people with one another due to their location;
(3) Regional characteristics: Characteristics of a place such as landform and climate, types of plants and animals, kinds of people who live there, and how they use the land; and
(4) Forces that change the earth: Such as human activities and natural forces.

Geographical studies are divided into:

1. Regional: Elements and characteristics of a place or region
2. Topical: One earth feature or one human activity occurring throughout the entire world
3. Physical: Earth's physical features, what creates and changes them, their relationships to each other as well as human activities
4. Human: Human activity patterns and how they relate to the environment including political, cultural, historical, urban, and social geographical fields of study.

Special research methods used by geographers include mapping, interviewing, field studies, mathematics, statistics, and scientific instruments.

HISTORY is the study of the past, especially the aspects of the human past, political and economic events as well as cultural and social conditions. Students study history through textbooks, research, field trips to museums and historical sights, and other methods. Most nations set the requirements in history to study the country's heritage, usually to develop an awareness and feeling of loyalty and patriotism. History is generally divided into the three main divisions: **(a) time periods, (b) nations, and (c) specialized topics.** Study is accomplished through research, reading, and writing.

POLITICAL SCIENCE is the study of political life, different forms of government including elections, political parties, and public administration. In addition, political science studies include values such as justice, freedom, power, and equality. There are six main fields of political-study in the United States:

1. Political theory and philosophy,
2. Comparative governments,
3. International relations,
4. Political behavior,
5. Public administration, and
6. American government and politics.

PSYCHOLOGY involves scientifically studying behavior and mental processes. The ways people and animals relate to each other are observed and recorded. Psychologists scrutinize specific patterns, which will enable them to discern and predict certain behaviors, using scientific methods to verify their ideas. In this way they have been able to learn how to help people fulfill their individual human potential and strengthen understanding between individuals as well as groups and in nations and cultures. The results of the research of psychologists have deepened our understanding of the reasons for people's behavior.

Psychology is not only closely connected to the natural science of biology and the medical field of psychiatry but it is also connected to the social science areas of anthropology and sociology which have to do with people in society. Along with the sociologists and anthropologists, psychologists also study humans in their social settings, analyzing their attitudes and relationships. The disciplines of anthropology psychology, and sociology often research the same kinds of problems but from different points of view, with the emphasis in psychology on individual behavior, how an individual's actions are influenced by feelings and beliefs.

In their research, psychologists develop hypotheses, and then test them using the scientific method. These methods used in psychological research include:

1   **naturalistic observation** which includes observing the behavior of animals and humans in their natural surroundings or environment

2   **systematic assessment,** which describes assorted ways to measure the feelings, thoughts, and personality traits of people using case histories, public opinion polls or surveys, and standardized tests. These three types of assessments enable psychologists to acquire information not available through naturalistic observations

3   **experimentation** enables psychologists to find and corroborate the cause-and-effect relationships in behavior, usually by randomly dividing the subjects into two groups: experimental group and control group

SOCIOLOGY is the study of human society: the individuals, groups, and institutions making up human society. It includes every feature of human social conditions. It deals with the predominant behaviors, attitudes, and types of relationships within a society, which is defined as a group of people with a similar cultural background living in a specific geographical area. Sociology is divided into five major areas of study:

1. Population studies: General social patterns of groups of people living in a certain
2. geographical area, Social behaviors: Changes in attitudes, morale, leadership,
3. conformity, and others,
4. Social institutions: Organized groups of people performing specific functions within a society such as churches, schools, hospitals, business organizations, and governments
5. Cultural influences: Including customs, knowledge, arts, religious beliefs, and language, and
6. Social change: Such as wars, revolutions, inventions, fashions, and other events or activities.

Sociologists use three major methods to test and verify theories:

(1) Surveys;
(2) Controlled experiments; and
(3) Field observation.

Skill 1.1.b   Be able to show knowledge and understanding of concepts, vocabulary, and the interrelationships of the disciplines.

The major disciplines within the social sciences are definitely intertwined and interrelated. Knowledge and expertise in one requires background that involves some or most of the others.

Anthropology is the field of study of human culture--how different groups of people live, how they have adapted to their physical environment, what they make or produce, and their relationship to other cultures, behavior, differences and similarities. To pursue the study of people, the anthropologist must know the history of the people being studied; their geography--physical environment; their governmental structure, organization, and its impact on the people; sociology is closely related to this field so knowledge and study in this area is helpful; their goods and produce and how they are used tie in with a background of economics.

Archaeology studies human cultures in the past, examining artifacts left behind to determine how certain people or groups lived their daily lives. Certainly, knowledge of history gives a background as a foundation of study. Geography makes its contribution by not only knowing where to look for remains but also how geographic conditions contributed to and affected the people or cultural groups being studied; how physical factors contributed to artifacts left behind.

Civics deals with what is required and expected of a region's citizens, their rights and responsibilities to government and each other. Knowledge of history gives the background and foundation and government or political science explains not only the organization and set-up of the government but also the impact of international relations on the country or area.

Economics is tied in mainly with history, geography, and political science. The different interrelationships include: History of economic theory and principles combined with historical background of areas; economic activities in the different countries, regions of the world and how international trade and relations are affected which leads to political science or government--how political organization and government affect an area's economic activities.

Geography is the study of the earth, its people, and how people adapt to life on earth and how they use its resources. It is undeniably connected to history, economics, political science, sociology, anthropology, and even a bit of archaeology. Geography not only deals with people and the earth today but also with:
How did it all begin?
What is the background of the people of an area?
What kind of government or political system do they have?
How does that affect their ways of producing goods and the distribution of them?
What kind of relationships do these people have with other groups?
How is the way they live their lives affected by their physical environment?
In what ways do they effect change in their way of living?
All of this is tied in with their physical environment, the earth and its people.

History is without doubt an integral part of every other discipline in the social sciences. Knowing historical background on anything and anyone anywhere goes a long way towards explaining that what happened in the past leads up to and explains the present.

Political Science is the study of government, international relations, political thought and activity, and comparison of governments. It is tied in with history (historical background), anthropology (how government affects a group's culture and relationship with other groups), economics (governmental influence and regulation of producing and distributing goods and products), and sociology (insight into how social developments affect political life). Other disciplines are also affected, as the study of political science is crucial to understanding the political processes and the influence of government, civic duties, and responsibilities of people.

Psychology is defined as scientifically studying mental processes and behavior. It is related to anthropology and sociology, two social sciences that also study people in society. All three closely consider relationships and attitudes of humans within their social settings. Anthropology considers humans within their cultures, how they live, what they make or produce, how different groups or cultures relate to each other. Sociology follows the angle of looking at behaviors, attitudes, conditions, and relationships in human society. Psychology focuses on individual behavior and how actions are influenced by feelings and beliefs.

Sociology studies human society with its attitudes, behaviors, conditions, and relationships with others. It is closely related to anthropology, especially applied to groups outside of one's region, nation, or hemisphere. History puts it in perspective with an historical background. Political Science is tied to sociology with the impact of political and governmental regulation of activities. Awareness of, influence of, and use of the physical environment as studied in geography also contributes to understanding. Economic activities are a part of human society. The field of psychology is also related.

Competency 1.2   Understand the use of analysis, interpretation, and evaluation in social science inquiry.

Primary sources include the following kinds of materials:

- Documents that reflect the immediate, everyday concerns of people: memoranda, bills, deeds, charters, newspaper reports, pamphlets, graffiti, popular writings, journals or diaries, records of decision-making bodies, letters, receipts, snapshots, etc.
- Theoretical writings which reflect care and consideration in composition and an attempt to convince or persuade. The topic will generally be deeper and have more persuasive value than is the case with "immediate" documents. These may include newspaper or magazine editorials, sermons, political speeches, philosophical writings, etc.
- Narrative accounts of events, ideas, trends, etc. written with intention by someone contemporary with the events described.
- Statistical data, although statistics may be misleading.
- Literature and nonverbal materials, novels, stories, poetry and essays from the period, as well as coins, archaeological artifacts, and art produced during the period.

Guidelines for the use of primary resources:

1. Be certain that you understand how language was used at the time of writing and that you understand the context in which it was produced.
2. Do not read history blindly; but be certain that you understand both explicit and implicit referenced in the material.
3. Read the entire text you are reviewing; do not simply extract a few sentences to read.
4. Although anthologies of materials may help you identify primary source materials, the full original text should be consulted.

Secondary sources include the following kinds of materials:

- Books written on the basis of primary materials about the period of time
- Books written on the basis of primary materials about persons who played a major role in the events under consideration
- Books and articles written on the basis of primary materials about the culture, the social norms, the language, and the values of the period
- Quotations from primary sources
- Statistical data on the period
- The conclusions and inferences of other historians
- Multiple interpretations of the ethos of the time

Guidelines for the use of secondary sources:

1. Do not rely upon only a single secondary source.
2. Check facts and interpretations against primary sources whenever possible.
3. Do not accept the conclusions of other historians uncritically.
4. Place greatest reliance on secondary sources created by the best and most respected scholars.
5. Do not use the inferences of other scholars as if they were facts.
6. Ensure that you recognize any bias the writer brings to his/her interpretation of history.
7. Understand the primary point of the book as a basis for evaluating the value of the material presented in it to your questions.

A synthesis of information from multiple sources requires an understanding of the content chosen for the synthesis, first of all. The writer of the synthesis will, no doubt, wish to incorporate his/her own ideas, particularly in any conclusions that are drawn, and show relationships to those of the chosen sources. That can only happen if the writer has a firm grip on what others have said or written. The focus is not so much on documentary methods but on techniques of critically examining and evaluating the ideas of others. Even so, careful documentation is extremely important in this type of presentation, particularly with regard to which particular edition is being read in the case of written sources; and date, location, etc., of online sources. The phrase "downloaded from such-and-such a website on such-and-such a date" is useful. If the conversation, interview, or speech is live, date, circumstances, and location must be indicated.

The purpose of a synthesis is to understand the works of others and to use that work in shaping a conclusion. The writer or speaker must clearly differentiate between the ideas that come from a source and his/her own.

Helping students become critical thinkers is an important objective of the social studies curriculum. The history, geography, and political science classes provide many opportunities to teach students to recognize and understand reasoning errors. Errors tend to fall into two categories: a) inadequate reasons; and b) misleading reasoning. Following are examples of each:

Inadequate reasons:

1. Faulty analogies: The two things being compared must be similar in all significant aspects if the reasoning is to be relied upon. If there is a major difference between the two, then the argument falls apart.
2. False cause (*Post Hoc Ergo Propter Hoc*): after this, therefore because of this. There must be a factual tie between the effect and its declared cause.
3. *Ad Hominen*: Attacking the person instead of addressing the issues.
4. Slippery Slope: The domino effect. This is usually prophetic in nature—predicting what will follow if a certain event occurs. This is only reliable when it is used in hindsight—not in predicting the future because no one is wise enough to know the future.
5. Hasty Conclusions: Leaping to conclusions when not enough evidence has been collected. A good example is the accusations made in the 1996 bombing at the summer Olympics in Atlanta. Not enough evidence had been collected and the wrong man was arrested.

Misleading reasoning:

1. The Red Herring: comes from a smoked fish being dragged across a trail to distract hunting dogs. Often used in politics—getting your opponent on the defensive about a different issue than the one under discussion.
2. *Ad Populum* or Jumping on the Bandwagon: "Everybody's doing it, so it must be right." Biggest is not necessarily best when it comes to following a crowd.
3. Appeal to Tradition: "We've always done it this way." Often used to squelch innovation.
4. The False Dilemma or the Either/Or Fallacy: No other alternative is possible except the extremes at each end. Used in politics a lot. The creative statesman finds other alternatives.

Competency 1.3   Understand basic political concepts, systems, and organizations and examine major features of national, state, and local government in the United States.

Skill 1.3.a   Explain the major concepts of the U.S. Constitution, separation of powers and Federal versus State authority.

In the United States, the three branches of the federal government mentioned earlier, the **Executive**, the **Legislative**, and the **Judicial**, divide up their powers thus:

Legislative – Article 1 of the Constitution established the legislative, or law-making branch of the government called the Congress. It is made up of two houses, the House of Representatives and the Senate. Voters in all states elect the members who serve in each respective House of Congress. The legislative branch is responsible for making laws, raising and printing money, regulating trade, establishing the postal service and federal courts, approving the President's appointments, declaring war and supporting the armed forces. The Congress also has the power to change the Constitution itself, and to *impeach* (bring charges against) the President. Charges for impeachment are brought by the House of Representatives, and are then tried in the Senate.

Executive – Article 2 of the Constitution created the executive branch of the government, headed by the President, who leads the country, recommends new laws, and can veto bills passed by the legislative branch. As the chief of state, the President is responsible for carrying out the laws of the country and the treaties and declarations of war passed by the legislative branch. The President also appoints federal judges and is commander-in-chief of the military when it is called into service. Other members of the executive branch include the Vice-President, also elected, and various cabinet members as he might appoint: ambassadors, presidential advisors, members of the armed forces, and other appointed and civil servants of government agencies, departments and bureaus. Though the President appoints them, they must be approved by the legislative branch.

Judicial – Article 3 of the Constitution established the judicial branch of government headed by the Supreme Court. The Supreme Court has the power to rule that a law passed by the legislature, or an act of the executive branch is illegal and unconstitutional. Citizens, businesses, and government officials can also, in an appeal capacity, ask the Supreme Court to review a decision made in a lower court if someone believes that the ruling by a judge is unconstitutional. The judicial branch also includes lower federal courts known as federal district courts that have been established by the Congress. These courts try law breakers and review cases referred from other courts.

Powers delegated to the federal government:

1. To tax.
2. To borrow and coin money
3. To establish postal service.
4. To grant patents and copyrights.
5. To regulate interstate and foreign commerce.
6. To establish courts.
7. To declare war.
8. To raise and support the armed forces.
9. To govern territories.
10. To define and punish felonies and piracy on the high seas.
11. To fix standards of weights and measures.
12. To conduct foreign affairs.

Powers reserved to the states:

1. To regulate intrastate trade.
2. To establish local governments.
3. To protect general welfare.
4. To protect life and property.
5. To ratify amendments.
6. To conduct elections.
7. To make state and local laws.

Concurrent powers of the federal government and states.

1. Both Congress and the states may tax.
2. Both may borrow money.
3. Both may charter banks and corporations.
4. Both may establish courts.
5. Both may make and enforce laws.
6. Both may take property for public purposes.
7. Both may spend money to provide for the public welfare.

Implied powers of the federal government.

1. To establish banks or other corporations, implied from delegated powers to tax, borrow, and to regulate commerce.
2. To spend money for roads, schools, health, insurance, etc. implied from powers to establish post roads, to tax to provide for general welfare and defense, and to regulate commerce.
3. To create military academies, implied from powers to raise and support an armed force.
4. To locate and generate sources of power and sell surplus, implied from powers to dispose of government property, commerce, and war powers.
5. To assist and regulate agriculture, implied from power to tax and spend for general welfare and regulate commerce.

Skill 1.3.b Be familiar with the history of the American electoral process.

The term **suffrage** means voting or the right to vote. Historically the right to vote has always been very limited. Elections have always been associated with democratic practices but various limitations have been placed on the right to vote throughout history. These have included property qualifications, poll taxes, residency requirements, and restrictions against the right of women to vote.

In 1787, the Constitution of the United States provided for the election of the chief executive in Article II, Section I, and members of the national legislature in Article I, Section II. A number of election abuses, however, led to the adoption of what was known as the Australian, or secret, ballot and the practice of registering voters prior to Election Day. Voting machines were first used in the United States in 1892. During the 19th century, the electorate in the United States grew considerably, most of the states franchised all white male adults, although the so-called poll tax was retained. (It was abolished by the 24th Amendment to the Constitution, ratified in 1964.) The 15th Amendment to the United States Constitution ratified in 1870, extended the vote to the former black slaves. In the period after the Civil War, known as Reconstruction, many blacks were elected to high office for the first time in American history. It was during the post-Civil War period that the primary system of selecting candidates for public office became widely used. By 1900, the system of primaries was regulated by law in most states. Women in the United States were granted the right to vote by the 19th Amendment to the Constitution which was ratified in 1920. The right to vote was extended to those eighteen years of age by the 26th Amendment to the Constitution in 1971.

The struggle over what is to be the fair method to ensure equal political representation for all different groups in the United States continues to dominate the national debate. This has revolved around the problems of trying to ensure proper racial and minority representation. Various civil rights acts, notable the **Voting Rights Act of 1965**, sought to eliminate the remaining features of unequal suffrage in the United States.

Most recently the question has revolved around the issue of what is called "Gerrymandering", which involves the adjustment of various electoral districts in order to achieve a predetermined goal. Usually this is used in regards to the problem of minority political representation. The fact that this sometimes creates odd and unusual looking districts, (this is where the practice gets its name), and most often the sole basis of the adjustments is racial, has led in recent years to the questioning of this practice being a fair, let alone constitutional, way for society to achieve its desired goals. This alone promises to be the major issue in national electoral politics for some time to come. The debate has centered on those of the "left" (Liberals), who favor such methods, and the "right" (Conservatives), who oppose them. Overall, most Americans would consider themselves in the "middle" (Moderates).

Skill 1.3.c   Be familiar with the history of political parties in the United States.

In regards to the American political system, it is important to realize that political parties are never mentioned in the United States Constitution. In fact, George Washington himself warned against the creation of "factions" in American politics that cause "jealousies and false alarms" and the damage they could cause to the body politic. Thomas Jefferson echoed this warning, yet he would come to lead a party himself.

Americans had good reason to fear the emergence of political parties. They had witnessed how parties worked in Great Britain. Parties, called "factions" in Britain, thus Washington's warning, were made up of a few people who schemed to win favors from the government. They were more interested in their own personal profit and advantage than in the public good. Thus, the new American leaders were very interested in keeping factions from forming. It was, ironically, disagreements between two of Washington's chief advisors, Thomas Jefferson and Alexander Hamilton, that spurred the formation of the first political parties in the newly formed United States of America.

The two parties that developed through the early 1790s were led by Jefferson as the Secretary of State and Alexander Hamilton as the Secretary of the Treasury. Jefferson and Hamilton were different in many ways. Not the least was their views on what should be the proper form of government of the United States. This difference helped to shape the parties that formed around them.

Hamilton wanted the federal government to be stronger than the state governments. Jefferson believed that the state governments should be stronger. Hamilton supported the creation of the first Bank of the United States, Jefferson opposed it because he felt that it gave too much power to wealthy investors who would help run it. Jefferson interpreted the Constitution strictly; he argued that nowhere did the Constitution give the federal government the power to create a national bank. Hamilton interpreted the Constitution much more loosely. He pointed out that the Constitution gave Congress the power to make all laws "necessary and proper" to carry out its duties. He reasoned that since Congress had the right to collect taxes, then Congress had the right to create the bank. Hamilton wanted the government to encourage economic growth. He favored the growth of trade, manufacturing, and the rise of cities as the necessary parts of economic growth. He favored the business leaders and mistrusted the common people. Jefferson believed that the common people, especially the farmers, were the backbone of the nation. He thought that the rise of big cities and manufacturing would corrupt American life.

Finally, Hamilton and Jefferson had their disagreements only in private. But when Congress began to pass many of Hamilton's ideas and programs, Jefferson and his friend, James Madison, decided to organize support for their own views. They moved quietly and very cautiously in the beginning.

In 1791, they went to New York telling people that they were going to just study its wildlife. Actually, Jefferson was more interested in meeting with several important New York politicians such as its governor George Clinton and Aaron Burr, a strong critic of Hamilton. Jefferson asked Clinton and Burr to help defeat Hamilton's program by getting New Yorkers to vote for Jefferson's supporters in the next election.

Before long, leaders in other states began to organize support for either Jefferson or Hamilton. Jefferson's supporters called themselves **Democratic-Republicans** (often this was shortened just to Republicans, though in actuality it was the forerunner of today's Democratic Party, not the Republican). Hamilton and his supporters were known as **Federalists** because they favored a strong federal government. The Federalists had the support of the merchants and ship owners in the Northeast and some planters in the South. Small farmers, craft workers, and some of the wealthier land owners supported Jefferson and the Democratic-Republicans.

Newspapers, then as now, influenced the growth of political parties. Newspaper publishers and editors took sides on the issues. Thus, from the very beginning, American newspapers and each new branch of the media have played an important role in helping to shape public opinion.

By the time Washington retired from office in 1796, the new political parties would come to play an important role in choosing his successor, with each putting up its own candidates for office. The election of 1796 was the first one in which political parties played a role. A role that, for better or worse, they have continued to play in various forms for all of American history. By the beginning of the 1800s, the Federalist Party, torn by internal divisions, began suffering a decline. The election in 1800 of Thomas Jefferson as President, Hamilton's bitter rival, and after its leader Alexander Hamilton was killed in 1804 in a duel with Aaron Burr, the Federalist Party began to collapse. By 1816, after losing a string of important elections, (Jefferson was reelected in 1804, and James Madison, a Democratic-Republican was elected in 1808), the Federalist party ceased to be an effective political force and soon passed off the national stage.

By the late 1820s, new political parties had grown up. The Democratic-Republican Party, or simply the Republican Party, had been the major party for many years, but differences within it about the direction the country was headed in caused a split after 1824. Those who favored strong national growth took the name **Whigs** after a similar party in Great Britain and united around then President John Quincy Adams. Many business people in the Northeast as well as some wealthy planters in the South supported it.

Those who favored slower growth and were more worker and small farmer oriented, went on to form the new **Democratic Party,** with Andrew Jackson being its first leader as well as becoming the first President from it. It is the forerunner of today's present party of the same name.

In the mid-1850s, the slavery issue was beginning to heat up and in 1854, those opposed to slavery, the Whigs, and some Northern Democrats opposed to slavery, united to form the **Republican Party**. Before the Civil War, the Democratic Party was more heavily represented in the South and was thus pro-slavery for the most part.

Thus, by the time of the Civil War, the present form of the major political parties had been formed. Though there would sometimes be drastic changes in ideology and platforms over the years, no other political parties would manage to gain enough strength to seriously challenge the "Big Two" parties.

In fact, they have shown themselves to be very adaptable to changing times. In many instances, they have managed to shut out other parties by simply adapting their platforms, such as in the 1930s during the Great Depression and in the years immediately preceding it. The Democratic Party adapted much of the Socialist Party platform and, under Franklin Roosevelt, put much of it into effect thus managing to eliminate it as any serious threat. Since the Civil War, no other political party has managed to gain enough support to either elect substantial members to Congress or elect a President, some have come closer than others, but barring any unforeseen circumstances, the absolute monopoly on national political debate seems very secure in the hands of the Republican and Democratic parties.

Time will tell if this is to remain so. For history and political science both teach us that the American people are quite willing to change their support from one area or group to another. Especially if it means a better way of doing things or will give them more opportunity and freedoms. As conservative as some might think Americans have become, there has always been and always will be, something of the revolutionary spirit about them.

Skill 1.3.d   Define the rights and responsibilities of United States citizens.

The terms "civil liberties" and "civil rights" are often used interchangeably, but there are some fine distinctions between the two terms. The term civil liberties is more often used to imply that the state has a positive role to play in assuring that all its' citizens will have equal protection and justice under the law with equal opportunities to exercise their privileges of citizenship and to participate fully in the life of the nation, regardless of race, religion, sex, color or creed. The term civil rights is used more often to refer to rights that may be described as guarantees that are specified as against the state authority implying limitations on the actions of the state to interfere with citizens' liberties. Although the term "civil rights" has thus been identified with the ideal of equality and the term "civil liberties" with the idea of freedom, the two concepts are really inseparable and interacting. Equality implies the proper ordering of liberty in a society so that one individual's freedom does not infringe on the rights of others.

The beginnings of civil liberties and the idea of civil rights in the United States go back to the ideas of the Greeks. Also the experience of the early British struggle for civil rights and to the very philosophies that led people to come to the New World in the first place. Religious freedom, political freedom, and the right to live one's life as one sees fit are basic to the American ideal. These were embodied in the ideas expressed in the Declaration of Independence and the Constitution.

All these ideas found their final expression in the United States Constitution's first ten amendments, known as the **Bill of Rights**. In 1789, the first Congress passed these first amendments and by December, 1791, three-fourths of the states at that time had ratified them. The Bill of Rights protects certain liberties and basic rights. James Madison who wrote the amendments said that the Bill of Rights does not give Americans these rights. People, Madison said, already have these rights. They are natural rights that belong to all human beings. The Bill of Rights simply prevents the governments from taking away these rights.

To summarize:

The first amendment guarantees the basic rights of freedom of religion, freedom of speech, freedom of the press, and freedom of assembly.

The next three amendments came out of the colonists' struggle with Great Britain. For example, the third amendment prevents Congress from forcing citizens to keep troops in their homes. Before the Revolution, Great Britain tried to coerce the colonists to house soldiers.

Amendments five through eight protect citizens who are accused of crimes and are brought to trial. Every citizen has the right to due process of law, (due process as defined earlier, being that the government must follow the same fair rules for everyone brought to trial.) These rules include the right to a trial by an impartial jury, the right to be defended by a lawyer, and the right to a speedy trial.

The last two amendments limit the powers of the federal government to those that are expressly granted in the Constitution, any rights not expressly mentioned in the Constitution, thus, belong to the states or to the people.

In regards to specific guarantees:

Freedom of Religion: Religious freedom has not been seriously threatened in the United States historically. The policy of the government has been guided by the premise that church and state should be separate. But when religious practices have been at cross purposes with attitudes prevailing in the nation at particular times, there has been restrictions placed on these practices. Some of these have been restrictions against the practice of polygamy that is supported by certain religious groups. The idea of animal sacrifice that is promoted by some religious beliefs is generally prohibited. The use of mind altering illegal substances that some use in religious rituals has been restricted. In the United States, all recognized religious institutions are tax-exempt in following the idea of separation of church and state, and therefore, there have been many quasi-religious groups that have in the past tried to take advantage of this fact. All of these issues continue, and most likely will continue to occupy both political and legal considerations for some time to come.

Freedom of Speech, Press, and Assembly: These rights historically have been given wide latitude in their practices, though there has been instances when one or the other have been limited for various reasons. The most classic limitation, for instance, in regards to freedom of speech, has been the famous precept that an individual is prohibited from yelling fire! in a crowded theatre. This prohibition is an example of the state saying that freedom of speech does not extend to speech that might endanger other people. There is also a prohibition against **slander,** or the knowingly stating of a deliberate falsehood against one party by another. Also there are many regulations regarding freedom of the press, the most common example are the various laws against **libel**, (or the printing of a known falsehood). In times of national emergency, various restrictions have been placed on the rights of press, speech and sometimes assembly.

The legal system in recent years has also undergone a number of serious changes, some would say challenges, with the interpretation of some constitutional guarantees.

America also has a number of organizations that put themselves out as champions of the fight for civil liberties and civil rights in this country. Much criticism, however, has been raised at times against these groups as to whether or not they are really protecting rights, or by following a specific ideology, perhaps are attempting to create "new" rights.

Or are simply in many cases, looking at the strict letter of the law, as opposed to what the law actually intends.

"Rights" come with a measure of responsibility and respect for the public order, all of which must be taken into consideration.

Overall, the American experience has been one of exemplary conduct in regards to the protection of individual rights. Where there has been a lag in its practice, notably the refusal to grant full and equal rights to blacks, the very fact of their enslavement, and the second class status of women for much of American history, negates the good that the country has done in other areas. With the exception of the American Civil War, the country has proved itself to be more or less resilient in being able, for the most part, peacefully, to change when it has not lived up to its' stated ideals in practice. What has been called "the virtual bloodless civil rights revolution" is a case in point.

Though much effort and suffering accompanied the struggle for civil rights, in the end it did succeed in spite of all. The foundation of society was actually changed in such a profound way that would have been unheard of in many other countries. The strong tradition of freedom and liberty that was and is the underlying feature of American society allows our country to be a leader in civil rights.

How best to move forward with ensuring civil liberties and civil rights for all continues to dominate the national debate. In recent times, issues seem to revolve not around individual rights, but what has been called "group rights" has been raised. At the forefront of the debate is whether some specific remedies like affirmative action, quotas, gerrymandering and various other forms of preferential treatment are actually fair or just as bad as the ills they are supposed to cure. At the present no easy answers seem to be forthcoming. It is a testament to the American system that it has shown itself able to enter into these debates, to find solutions and tended to come out stronger.

The fact that the United States has the longest single constitutional history in the modern era is just one reason to be optimistic about the future of American liberty.

Competency 1.4 Understand economic concepts and systems and the operation of the U.S. and world economies.

Skill 1.4.a   Be able to apply the principles of consumer economics.

A **consumer** is a person who uses goods and services and, in a **capitalist** or free enterprise economy, decides with other consumers what is produced by what they choose to buy. The terms **"supply and demand"** are used to explain the influence of consumers on production. This law or principle of supply and demand means that prices of goods rise due to an increased demand and fall when there is an increase in the supply of goods.

Due to unstable economies, inflation, job insecurity due to downsizing, bankruptcy and other factors, having cash on hand while buying is less prevalent than having **credit cards.** These cards are frequently referred to as "plastic money" but in reality are not money. They are a convenient tool for receiving a short-term loan from the financial institutions issuing the cards. These popular pieces of plastic aid consumers in such economic activities as purchasing items on "installment plans." Financial institutions are not the only ones issuing credit cards. Oil companies, airlines, national automobile manufacturers, and large corporations are just some of the backers of credit cards. Department store charge cards do not enable the holder to obtain money from an **Automated Teller Machine (ATM)** but do enable one to buy on credit or on the installment plan. Automobile dealerships, banks, credit unions, loan companies all, in similar ways, make it possible for just about anyone to purchase on installment and drive a car. Mortgages allow people to pay for their own homes or condominiums.

Skill 1.4.b   Show an understanding of the role of markets.

A "market" is an economic term to describe the places and situations in which goods and services are bought and sold. In a capitalistic free enterprise economy, the market prices of goods and services rise and fall according to decreases and increases in the supply and demand and the degree of competition.

In an economic system, there is also a "market" for land, capital, and labor. The labor market, for example, is studied by economists in order to better understand trends in jobs, productivity of workers, activities of labor unions, and patterns of employment. Potential customers for a product or service are called a **market** and are the subject of **market research** to determine who would possibly make use of whatever is offered to customers.

Other types of markets, which are part of countries' economic systems, include the following:

Stock Market

This is part of a capitalistic free enterprise system and is one of significant investment and speculation. Any changes in the prices of stocks are seriously affected by those who buy stocks when their prices are rising and sell them when their prices are falling. Business planners quite often regard the stock market as a barometer of the degree of confidence investors have in the conditions of businesses in the future. When the stock market is a rising "bull" market, economists and investors see it as the public showing confidence in the future of business. At the same time, when the market is a falling "bear" market, it is an indication of a lack of confidence. In unstable economic conditions, one or more conditions and situations can seriously affect the stock market's rise and fall. The "bottom line" is that these fluctuations are directly tied to and directly affected by investment changes.

"Black" Market

This illegal market has in the past and even today exists in countries where wage and price controls are in place and enforced by law. In these markets, goods and products are priced and sold above legal limits, especially if the maximum legal price is much less than free-market price. The black market thrives when certain products are unavailable in the regulated market and there is a demand for them, or if wage and price controls are in place for an extended period.

Common Market

This market, also known as the European Economic Community (EEC), began in 1958 and is comprised of several European nations. Its major purpose was to remove all restrictive tariffs and import quotas in order to encourage and facilitate free trade among member nations. Included were efforts to move workers and services without restrictions.

Skill 1.4.c   Be familiar with other economic systems.

Those other important modern economic and ideological systems that have had the greatest effect in modern era are, *Socialism, Communism,* and *Fascism.* Each will be examined in its turn.

Socialism – This is a fairly recent political phenomenon though its roots can be traced pretty far back in time in many respects. At the core, both socialism and communism are fundamentally economic philosophies that advocate public rather than private ownership, especially over means of production, yet even here, there are many distinctions. Karl Marx basically concentrated his attention on the industrial worker and on state domination over the means of production.

In practice, this Marxian dogma has largely been followed the most in those countries that profess to be Communist. In conjunction with massive programs for the development of heavy industry, this emphasis on production regardless of the wants or comforts of the individual in the given society. Socialism by contrast, usually occurring where industry has already been developed, has concerned itself more with the welfare of the individual and the fair distribution of whatever wealth is available.

Communism has a rigid theology, and a bible (*Das Capital*), that sees Communism emerging as a result of almost cosmic laws. Modern socialism is much closer to the ground. It too sees change in human society and hopes for improvement, but there is no unchanging millennium at the end of the road. Communism is sure that it will achieve the perfect state and in this certainty it is willing to use any and all means, however ruthless, to bring it about.
Socialism on the other hand, confident only that the human condition is always changing, makes no easy approximation between ends and means and so cannot justify brutalities. This distinction in philosophy, of course, makes for an immense conflict in methods. Communism, believing that revolution is inevitable, works toward it by emphasizing class antagonisms. Socialism, while seeking change, insists on the use of democratic procedures within the existing social order of a given society. In it, the upper classes and capitalists are not to be violently overthrown but instead to be won over by logical persuasion.

It is interesting to note that in every perfect, idealized community or society that people have dreamed about throughout history, where human beings are pictured living in a special harmony that transcends their natural instincts, there has been a touch of socialism. This tendency was especially found in the *Utopian-Socialists* of the early 19th century, whose basic aim was the repudiation of the private-property system with its economic inefficiency and social injustice. Their criticisms rather than any actual achievements would linger after them. Like Marx, they envisioned industrial capitalism as becoming more and more inhumane and oppressive. They could not imagine the mass of workers prospering in such a system. Yet the workers soon developed their own powerful organizations and institutions. They began to bend the economic system to their own benefit. Thus a split did occur. First, between those who after the growing success of the labor movement rejected the earlier utopian ideas as being impractical. Second, those who saw in this newfound political awareness of the working class the key to organizing a realistic ability of revolution, who saw this as inevitable based on their previous observations and study of history. Having reached a point where it has managed to jeopardize its very own survival, the inevitable revolution of those opposed to the present capitalist system had to occur, history has proven this so, and history is always right and irrefutable.

These believers in the absolute correctness of this doctrine gathered around Marx in what he called *Scientific Socialism*. In contempt to all other kinds which he considered not to be scientific, and therefore, useless as a realistic political philosophy.

The next split would occur between those who believed in the absolute inevitability of the coming revolution (the *Revolutionary Socialists* or as they came to be known, the *Communists*), and those while accepting the basic idea that the current capitalist system could not last, saw in the growing political awareness of the working class the beginnings of an ability to effect peaceful and gradual change in the social order. They believed this is better in the long run for everyone concerned as opposed to a cataclysmic, apocalyptic uprising (the *Democratic-Socialists*).

Major strides for the *Democratic-Socialists* were made before the First World War. A war that the Socialists, by philosophy pacifists, initially resisted, giving only reluctant support only once the struggle had begun. During the conflict, public sentiment against pacifism tended generally to weaken the movement, but with peace, reaction set in. The cause of world socialism leaped forward, often overcompensating by adhering to revolutionary communism which in the Revolution of 1917 had taken hold of in Russia. The between wars period saw the sudden spurt of socialism, whether their leanings were democratic or not, all socialists were bound together for a time in their resistance to fascism.

The decade following World War II saw tremendous growth in socialism. Economic planning and the nationalization of industry was undertaken in many countries and to this day have not been repudiated, though a subsequent return to self-confidence in the private business community and among voters, in general, has frequently weakened the socialist majority or reduced it to the status of an opposition party. This political balance leaves most industrialized countries with a mixed socialist-capitalist economy. So long as there is no major world-wide depression, this situation may remain relatively stable. The consequences of World War II, particularly the independence of former European colonies, has opened vast new areas for the attempted development of socialist forms. Most have tried to aspire to the democratic type but very few have succeeded except where democratic traditions were strong.

Socialism though concentrating on economic relationships, has always considered itself a complete approach to human society. In effect, a new belief system and thus a world rather than a national movement.

In this respect as well, it owes much to Great Britain for it was in London in 1864 that the first *Socialist International* was organized by Karl Marx. This radical leftist organization died off after limping along for twelve years, by which time its headquarters had moved to New York.

After the passage of about another twelve years, the *Second Socialist International* met in Paris to celebrate the anniversary of the fall of the Bastille in the French Revolution. By this time, serious factions were developing. There were the **Anarchists**, who wanted to tear down everything, **Communists** who wanted to tear down the established order and build another in its place, and the **Democratic-Socialist** majority who favored peaceful political action.

Struggling for internal peace and cohesion right up to the First World War, socialism would remain largely ineffectual at this critical international time. Peace brought them all together again in Bern, Switzerland, but by this time the Soviet Union had been created, and the Russian Communists refused to attend the meeting on the ground that the Second Socialist International opposed the type of dictatorship it saw as necessary in order to achieve revolutions. Thus the *Communist International* was created in direct opposition to the Socialist International. While the socialists went on to advocate the "triumph of democracy, firmly rooted in the principles of liberty". The main objective of this new Socialist International was to maintain the peace, an ironic and very elusive goal in the period between the two world wars.

The Nazi attack on Poland in September, 1939, completely shattered the organization. In 1946, however a new *Socialist Information and Liaison Office* was set up to reestablish old contacts, and in 1951 the Communist International was revived with a conference in Frankfurt, Germany. At which time, it adopted a document entitled "Aims and Tasks of Democratic Socialism". A summary of these objectives gives a good picture of modern Democratic-Socialism as it exists on paper in its ideal form.

As always, the first principle is nationalized ownership of the major means of production and distribution. Usually public ownership is deemed appropriate for the strategically important services, public utilities, banking and resource industries such as coal, iron, lumber and oil. Farming has never been considered well adapted to public administration and has usually been excluded from nationalization. From this takeover of the free enterprise system, socialists expect a more perfect freedom to evolve. Offering equal opportunity for all, the minimizing of class conflict, better products for less cost, and security from physical want or need.

At the international level, socialism seeks a world of free peoples living together in peace and harmony for the mutual benefit of all. That freedom, at least from colonial rule, has largely been won. Peace throughout the world, however, is still as far off in most respects as it has ever been. According to the socialist doctrine, putting an end to capitalism will do much to reduce the likelihood of war. Armies and business are seen to need each other in a marriage of the weapons-mentality and devotion to private profit through the economic exploitation of weaker countries.

The United States remains the bastion of the free enterprise system. Socialism in the United States has long been regarded historically as a "menace" to the "American way". There is no question that socialists do argue for change. Capitalism in their opinion makes for unfair distribution of wealth, causing private affluence and public squalor. They also hold it responsible for environmental pollution and economic inflation. By curbing the absolute freedom of the private businessman or corporation, socialism hopes to satisfy all human necessities at the price of individual self-indulgence. Anti-trust legislation, the graduated income tax, and Social Security have all moved the United States toward the idea of the "welfare state", which recognizes as its prime objective full employment and a minimum living standard for all, whether employed or not. Even such taken for granted features of modern life as public schools and the federal postal service are relatively recent and socialistic innovations. Socialists applaud these programs, but, in what they regard as a sick society, these remedies seem to them only so much aspirin where major surgery is needed.

While communism and socialism arose in reaction to the excesses of 19th century capitalism, all three have matured in the past 100 years. Capitalism has mellowed, while a sibling rivalry may continue to exist between communism and socialism. Officially, communism clings to the idea of revolution and the seizing of capitalist property by the state without compensation, socialism accepts gradualism, feeling that a revolution, particularly in an industrial society would be ruinous. In fact, socialists and in some situations even communists, have come to realize that not all economic institutions function better in public hands. Private responsibility frequently offers benefits that go to the public good. This is particularly true in the agricultural sector, where personal ownership and cultivation of land have always been deeply ingrained.

All socialism denies certain freedoms, sometimes hidden in what it considers favorable terms. It deprives the minority of special economic privileges for the benefit of majority. The more left-wing, communistic socialism may deny the democratic process entirely. Traditionally defined, democracy holds to the idea that the people, exercising their majority opinion at the polls, will arrive at the common good by electing representative individuals to govern them. Communists would interpret this to mean the tyranny of an uneducated majority obliged to decide between a politically selected group of would-be leaders.

There is no question that the democratic process has its limitations, but for want of a better method, contemporary socialism accepts democracy as a major principle.

The expressed goals of modern socialism are commendable, but goals of course are easy to state, especially when there is no real opportunity to carry them out in actual fact. The gulf between theory and practice is often insurmountable, the situation thus remains whether given the chance socialism can bring about a better world than now exists.

Nowhere today does socialism exist in a pure and unchallenged form, but in many nations it has made impressive gains.

Communism – It comes next and is, in fact, a direct outgrowth of socialism. In 1848, Karl Marx (with Freidrich Engels) began his *Communist Manifesto* with the prophetic sentence *"a specter is haunting Europe, the specter of communism"*. Little more than a century later, nearly one third of the world's population would live under governments professing communism. Even with the collapse of the Soviet Union and the Eastern Communist Block, China with nearly one fourth of the world's population, not to mention North Korea and Cuba, still claim to follow the communist ideal. Yet, in these societies, not one of them could say that they have achieved, (through massive toil, treachery and bloodshed), the ideal state that communism was supposed to create.

Marx took the name for his ideal society from the *French Communes*, feudal villages that held land and produce in common. But he was not satisfied with villages. His dream was of newly industrialized Europe shaped into a communist world. As he saw it, other systems would give way, or if they fought back, would be destroyed. With the birth of the industrial age in the early 19th century, privately owned factories employed larger and larger work forces. The owners of these factories made vast profits, which they plowed back into building more factories. The workers were becoming mere tools in a huge anonymous crowd, alienated from the product of their toil. Labor was hard, often dangerous, and poorly rewarded.

This was the economic system of capitalism in its formative years, and Marx saw it leading only to increased enrichment of the owners of great businesses and to the eventual enslavement of the working class. Marx exhorted the workers to revolt. He urged them in his writings to seize the factories from the capitalists, not in order to become capitalist themselves, but in order to place the means of production in the hands of the community for the benefit of all its citizens. This intermediate society controlling the means of production is called the *"Dictatorship of the Proletariat"*. It is what the Soviet Union and other so-called communist nations achieved, but it is not communism. True communism comes only with the further step of the state giving ownership back to the people, who then continue to live together in abundance without supervision from a ruling class.

Pure Communism does not now, (in those few countries that still profess it), nor has it ever, existed in actual fact. Perhaps it never will. It is a Neverland of absolute bliss, heaven on Earth, the Garden of Eden revisited, this time for all to enjoy.

So, despite endless writing on the subject of communism, almost all of its verbiage has been devoted to the struggle to achieve socialism. Today for the commissar who drives the worker, and the peasant who pulls the load, communism still remains the goal, the end of the struggle. Though Marx and his disciples have insisted and continue to insist that socialism is only a stop on the way to communism, they have not dared to describe this final paradise on Earth except in the haziest of ways.

With the final achievement of communism, greed and competition will presumably cease. Each person will contribute according to their ability and receive according to their need. There will be no cause for crime or vice of any kind. No race or class rivalry, no grounds for war, and no reason for government.

Perfection indeed, but unhappily not yet of this world. In fact, it is not measurably nearer today anywhere than when Marx first conceived it.

In fact, as has been examined earlier, the fact that it can never really occur, has not stopped it from being believed in some quarters.

Fascism – The last important historical economic system to arise. It has been called a reaction against the last two ideologies discussed. It can, at times, cooperate with a Monarchy if it has to.

In general, Fascism is the effort to create, by dictatorial means, a viable national society in which competing interests were to be adjusted to each other by being entirely subordinated to the service of the state. The following features have been characteristic of Fascism in its various manifestations: **(1)** An origin at a time of serious economic disruption and of rapid and bewildering social change. **(2)** A philosophy that rejects democratic and humanitarian ideals and glorifies the absolute sovereignty of the state, the unity and destiny of the people, and their unquestioning loyalty and obedience to the dictator. **(3)** An aggressive nationalism which calls for the mobilization and regimentation of every aspect of national life and makes open use of violence and intimidation. **(4)** The simulation of mass popular support, accomplished by outlawing all but a single political party and by using suppression, censorship, and propaganda. **(5)** A program of vigorous action including economic reconstruction, industrialization, pursuit of economic self-sufficiency, territorial expansion and war which is dramatized as bold, adventurous, and promising a glorious future.

Fascist movements often had socialists origins. For example, in Italy, where fascism first arose in place of socialism, **Benito Mussolini**, sought to impose what he called "*corporativism*". A fascist "*corporate*" state would, in theory, run the economy for the benefit of the whole country like a corporation. It would be centrally controlled and managed by an elite who would see that its benefits would go to everyone.

Fascism has always declared itself the uncompromising enemy of communism, with which, however, fascist actions have much in common. (In fact, many of the methods of organization and propaganda used by fascists were taken from the experience of the early Russian communists, along with the belief in a single strong political party, secret police, etc.) The propertied interests and the upper classes, fearful of revolution, often gave their support to fascism on the basis of promises by the fascist leaders to maintain the status quo and safeguard property. (In effect, accomplishing a revolution from above with their help as opposed from below against them. However, fascism did consider itself a revolutionary movement of a different type).

Once established, a fascist regime ruthlessly crushes communist and socialist parties as well as all democratic opposition. It regiments the propertied interests to its national goals and wins the potentially revolutionary masses to fascist programs by substituting a rabid nationalism for class conflict. Thus fascism may be regarded as an extreme defensive expedient adopted by a nation faced with the sometimes illusionary threat of communist subversion or revolution. Under fascism, capital is regulated as much as labor and fascist contempt for legal or constitutional guarantees effectively destroyed whatever security the capitalistic system had enjoyed under pre-fascist governments.

In addition, fascist or similar regimes are at times anti-Communist. This is evidenced by the Soviet-German treaty of 1939. During the period of alliance created by the treaty, Italy and Germany and their satellite countries ceased their anti-Communist propaganda. They emphasized their own revolutionary and proletarian origins and attacked the so-called plutocratic western democracies.

The fact that fascist countries sought to control national life by methods identical to those of communist governments make such nations vulnerable to communism after the fascist regime is destroyed.

In theory at least, the chief distinction between fascism and communism is that fascism is *nationalist*, exalting the interests of the state and glorifying war between nations, whereas, communism is *internationalist,* exalting the interests of a specific economic class (the proletariat) and glorifying world wide class warfare. In practice, however, this fundamental distinction loses some of its validity. For in its heyday, fascism was also an internationalist movement. A movement dedicated to world conquest, (like communism), as evidenced by the events prior to and during the Second World War. At the same time, many elements in communism as it evolved came to be very nationalistic as well.

Skill 1.4.d   Be able to understand and illustrate global economic concepts.

"Globalism" is defined as the principle of the interdependence of all the world's nations and their peoples. Within this global community, every nation, in some way to a certain degree, is dependent on other nations. Since no one nation has all of the resources needed for production, trade with other nations is required to obtain what is needed for production, to sell what is produced or to buy finished products, to earn money to maintain and strengthen the nation's economic system.

Developing nations receive technical assistance and financial aid from developed nations. Many international organizations have been set up to promote and encourage cooperation and economic progress among member nations. Through the elimination of such barriers to trade as tariffs, trade is stimulated resulting in increased productivity, economic progress, increased cooperation and understanding on diplomatic levels.

Those nations not part of an international trade organization not only must make those economic decisions of what to produce, how and for whom, but must also deal with the problem of tariffs and quotas on imports. Regardless of international trade memberships, economic growth and development are vital and affect all trading nations. Businesses, labor, and governments share common interests and goals in a nation's economic status. International systems of banking and finance have been devised to assist governments and businesses in setting the policy and guidelines for the exchange of currencies.

Competency 1.5   Understand basic tools and methods of geographic inquiry and apply knowledge of cultural and physical geography.

Skill 1.5.a   Know the earth's physical features and be able to give examples and their locations.

The earth's surface is made up of 70% water and 30% land. Physical features of the land surface include mountains, hills, plateaus, valleys, and plains. Other minor landforms include deserts, deltas, canyons, mesas, basins, foothills, marshes and swamps. Earth's water features include oceans, seas, lakes, rivers, and canals.

Mountains are landforms with rather steep slopes at least 2,000 feet or more above sea level. Mountains are found in groups called mountain chains or mountain ranges. At least one range can be found on six of the earth's seven continents. North America has the Appalachian and Rocky Mountains; South America the Andes; Asia the Himalayas; Australia the Great Dividing Range; Europe the Alps; and Africa the Atlas, Ahaggar, and Drakensburg Mountains.

Hills are elevated landforms rising to an elevation of about 500 to 2000 feet. They are found everywhere on earth including Antarctica where they are covered by ice.

Plateaus are elevated landforms usually level on top. Depending on location, they range from being an area that is very cold to one that is cool and healthful. Some plateaus are dry because they are surrounded by mountains that keep out any moisture. Some examples include the Kenya Plateau in East Africa, which is very cool. The plateau extending north from the Himalayas is extremely dry while those in Antarctica and Greenland are covered with ice and snow.

Plains are described as areas of flat or slightly rolling land, usually lower than the landforms next to them. Sometimes called lowlands (and sometimes located along **seacoasts)** they support the majority of the world's people. Some are found inland and many have been formed by large rivers. This resulted in extremely fertile soil for successful cultivation of crops and numerous large settlements of people. In North America, the vast plains areas extend from the Gulf of Mexico north to the Arctic Ocean and between the Appalachian and Rocky Mountains. In Europe, rich plains extend east from Great Britain into central Europe on into the Siberian region of Russia. Plains in river valleys are found in China (the Yangtze River valley), India (the Ganges River valley), and Southeast Asia (the Mekong River valley).

Valleys are land areas that are found between hills and mountains. Some have gentle slopes containing trees and plants; others have very steep walls and are referred to as canyons. One famous example is Arizona's Grand Canyon of the Colorado River.

Deserts are large dry areas of land receiving ten inches or less of rainfall each year. Among the better known deserts are Africa's large Sahara Desert, the Arabian Desert on the Arabian Peninsula, and the desert Outback covering roughly one third of Australia.

Deltas are areas of lowlands formed by soil and sediment deposited at the mouths of rivers. The soil is generally very fertile and most fertile river deltas are important crop-growing areas. One well-known example is the delta of Egypt's Nile River, known for its production of cotton.

Mesas are the flat tops of hills or mountains usually with steep sides. Sometimes plateaus are also called mesas. Basins are considered to be low areas drained by rivers or low spots in mountains. Foothills are generally considered a low series of hills found between a plain and a mountain range. Marshes and swamps are wet lowlands providing growth of such plants as rushes and reeds.

Oceans are the largest bodies of water on the planet. The four oceans of the earth are the **Atlantic Ocean**, one-half the size of the Pacific and separating North and South America from Africa and Europe; the **Pacific Ocean**, covering almost one-third of the entire surface of the earth and separating North and South America from Asia and Australia; the **Indian Ocean**, touching Africa, Asia, and Australia; and the ice-filled **Arctic Ocean,** extending from North America and Europe to the North Pole. The waters of the Atlantic, Pacific, and Indian Oceans also touch the shores of Antarctica.

Seas are smaller than oceans and are surrounded by land. Some examples include the Mediterranean Sea found between Europe, Asia, and Africa; and the Caribbean Sea, touching the West Indies, South and Central America. A lake is a body of water surrounded by land. The Great Lakes in North America are a good example.

Rivers, considered a nation's lifeblood, usually begin as very small streams, formed by melting snow and rainfall, flowing from higher to lower land, emptying into a larger body of water, usually a sea or an ocean. Examples of important rivers for the people and countries affected by and/or dependent on them include the Nile, Niger, and Zaire Rivers of Africa; the Rhine, Danube, and Thames Rivers of Europe; the Yangtze, Ganges, Mekong, Hwang He, and Irrawaddy Rivers of Asia; the Murray-Darling in Australia; and the Orinoco in South America. River systems are made up of large rivers and numerous smaller rivers or tributaries flowing into them. Examples include the vast Amazon Rivers system in South America and the Mississippi River system in the United States.

Canals are man-made water passages constructed to connect two larger bodies of water. Famous examples include the **Panama Canal** across Panama's isthmus connecting the Atlantic and Pacific Oceans and the **Suez Canal** in the Middle East between Africa and the Arabian peninsula connecting the Red and Mediterranean Seas.

Skill 1.5.b   Know the difference between climate and weather and the descriptions and locations of different types of climates.

Weather is the condition of the air which surrounds the day-to-day atmospheric conditions including temperature, air pressure, wind and moisture or precipitation which includes rain, snow, hail, or sleet.

Climate is average weather or daily weather conditions for a specific region or location over a long or extended period of time. Studying the climate of an area includes information gathered on the area's monthly and yearly temperatures and its monthly and yearly amounts of precipitation. In addition, a characteristic of an area's climate is the length of its growing season. Four reasons for the different climate regions on the earth are differences in:

1. Latitude,
2. The amount of moisture,
3. Temperatures in land and water, and
4. The earth's land surface.

There are many different climates throughout the earth. It is most unusual if a country contains just one kind of climate. Regions of climates are divided according to latitudes:

0 - 23 1/2 degrees are the "low latitudes"
23 1/2 - 66 1/2 degrees are the "middle latitudes"
66 1/2 degrees to the Poles are the "high latitudes"

The **low latitudes** are comprised of the rainforest, savanna, and desert climates. The tropical rainforest climate is found in equatorial lowlands and is hot and wet. There is sun, extreme heat and rain--everyday. Although daily temperatures rarely rise above 90 degrees F, the daily humidity is always high, leaving everything sticky and damp. North and south of the tropical rainforests are the tropical grasslands called "savannas," the "lands of two seasons"--a winter dry season and a summer wet season. Further north and south of the tropical grasslands or savannas are the deserts. These areas are the hottest and driest parts of the earth receiving less than 10 inches of rain a year. These areas have extreme temperatures between night and day. After the sun sets, the land cools quickly dropping the temperature as much as 50 degrees F.

The **middle latitudes** contain the Mediterranean, humid-subtropical, humid-continental, marine, steppe, and desert climates. Lands containing the Mediterranean climate are considered "sunny" lands found in six areas of the world: lands bordering the Mediterranean Sea, a small portion of southwestern Africa, areas in southern and southwestern Australia, a small part of the Ukraine near the Black Sea, central Chile, and Southern California. Summers are hot and dry with mild winters. The growing season usually lasts all year and what little rain falls are during the winter months. What is rather unusual is that the Mediterranean climate is located between 30 and 40 degrees north and south latitude on the western coasts of countries.

The humid **subtropical climate** is found north and south of the tropics and is moist indeed. The areas having this type of climate are found on the eastern side of their continents and include Japan, mainland China, Australia, Africa, South America, and the United States--the southeastern coasts of these areas. An interesting feature of their locations is that warm ocean currents are found there. The winds that blow across these currents bring in warm moist air all year round. Long, warm summers; short, mild winters; a long growing season allow for different crops to be grown several times a year. All contribute to the productivity of this climate type which supports more people than any of the other climates.

The **marine climate** is found in Western Europe, the British Isles, the U.S. Pacific Northwest, the western coast of Canada and southern Chile, along with southern New Zealand and southeastern Australia. A common characteristic of these lands is that they are either near water or surrounded by it. The ocean winds are wet and warm bringing a mild, rainy climate to these areas. In the summer, the daily temperatures average at or below 70 degrees F. During the winter, because of the warming effect of the ocean waters, the temperatures rarely fall below freezing.

In northern and central United States, northern China, south central and southeastern Canada, and the western and southeastern parts of the former Soviet Union is found the **"climate of four seasons,"** the **humid continental climate--spring,** summer, fall, and winter. Cold winters, hot summers, and enough rainfall to grow a variety of crops are the major characteristics of this climate. In areas where the humid continental climate is found are some of the world's best farmlands as well as important activities such as trading and mining. Differences in temperatures throughout the year are determined by the distance a place is inland, away from the coasts.

The **steppe or prairie climate** is located in the interiors of the large continents like Asia and North America. These dry flatlands are far from ocean breezes and are called prairies or the Great Plains in Canada and the United States and steppes in Asia. Although the summers are hot and the winters are cold as in the humid continental climate, the big difference is rainfall. In the steppe climate, rainfall is light and uncertain, 10 to 20 inches a year mainly in spring and summer and is considered normal. Where rain is more plentiful, grass grows; in areas of less, the steppes or prairies gradually become deserts. These are found in the Gobi Desert of Asia, central and western Australia, southwestern United States, and in the smaller deserts found in Pakistan, Argentina, and Africa south of the Equator.

The two major climates found in the high latitudes are **"tundra" and "taiga."** The word "tundra" meaning "marshy plain" is a Russian word and aptly describes the climatic conditions in the northern areas of Russia, Europe, and Canada. Winters are extremely cold and very long. Most of the year the ground is frozen but becomes rather mushy during the very short summer months. Surprisingly less snow falls in the area of the tundra than in the eastern part of the United States. However, due to the harshness of the extreme cold, very few people live there and no crops can be raised. Despite having a small human population, many plants and animals are found there.

The **"taiga"** is the northern forest region and is located south of the tundra. In fact, the Russian word "taiga" means 'forest." The world's largest forestlands are found here along with vast mineral wealth and forbearing animals. The climate is extreme that very few people live here, not being able to raise crops due to the extremely short growing season. The winter temperatures are colder and the summer temperatures are hotter than those in the tundra are because the taiga climate region is farther from the waters of the Arctic Ocean. The taiga is found in the northern parts of Russia, Sweden, Norway, Finland, Canada, and Alaska with most of their lands covered with marshes and swamps.

In certain areas of the earth there exists a type of climate unique to areas with high mountains, usually different from their surroundings. This type of climate is called a **"vertical climate"** because the temperatures, crops, vegetation, and human activities change and become different as one ascends the different levels of elevation. At the foot of the mountain, a hot and rainy climate is found with the cultivation of many lowland crops. As one climbs higher, the air becomes **cooler,** the climate changes sharply and different economic activities change, such as grazing sheep and growing corn. At the top of many mountains, snow is found year round.

Skill 1.5.c Be able to explain how physical and political locations are determined and give examples.

Physical **locations** of the earth's surface features include the four major hemispheres and the parts of the earth's continents in them. Political **locations** are the political divisions, if any, within each continent. Both physical and political locations are precisely determined in two *ways:* (1) Surveying is done to determine boundary lines and distance from other features. (2) Exact locations are precisely determined by imaginary lines of **latitude (parallels)** and **longitude** (meridians). The intersection of these lines at right angles forms a grid, making it impossible to pinpoint an exact location of any place using any two grip coordinates.

The **Eastern Hemisphere,** located between the North and South Poles and between the Prime Meridian (0 degrees longitude) east to the International Date Line at 180 degrees longitude, consists of most of Europe, all of Australia, most of Africa, and all of Asia, except for a tiny piece of the easternmost part of Russia that extends east of 180 degrees longitude.

The **Western Hemisphere,** located between the North and South Poles and between the Prime Meridian (0 degrees longitude) west to the International Date Line at 180 degrees longitude, consists of all of North and South America, a tiny part of the easternmost part of Russia that extends east of 180 degrees longitude, and a part of Europe that extends west of the Prime Meridian (0 degrees longitude).

The **Northern Hemisphere,** located between the North Pole and the Equator, contains all of the continents of Europe and North America and parts of South America, Africa, and most of Asia.

The **Southern Hemisphere,** located between the South Pole and the Equator, contains all of Australia, a small part of Asia, about one-third of Africa, most of South America, and all of Antarctica.

Of the **seven continents,** only one contains just one entire country and is the only island continent, **Australia.** Its political divisions consist of six states and one territory: Western Australia, South Australia, Tasmania, Victoria, New South Wales, Queensland, and Northern Territory.

Africa is made up of 54 separate countries, the major ones being Egypt, Nigeria, South Africa, Zaire, Kenya, Algeria, Morocco, and the large island of Madagascar.

Asia consists of 49 separate countries, some of which include China, Japan, India, Turkey, Israel, Iraq, Iran, Indonesia, Jordan, Vietnam, Thailand, and the Philippines.

Europe's 43 separate nations include France, Russia, Malta, Denmark, Hungary, Greece, Bosnia and Herzegovina.

North America consists of Canada and the United States of America and the island nations of the West Indies and the "land bridge" of Middle America, including Cuba, Jamaica, Mexico, Panama, and others.

Thirteen separate nations together occupy the continent of **South America,** among them such nations as Brazil, Paraguay, Ecuador, and Suriname.

The continent of **Antarctica** has no political boundaries or divisions but is the location of a number of science and research stations managed by nations such as Russia, Japan, France, Australia, and India.

Skill 1.5.d Be able to show an understanding of the relationship of geography to culture.

Social scientists use the term **culture** to describe the way of life of a group of people. This would include not only art, music, and literature but also beliefs, customs, languages, traditions, inventions--in short, any way of life whether complex or simple. The term geography is defined as the study of earth's features and living things as to their location, relationship with each other, how they came to be there, and why so important.

Physical geography is concerned with the locations of such earth features as climate, water, and land; how these relate to and affect each other and human activities; and what forces shaped and changed them. All three of these earth features affect the lives of all humans having a direct influence on what is made and produced, where it occurs, how it occurs, and what makes it possible. The combination of the different climate conditions and types of landforms and other surface features work together all around the earth to give the many varied cultures their unique characteristics and distinctions.

Cultural geography studies the location, characteristics, and influence of the physical environment on different cultures around the earth. Also included in these studies are comparisons and influences of the many varied cultures. Ease of travel and up-to-the-minute, state-of-the-art communication techniques ease the difficulties of understanding cultural differences making it easier to come in contact with them.

Competency 1.6 Understand concepts, terms, and theories related to human behavior and development.

Skill 1.6.a Be able to explain basic psychological concepts

PSYCHOLOGY involves scientifically studying behavior and mental processes. The ways people and animals relate to each other are observed and recorded. Psychologists scrutinize specific patterns, which will enable them to discern and predict certain behaviors, using scientific methods to verify their ideas. In this way they have been able to learn how to help people fulfill their individual human potential and strengthen understanding between individuals as well as groups and in nations and cultures. The results of the research of psychologists have deepened our understanding of the reasons for people's behavior.

Psychology is not only closely connected to the natural science of biology and the medical field of psychiatry but it is also connected to the social science areas of anthropology and sociology which have to do with people in society. Along with the sociologists and anthropologists, psychologists also study humans in their social settings, analyzing their attitudes and relationships. The disciplines of anthropology psychology, and sociology often research the same kinds of problems but from different points of view, with the emphasis in psychology on individual behavior, how an individual's actions are influenced by feelings and beliefs.

In their research, psychologists develop hypotheses, and then test them using the scientific method. These methods used in psychological research include:

(1) **naturalistic observation** which includes observing the behavior of animals and humans in their natural surroundings or environment

(2) **systematic assessment,** which describes assorted ways to measure the feelings, thoughts, and personality traits of people using case histories, public opinion polls or surveys, and standardized tests. These three types of assessments enable psychologists to acquire information not available through naturalistic observations

(3) **experimentation** enables psychologists to find and corroborate the cause-and-effect relationships in behavior, usually by randomly dividing the subjects into two groups: experimental group and control group

Competency 1.7 Understand concepts, terms, and theories related to the study of cultures, the structure and organization of human societies, and the process of social interaction.

Skill 1.7.a Be able to explain basic sociological concepts.

SOCIOLOGY is the study of human society: the individuals, groups, and institutions making up human society. It includes every feature of human social conditions. It deals with the predominant behaviors, attitudes, and types of relationships within a society, which is defined as a group of people with a similar cultural background living in a specific geographical area. Sociology is divided into five major areas of study:

1) Population studies: General social patterns of groups of people living in a certain
2) geographical area, Social behaviors: Changes in attitudes, morale, leadership,
3) conformity, and others,
4) Social institutions: Organized groups of people performing specific functions within a society such as churches, schools, hospitals, business organizations, and governments
5) Cultural influences: Including customs, knowledge, arts, religious beliefs, and language, and
6) Social change: Such as wars, revolutions, inventions, fashions, and other events or activities.

Sociologists use three major methods to test and verify theories:

(1) Surveys;
(2) Controlled experiments; and
(3) Field observation.

Skill 1.7.b Be able to explain basic anthropological concepts.

ANTHROPOLOGY is the scientific study of human culture and humanity, the relationship between man and his culture. Anthropologists study different groups, how they relate to other cultures, and patterns of behavior, similarities and differences. Their research is two-fold: cross-cultural and comparative. The major method of study is referred to as "participant observation." The anthropologist studies and learns about the people being studied by living among them and participating with them in their daily lives. Other methods may be used but this is the most characteristic method used.

Skill 1.7.c   Be able to explain basic archaeological concepts.

ARCHAEOLOGY is the scientific study of past human cultures by studying the remains they left behind--objects such as pottery, bones, buildings, tools, and artwork. Archaeologists locate and examine any evidence to help explain the way people lived in past times. They use special equipment and techniques to gather the evidence and make special effort to keep detailed records of their findings because a lot of their research results in destruction of the remains being studied. The first step is to locate an archaeological site using various methods. Next, surveying the site takes place starting with a detailed description of the site with notes, maps, photographs, and collecting artifacts from the surface. Excavating follows either by digging for buried objects or by diving and working in submersible decompression chambers, when underwater. They record and preserve the evidence for eventual classification, dating, and evaluating their find.

SUBAREA II: HISTORY COMMON CORE

Competency 2.1 Understand basic historical terms and concepts, comparative history, and the interpretive nature of history.

HISTORY is the study of the past, especially the aspects of the human past, political and economic events as well as cultural and social conditions. Students study history through textbooks, research, field trips to museums and historical sights, and other methods. Most nations set the requirements in history to study the country's heritage, usually to develop an awareness and feeling of loyalty and patriotism. History is generally divided into the three main divisions: (a) time periods, (b) nations, and (c) specialized topics. Study is accomplished through research, reading, and writing.

History is without doubt an integral part of every other discipline in the social sciences. Knowing historical background on anything and anyone anywhere goes a long way towards explaining that what happened in the past leads up to and explains the present.

Causality: The reason something happens, its cause, is a basic category of human thinking. We want to know the causes of some major event in our lives. Within the study of history, causality is the analysis of the reasons for change. The question we are asking is why and how a particular society or event developed in the particular way it did given the context in which it occurred.

Conflict: Conflict within history is opposition of ideas, principles, values or claims. Conflict may take the form of internal clashes of principles or ideas or claims within a society or group or it may take the form of opposition between groups or societies.

Bias: A prejudice or a predisposition either toward or against something. In the study of history, bias can refer to the persons or groups studied, in terms of a society's bias toward a particular political system, or it can refer to the historian's predisposition to evaluate events in a particular way.

Interdependence: A condition in which two things or groups rely upon one another; as opposed to independence, in which each thing or group relies only upon itself.

Identity: The state or perception of being a particular thing or person. Identity can also refer to the understanding or self-understanding of groups, nations, etc.

Nation-state: A particular type of political entity that provides a sovereign territory for a specific nation in which other factors also unites the citizens (e.g., language, race, ancestry, etc.).

Culture: the civilization, achievements, and customs of the people of a particular time and place.

Herodotus was the first major Greek historian who wrote the account of the wars between the Greeks and Persians; often called the "Father of History".

Thucydides wrote an authentic account of the war between Athens and Sparta titled "History of the Peloponnesian War".

Livy was a Roman historian who wrote "History from the Founding of the City".

Eusebius wrote "Ecclesiastical History", a history of Christianity showing God's control of human events.

Bede was the Middle Ages' greatest historian who wrote "Ecclesiastical History of the English Nation" (731 A.D.) and still considered the principal source for English history up to that time.

Ibn Khaldun was a great Arab historian who wrote a seven-volume study of world civilization entitled "Universal History".

Edward Gibbon was a British scholar who wrote the masterpiece "History of the Decline and Fall of the Roman Empire" which showed bias against Christianity and blamed Christianity partly for the fall of the Roman Empire.

Leopold von Ranke is considered the "Father of Modern History" who conceived the basic methods modern historians used to analyze and evaluate historical documents and introduced seminars to train future historians in how to do research.

Specialized fields of historical study include the following:

- Social history – the approach to the study of history that views a period of time through the eyes of everyday people and is focused on emerging trends.
- Archaeology: study of prehistoric and historic human cultures through the recovery, documentation and analysis of material remains and environmental data.
- Art History: the study of changes in and social context of art.
- Big History: study of history on a large scale across long time frames (since the Big Bang and up to the future) through a multi-disciplinary approach.
- Chronology: science of localizing historical events in time.
- Cultural history: the study of culture in the past.
- Diplomatic history: the study of international relations in the past.
- Economic History: the study of economies in the past.

Military History: the study of warfare and wars in history and what is sometimes considered to be a sub-branch of military history, Naval History.
- Paleography: study of ancient texts.
- Political history: the study of politics in the past.
- Psychohistory: study of the psychological motivations of historical events.
- Historiography of science: study of the structure and development of science.
- Social History: the study of societies in the past.
- World History: the study of history from a global perspective.

Varying perspectives on the study of history may be summarized by one of three definitions:

1. History is the study of what persons have done and said and thought in the past.
2. History is a creative attempt to reconstruct the lives and thoughts of particular persons who lived at specific times (biography).
3. History is the study of the social aspects of humans, both past and present.

The first definition essentially applies to the *narrative school of history*. This approach attempts to provide a general account of the most important things people have said, done, written, etc. in the past. Several schools fall within this category:

- The political-institutional school believes that what has occurred in government and law is the most important.
- The school of intellectual history (the history of ideas) finds greatest importance in the emergence of higher thought and feeling (including philosophy, art, science, literature).
- Economic historians are most concerned with the way humans have controlled the environment and made a living.
- Cultural historians focus on the development of ideas within the total context of a social, economic, and political situation.

The second definition above understands history as biography of important persons. These historians fall into one of two schools:

- Psychologizing approaches – historians who believe the motivations and actions of people in the past can be understood and explained in terms of modern psychological theories.
- Non-psychologizing approaches – historians who believe it is impossible to psychoanalyze people who are dead and that people of the past must be understood in terms of the theories of personality and motivation that were accepted at the time.

The third definition above essentially equates history with sociology. This approach believes it is possible to study history to observe forms of social change that are relevant to current social problems. This group is also divided:

- One group uses the Marxist doctrine of dialectical materialism to explain social change.
- Another group believes that each society is unique and distinctive.
- Comparative sociological historians study history to identify consistent patterns that run through all or several societies.

Competency 2.2   Understand major trends, key turning points, and the roles of influential individuals and groups in U.S. history.

Skill 2.2.a   Understand the importance and results of the Age of Exploration.

The Age of Exploration actually had its beginnings centuries before exploration actually took place. The rise and spread of Islam in the seventh century and its subsequent control over the holy city of Jerusalem led to the European so-called holy wars, the Crusades, to free Jerusalem and the Holy Land from this control. Even though, as a whole, the Crusades were not a success, those who survived and returned to their homes and countries in Western Europe brought back with them new products such as silks, spices, perfumes, new and different foods - luxuries unheard of that gave new meaning to colorless, drab, dull lives.

New ideas, new inventions, and new methods also went to Western Europe with the returning Crusaders and from these new influences was the intellectual stimulation which led to the period known as the Renaissance. Revival of interest in classical Greece led to increased interest in art, architecture, literature, science, astronomy, medicine and increased trade between Europe and Asia plus the invention of the printing press to give the spread of knowledge a big push was all that was needed to start exploring.

For many centuries, various mapmakers made many maps and charts, which in turn stimulated curiosity and the seeking of more knowledge. At the same time, the Chinese were using the magnetic compass in their sailings. Pacific islanders were going from island to island, covering thousands of miles in open canoes navigating by sun and stars. Arab traders were sailing all over the Indian Ocean in their dhows. The trade routes between Europe and Asia were slow, difficult, dangerous, and very expensive. Between sea voyages on the Indian Ocean and Mediterranean Sea and the camel caravans in central Asia and the Arabian Desert, the trade was still controlled by the Italian merchants in Genoa and Venice. It would take months and even years for the exotic luxuries of Asia to reach the markets of Western Europe. A faster, cheaper way had to be found. A way had to be found which would by-pass and end the control of the Italian merchants.

Prince Henry of Portugal (also called the Navigator) encouraged, supported, and financed the Portuguese seamen who led in the search for an all-water route to Asia. A shipyard was built along with a school teaching navigation. New types of sailing ships were built which would carry the seamen safely through the ocean waters. Experiments were conducted using newer maps, newer navigational methods, and newer instruments. These included the astrolabe and the compass enabling sailors to determine direction as well as latitude and longitude for exact location.

Although Prince Henry died in 1460, the Portuguese kept on, sailing along and exploring Africa's west coastline. In 1488, Bartholomew Diaz and his men sailed around Africa's southern tip and were headed toward Asia. Diaz wanted to push on but turned back because his men were discouraged and weary from the long months at sea, extremely fearful of the unknown, and just refusing to travel any further.

However, the Portuguese were finally successful ten years later in 1498 when Vasco da Gama and his men, continuing the route of Diaz, rounded Africa's Cape of Good Hope, sailing across the Indian Ocean, reaching India's port of Calicut (Calcutta). Although, six years earlier, Columbus had reached the New World and an entire hemisphere, da Gama had proved Asia could be reached from Europe by sea.

Of course, everyone knows that Columbus' first Trans-Atlantic voyage was to try to prove his theory or idea that Asia could be reached by sailing west. And to a certain extent, his idea was true. It could be done but only after figuring how to go around or across or through the landmass in between. Long after Spain dispatched explorers and her famed conquistadors to gather the wealth for the Spanish monarchs and their coffers, the British were searching valiantly for the "Northwest Passage," a land-sea route across North America and the eventual open sea to the wealth of Asia. It wasn't until after the Lewis and Clark Expedition when Captains Meriwether Lewis and William Clark proved conclusively that there simply was no Northwest Passage. It did not exist.

However, this did not deter exploration and settlement. **Spain, France, and England** along with some participation by the **Dutch** led the way with expanding Western European civilization in the New World. These three nations had strong monarchial governments and were struggling for dominance and power in Europe. With the defeat of Spain's mighty Armada in 1588, England became undisputed mistress of the seas. Spain lost its power and influence in Europe and it was left to France and England to carry on the rivalry, leading to eventual British control in Asia as well.

Spain's influence was in Florida, the Gulf Coast from Texas all the way west to California and south to the tip of South America and some of the islands of the West Indies. French control centered from New Orleans north to what is now northern Canada including the entire Mississippi Valley, the St. Lawrence Valley, the Great Lakes, and the land that was part of the Louisiana Territory. A few West Indies islands were also part of France's empire. England settled the eastern seaboard of North America, including parts of Canada and from Maine to Georgia. Some West Indies islands also came under British control. The Dutch had New Amsterdam for a period but later ceded it into British hands. One interesting aspect of all of this was that each of these nations, especially England, laid claim to land that extended partly or all the way across the continent, regardless of the fact that the others claimed the same land. The wars for dominance and control of power and influence in Europe would undoubtedly and eventually extend to the Americas, especially North America.

The importance of the Age of Exploration was not only the discovery and colonization of the New World, but also better maps and charts; new accurate navigational instruments; increased knowledge; great wealth; new and different foods and items not known in Europe; a new hemisphere as a refuge from poverty, persecution, a place to start a new and better life; and proof that Asia could be reached by sea and that the earth was round; ships and sailors would not sail off the edge of a flat earth and disappear forever into nothingness.

Skill 2.2.b   Know the significance of the Colonial Period.

The part of North America claimed by France was called New France and consisted of the land west of the Appalachian Mountains. This area of claims and settlement included the St. Lawrence Valley, the Great Lakes, the Mississippi Valley, and the entire region of land westward to the Rockies. They established the permanent settlements of Montreal and New Orleans, thus giving them control of the two major gateways into the heart of North America, the vast, rich interior. The St. Lawrence River, the Great Lakes, and the Mississippi River along with its tributaries made it possible for the French explorers and traders to roam at will, virtually unhindered in exploring, trapping, trading, and furthering the interests of France.

Most of the French settlements were in Canada along the St. Lawrence River. Only scattered forts and trading posts were found in the upper Mississippi Valley and Great Lakes region. The rulers of France originally intended New France to have vast estates owned by nobles and worked by peasants with the peasants living on the estates in compact farming villages--the New World version of the Old World's medieval system of feudalism. However, it didn't work out that way. Each of the nobles wanted his estate to be on the river for ease of transportation. The peasants working the estates wanted the prime waterfront location, also. The result of all this real estate squabbling was that New France's settled areas wound up mostly as a string of farmhouses stretching from Quebec to Montreal along the St. Lawrence and Richelieu Rivers.

In the non-settled areas in the interior were the **French fur traders.** They made friends with the friendly tribes of Indians, spending the winters with them getting the furs needed for trade. In the spring, they would return to Montreal in time to take advantage of trading their furs for the products brought by the cargo ships from France, which usually arrived at about the same time. Most of the wealth for New France and its "Mother Country" was from the fur trade, which provided a livelihood for many, many people. Manufacturers and workmen back in France, ship-owners and merchants, as well as the fur traders and their Indian allies all benefited. However, the freedom of roaming and trapping in the interior was a strong enticement for the younger, stronger men and resulted in the French not strengthening the areas settled along the St. Lawrence.

Into the 18th century, the rivalry with the British was getting stronger and stronger. New France was united under a single government and enjoyed the support of many Indian allies. The French traders were very diligent in not destroying the forests and driving away game upon which the Indians depended for life. It was difficult for the French to defend all of their settlements as they were scattered over half of the continent. However, by the early 1750s, in Western Europe, France was the most powerful nation. Its armies were superior to all others and its navy was giving the British stiff competition for control of the seas. The stage was set for confrontation in both Europe and America.

Spanish settlement had its beginnings in the Caribbean with the establishment of colonies on Hispaniola (at Santo Domingo which became the capital of the West Indies), Puerto Rico, and Cuba. There were a number of reasons for Spanish involvement in the Americas, to name just a few:

- the spirit of adventure
- the desire for land
- expansion of Spanish power, influence, and empire
- the desire for great wealth
- expansion of Roman Catholic influence and conversion of native peoples

The first permanent settlement in what is now the United States was in 1565 at **St. Augustine,** Florida. A later permanent settlement in the southwestern United States was in 1609 at Santa Fe, New Mexico. At the peak of Spanish power, the area in the United States claimed, settled, and controlled by Spain included Florida and all land west of the Mississippi River--quite a piece of choice real estate. Of course, France and England also lay claim to the same areas. Nonetheless, ranches and missions were built and the Indians who came in contact with the Spaniards were introduced to animals, plants, and seeds from the Old World that they had never seen before. Animals brought in included: horses, cattle, donkeys, pigs, sheep, goats, and poultry.

Barrels were cut in half and filled with earth to transport and transplant trees bearing:

> apples olives
> oranges lemons
> limes figs
> cherries apricots
> pears almonds
> walnuts

Even sugar cane and flowers made it to America along with bags bringing seeds of wheat, barley, rye, flax, lentils, rice, and peas.

All Spanish colonies belonged to the King of Spain. He was considered **an absolute monarch** with complete or absolute power and claimed rule by divine right, the belief being God had given him the right to rule and he answered only to God for his actions. His word was final, was the law. The people had no voice in government. The land, the people, the wealth all belonged to him to use as he pleased. He appointed personal representatives, or viceroys, to rule for him in his colonies. They ruled in his name with complete authority. Since the majority of them were friends and advisers, they were richly rewarded with land grants, gold and silver, privileges of trading, and the right to operate the gold and silver mines.

For the needed labor in the mines and on the plantations, Indians were used first as slaves. However, they either rapidly died out due to a lack of immunity from European diseases or escaped into nearby jungles or mountains. As a result, African slaves were brought in, especially to the islands of the West Indies. Some historians state that Latin American slavery was less harsh than in the later English colonies in North America.

Three reasons are given:

1. The following of a slave code based on ancient Roman laws;

2. The efforts of the Roman Catholic Church to protect and defend slaves because of efforts to convert them;

3. The lack of prejudice due to racial mixtures in of Spain controlled at one time by dark-skinned Moors from North Africa.

Regardless, slavery was still slavery and was very harsh--cruelly denying dignity and human worth and leading to desperate resistance.

Spain's control over her New World colonies lasted more than 300 years, longer than England or France. To this day, Spanish influence remains in names of places, art, architecture, music, literature, law, and cuisine. The Spanish settlements in North America were not commercial enterprises but were for protection and defense of the trading and wealth from their colonies in Mexico and South America. The Russians hunting seals came down the Pacific coast; the English moved into Florida and west into and beyond the Appalachians; and the French traders and trappers were making their way from Louisiana and other parts of New France into Spanish territory. The Spanish never realized or understood that self-sustaining economic development and colonial trade was so important. Consequently, the Spanish settlements in the U.S. never really prospered.

The nation had only itself to blame for this. The treasure and wealth found in Spanish New World colonies went back to Spain to be used to buy whatever goods and products were needed instead of setting up industries to make what was needed. As the amount of gold and silver was depleted, Spain could not pay for the goods needed and was unable to produce goods for themselves. Also, at the same time, Spanish treasure ships at sea were being seized by English and Dutch "pirates" taking the wealth to the coffers of their own countries.

Before 1763, when England was rapidly on the way to becoming the most powerful of the three major Western European powers, its thirteen colonies, located between the Atlantic Ocean and the Appalachian Mountains, physically occupied the least amount of land. Moreover, it is interesting that even before the Spanish Armada was defeated, two Englishmen, Sir Humphrey Gilbert and his half-brother Sir Walter Raleigh were unsuccessful in their attempts to build successful permanent colonies in the New World.

Nonetheless, the thirteen English colonies were successful and, by the time they had gained their independence from Britain, were more than able to govern themselves. They had a rich historical heritage of law, tradition, and documents leading the way to constitutional government conducted according to laws and customs. The settlers in the British colonies highly valued individual freedom, democratic government, and getting ahead through hard work.

The English colonies, with only a few exceptions, were considered commercial ventures to make a profit for the crown or the company or whoever financed its beginnings. One was strictly a philanthropic enterprise and three others were primarily for religious reasons but the other nine were started for economic reasons. Settlers in these unique colonies came for different reasons:

- religious freedom
- political freedom
- economic prosperity
- land ownership

The colonies were divided generally into the three regions of New England, Middle Atlantic, and Southern. The culture of each was distinct and affected attitudes, ideas towards politics, religion, and economic activities. The geography of each region also contributed to its unique characteristics.

The **New England colonies** consisted of Massachusetts, Rhode Island, Connecticut, and New Hampshire. Life in these colonies was centered on the towns. What farming was done was by each family on its own plot of land but a short summer growing season and limited amount of good soil gave rise to other economic activities such as manufacturing, fishing, shipbuilding, and trade. The vast majority of the settlers shared similar origins, coming from England and Scotland. Towns were carefully planned and laid out the same way. The form of government was the town meeting where all adult males met to make the laws. The legislative body, the General Court, consisted of an upper and lower house.

The **Middle or Middle Atlantic colonies** included New York, New Jersey, Pennsylvania, Delaware, and Maryland. New York and New Jersey were at one time the Dutch colony of New Netherland and Delaware at one time was New Sweden. These five colonies, from their beginnings were considered "melting pots" with settlers from many different nations and backgrounds. The main economic activity was farming with the settlers scattered over the countryside cultivating rather large farms. The Indians were not as much of a threat as in New England so they did not have to settle in small farming villages. The soil was very fertile, the land was gently rolling, and a milder climate provided a longer growing season.

These farms produced a large surplus of food, not only for the colonists themselves but also for sale. This colonial region became known as the "breadbasket" of the New World and the New York and Philadelphia seaports were constantly filled with ships being loaded with meat, flour, and other foodstuffs for the West Indies and England.

There were other economic activities such as shipbuilding, iron mines, and factories producing paper, glass, and textiles. The legislative body in Pennsylvania was unicameral or consisted of one house. In the other four colonies, the legislative body had two houses. Also units of local government were in counties and towns.

The **Southern colonies** were Virginia, North and South Carolina, and Georgia. Virginia was the first permanent successful English colony and Georgia was the last. The year 1619 was a very important year in the history of Virginia and the United States with three very significant events. First, sixty women were sent to Virginia to marry and establish families; second, twenty Africans, the first of thousands, arrived; and third, most importantly, the Virginia colonists were granted the right to self-government and they began by electing their own representatives to the House of Burgesses, their own legislative body.

The major economic activity in this region was farming. Here too the soil was very fertile and the climate was very mild with an even longer growing season. The large plantations eventually requiring large numbers of slaves were found in the coastal or tidewater areas. Although the wealthy slave-owning planters set the pattern of life in this region, most of the people lived inland away from coastal areas. They were small farmers and very few, it any, owned slaves.

The settlers in these four colonies came from diverse backgrounds and cultures. Virginia was colonized mostly by people from England while Georgia was started as a haven for debtors from English prisons. Pioneers from Virginia settled in North Carolina while South Carolina welcomed people from England and Scotland, French Protestants, Germans, and emigrants from islands in the West Indies. Products from farms and plantations included rice, tobacco, indigo, cotton, some corn and wheat. Other economic activities included lumber and naval stores (tar, pitch, rosin, and turpentine) from the pine forests and fur trade on the frontier. Cities such as Savannah and Charleston were important seaports and trading centers.

In the colonies, the daily life of the colonists differed greatly between the coastal settlements and the inland or interior. The Southern planters and the people living in the coastal cities and towns had a way of life similar to that of towns in England. The influence was seen and heard in the way people dressed and talked; the architectural styles of houses and public buildings; and the social divisions or levels of society. Both the planters and city dwellers enjoyed an active social life and had strong emotional ties to England.
On the other hand, life inland on the frontier had marked differences. All facets of daily living--clothing, food, home, economic and social activities--were all connected to what was needed to sustain life and survive in the wilderness.

Everything was produced practically themselves. They were self-sufficient and extremely individualistic and independent. There were little, if any, levels of society or class distinctions as they considered themselves to be the equal to all others, regardless of station in life. The roots of equality, independence, individual rights and freedoms were extremely strong and well developed. People were not judged by their fancy dress, expensive house, eloquent language, or titles following their names.

The colonies had from 1607 to 1763 to develop, refine, practice, experiment, and experience life in a rugged, uncivilized land. The Mother Country had virtually left them on their own to take care of themselves all that time. So when in 1763 Britain decided she needed to regulate and "mother" the "little ones," to her surprise, she had a losing fight on her hands.

Skill 2.2.c   Explain the crucial effects of the period of the American Revolution.

By the 1750s in Europe, Spain was "out of the picture," no longer the most powerful nation and not even a contender. The remaining rivalry was between Britain and France. For nearly 25 years, between 1689 and 1748, a series of "armed conflicts" involving these two powers had been taking place. These conflicts had spilled over into North America. The War of the League of Augsburg in Europe, 1689 to 1697, had been King William's War. The War of the Spanish Succession, 1702 to 1713, had been Queen Anne's War. The War of the Austrian Succession, 1740 to 1748, was called King George's War in the colonies. The two nations fought for possession of colonies, especially in Asia and North America, and for control of the seas, but none of these conflicts was decisive.

The final conflict, which decided once and for all who was the most powerful, began in North America in 1754, in the Ohio River Valley. It was known in America as the French and Indian War and in Europe as the Seven Years War, since it began there in 1756. In America, both sides had advantages and disadvantages. The British colonies were well established and consolidated in a smaller area. British colonists outnumbered French colonists 23 to 1. Except for a small area in Canada, French settlements were scattered over a much larger area (roughly half of the continent) and were smaller. However, the French settlements were united under one government and were quick to act and cooperate when necessary.
In addition, the French had many more Indian allies than the British. The British colonies had separate, individual governments and very seldom cooperated, even when needed. In Europe, at that time, France was the more powerful of the two nations.

Both sides had stunning victories and humiliating defeats. If there was one person who could be given the credit for British victory, it would have to be William Pitt. He was a strong leader, enormously energetic, supremely self-confident, and determined on a complete British victory. Despite the advantages and military victories of the French, Pitt succeeded. In the army he got rid of the incompetents and replaced them with men who could do the job. He sent more troops to America, strengthened the British navy, gave to the officers of the colonial militias equal rank to the British officers - in short, he saw to it that Britain took the offensive and kept it to victory. Of all the British victories, perhaps the most crucial and important was winning Canada.

The French depended on the St. Lawrence River for transporting supplies, soldiers, and messages-the link between New France and the Mother Country. Tied into this waterway system was the connecting links of the Great Lakes, Mississippi River and its tributaries along which were scattered French forts, trading posts, and small settlements. When, in 1758, the British captured Louisburg on Cape Breton Island, New France was doomed. Louisburg gave the British navy a base of operations preventing French reinforcements and supplies getting to their troops. Other forts fell to the British: Frontenac, Duquesne, Crown Point, Ticonderoga, Niagara, those in the upper Ohio Valley, and, most importantly, Quebec and finally Montreal. Spain entered the war in 1762 to aid France but it was too late. British victories occurred all around the world: in India, in the Mediterranean, and in Europe.

In 1763 in Paris, Spain, France, and Britain met to draw up the Treaty. Great Britain got most of India and all of North America east of the Mississippi River, except for New Orleans. Britain received from Spain control of Florida and returned to Spain Cuba and the islands of the Philippines, taken during the war. France lost nearly all of its possessions in America and India and was allowed to keep four islands: Guadeloupe, Martinique, Haiti on Hispaniola, and Miquelon and St. Pierre. France gave Spain New Orleans and the vast territory of Louisiana, west of the Mississippi River. Britain was now the most powerful nation--period.

Where did all of this leave the British colonies? Their colonial militias had fought with the British and they too benefited. The militias and their officers gained much experience in fighting which was very valuable later. The thirteen colonies began to realize that cooperating with each other was the only way to defend themselves. They didn't really understand that, until the war for independence and setting up a national government, but a start had been made. At the start of the war in 1754, Benjamin Franklin proposed to the thirteen colonies that they unite permanently to be able to defend themselves. This was after the French and their Indian allies had defeated Major George Washington and his militia at Fort Necessity. This left the entire northern frontier of the British colonies vulnerable and open to attack.

Delegates from seven of the thirteen colonies met at Albany, New York, along with the representatives from the Iroquois Confederation and British officials. Franklin's proposal, known as the Albany Plan of Union, was totally rejected by the colonists, along with a similar proposal from the British. They simply did not want each of the colonies to lose its right to act independently. However, the seed was planted.

The war for independence occurred due to a number of changes, the two most important ones being economic and political. By the end of the French and Indian War in 1763, Britain's American colonies were thirteen out of a total of thirty-three scattered around the earth. Like all other countries, Britain strove for having a strong economy and a favorable balance of trade. To have that delicate balance a nation needs wealth, self-sufficiency, and a powerful army and navy. This is where the overseas colonies appeared. They would provide raw materials for the industries in the Mother Country, be a market for the finished products by buying them and assist the Mother Country in becoming powerful and strong (as in the case of Great Britain) by having a strong merchant fleet which would be a school for training for the Royal Navy and provide places as bases of operation for the Royal Navy.

The foregoing explained the major reason for British encouragement and support of colonization, especially in North America. So between 1607 and 1763, at various times for various reasons, the British Parliament enacted different laws to assist the government in getting and keeping this trade balance. One series of laws required that most of the manufacturing be done only in England, such as: prohibition of exporting any wool or woolen cloth from the colonies, no manufacture of beaver hats or iron products. The colonists weren't concerned as they had no money and no highly skilled labor to set up any industries, anyway.

The Navigation Acts of 1651 put restrictions on shipping and trade within the British Empire by requiring that it was allowed only on British ships. This increased the strength of the British merchant fleet and greatly benefited the American colonists. Since they were British citizens, they could have their own vessels, building and operating them as well. By the end of the war in 1763, the shipyards in the colonies were building one third of the merchant ships under the British flag. There were quite a number of wealthy, American, colonial merchants.

The Navigation Act of 1660 restricted the shipment and sale of colonial products to England only. In 1663 another Navigation Act stipulated that the colonies had to buy manufactured products only from England and that any European goods going to the colonies had to go to England first. These acts were a protection from enemy ships and pirates and from competition from European rivals.

The New England and Middle Atlantic colonies felt threatened by these laws as they had started producing many of the products already being produced in Britain. But they soon found new markets for their goods and began what was known as a "triangular trade." Colonial vessels started the first part of the triangle by sailing for Africa loaded with kegs of rum from colonial distilleries. On Africa's West Coast, the rum was traded for either gold or slaves. The second part of the triangle was from Africa to the West Indies where slaves were traded for molasses, sugar, or money. The third part of the triangle was home, bringing sugar or molasses (to make more rum), gold, and silver.

The major concern of the British government was that the trade violated the 1733 Molasses Act. Planters had wanted the colonists to buy all of their molasses in the British West Indies but these islands could give the traders only about one eighth of the amount of molasses needed for distilling the rum. The colonists were forced to buy the rest of what they needed from the French, Dutch, and Spanish islands, thus evading the law by not paying the high duty on the molasses bought from these islands. If Britain had enforced the Molasses Act, economic and financial chaos and ruin would have occurred. Nevertheless, for this act and all the other mercantile laws, the government followed the policy of "salutary neglect," deliberately failing to enforce the laws.

In 1763, after the war, money was needed to pay the British war debt, for the defense of the empire, and to pay for the governing of 33 colonies scattered around the earth. It was decided to adopt a new colonial policy and pass laws to raise revenue. After all, it was reasoned, the colonists were subjects of the king and since the king and his ministers had spent a great deal of money defending and protecting them (this especially for the American colonists), it was only right and fair that the colonists should help pay the costs of defense, especially theirs. The earlier laws passed had been for the purposes of regulating production and trade which generally put money into colonial pockets. These new laws would take some of that rather hard-earned money out of their pockets and it would be done, in colonial eyes, unjustly and illegally.

Before 1763, except for trade and supplying raw materials, the colonies had been left pretty much to themselves. England looked on them merely as part of an economic or commercial empire. Little consideration was given as to how they were to conduct their daily affairs, so the colonists became very independent, self-reliant, and extremely skillful at handling those daily affairs. This, in turn, gave rise to leadership, initiative, achievement, and vast experience. In fact, there was a far greater degree of independence and self-government in the British colonies in America than could be found in Britain or the major countries on the Continent or any other colonies anywhere. There were a number of reasons for this:

1. The religious and scriptural teachings of previous centuries put forth the worth of the individual and equality in God's sight. Keep in mind that freedom of worship and freedom from religious persecution were major reasons to live in the New World.
2. European Protestants, especially Calvinists, believed and taught the idea that government originates from those governed, that rulers are required to protect individual rights and that the governed have the right and privilege to choose their rulers.
3. Trading companies put into practice the principle that their members had the right to make the decisions and shape the policies affecting their lives.
4. The colonists believed and supported the idea that a person's property should not be taken without his consent, based on that treasured English document, Magna Carta, and English common law.
5. From about 1700 to 1750, population increases in America came about through immigration and generations and generations of descendants of the original settlers. The immigrants were mainly Scots-Irish who hated the English, Germans who cared nothing about England, and black slaves who knew nothing about England. The descendants of the original settlers had never been out of America at any time.

6. In America, as new towns and counties were formed, there began the practice' of representation in government. Representatives to the colonial legislative assemblies were elected from the district in which they lived, chosen by qualified property-owning male voters, and representing the interests of the political district from which they were elected. One thing to remember: each of the 13 colonies had a royal governor appointed by the king, representing his interests in the colonies. Nevertheless, the colonial legislative assemblies controlled the purse strings having the power to vote on all issues involving money to be spent by the colonial governments.

Contrary to this was the governmental set-up in England. Members of Parliament were not elected to represent their own districts. They were considered representative of classes, not individuals. If some members of a professional or commercial class or some landed interests were able to elect representatives, then those classes or special interests were represented. It had nothing at all to do with numbers or territories. Some large population centers had no direct representation at all, yet the people there considered themselves represented by men elected from their particular class or interest somewhere else. Consequently, it was extremely difficult for the English to understand why the American merchants and landowners claimed they were not represented because they themselves did not vote for members of Parliament.

The colonists' protest of "no taxation without representation" was meaningless to the English. Parliament represented the entire nation, was completely unlimited in legislation, and had become supreme; and the colonists were incensed at the English attitude of "of course you have representation--everyone does." The colonists considered their colonial legislative assemblies equal to Parliament, totally unacceptable in England, of course. There were two different environments of the older traditional British system in the Mother Country and in America, new ideas and different ways of doing things. In a new country, a new environment has little or no tradition, institutions or vested interests. New ideas and traditions grew extremely fast pushing aside what was left of the old ideas and old traditions. By 1763, Britain had changed its perception of its American colonies to their being a "territorial" empire. The stage was set and the conditions were right for a showdown.

It all began in 1763 when Parliament decided to have a standing army in North America to reinforce British control. In 1765, the Quartering Act was passed requiring the colonists to provide supplies and living quarters for the British troops. In addition, efforts by the British were made to keep the peace by establishing good relations with the Indians. Consequently, a proclamation was issued which prohibited any American colonists from making any settlements west of the Appalachians until provided for through treaties with the Indians. The Sugar Act of 1764 required efficient collection of taxes on any molasses that were brought into the colonies and gave British officials free license to conduct searches of the premises of anyone suspected of violating the law. The colonists were taxed on newspapers, legal documents, and other printed matter under the Stamp Act of 1765. Although a stamp tax was already in use in England, the colonists would have none of it and after the ensuing uproar of rioting and mob violence, Parliament repealed the tax.

Of course, great exultation, jubilance, and wild joy resulted when news of the repeal reached America. However, what no one noticed was the small, quiet Declaratory Act attached to the repeal. This act plainly, unequivocally stated that Parliament still had the right to make all laws for the colonies and denied their right to be taxed only by their own colonial legislatures--a very crucial, important piece of legislation but virtually overlooked and unnoticed at the time. Other acts leading up to armed conflict included the Townshend Acts passed in 1767 taxing lead, paint, paper, and tea brought into the colonies. This really increased anger and tension resulting in the British sending troops to New York City and Boston.

In Boston, mob violence provoked retaliation by the troops thus bringing about the deaths of five people and the wounding of eight others. The so-called Boston Massacre shocked Americans and British alike. Subsequently, in 1770, Parliament voted to repeal all the provisions of the Townshend Acts with the exception of the tea tax. In 1773, the tax on tea sold by the British East India Company was substantially reduced, fueling colonial anger once more. This gave the company an unfair trade advantage and forcibly reminded the colonists of the British right to tax them. Merchants refused to sell the tea; colonists refused to buy and drink it; and a shipload of it was dumped into Boston Harbor--a most violent Tea Party.

In 1774, the passage of the Quebec Act extended the limits of that Canadian colony's boundary southward to include territory located north of the Ohio River. However, the punishment for Boston's Tea Party came in the same year with the Intolerable Acts. Boston's port was closed; the royal governor of the colony of Massachusetts was given increased power, and the colonists were compelled to house and feed the British soldiers. The propaganda activities of the patriot organizations Sons of Liberty and Committees of Correspondence kept the opposition and resistance before everyone. Delegates from twelve colonies met in Philadelphia September 5, 1774, in the First Continental Congress. They definitely opposed acts of lawlessness and wanted some form of peaceful settlement with Britain. They maintained American loyalty to the Mother Country and affirmed Parliament's power over colonial foreign affairs.

They insisted on repeal of the Intolerable Acts and demanded ending all trade with Britain until this took place. The reply from George III, last king of America, was an insistence of colonial submission to British rule or be crushed. With the start of the Revolutionary War April 19, 1775, the Second Continental Congress began meeting in Philadelphia May 10 that year to conduct the business of war and government for the next six years.

Interestingly, one historian explained that the British were interested only in raising money to pay war debts, regulate the trade and commerce of the colonies, and look after business and financial interests between the Mother Country and the rest of her empire. The establishment of overseas colonies was first and foremost a commercial enterprise, not a political one. The political aspect was secondary and assumed. The British took it for granted that Parliament was supreme, was recognized so by the colonists, and were very resentful of the colonial challenge to Parliament's authority. They were contemptuously indifferent to politics in America and had no wish to exert any control over it but as resistance and disobedience swelled and increased in America, the British increased their efforts to punish them and put them in their place.

The British had been extremely lax and totally inconsistent in enforcement of the mercantile or trade laws passed in the years before 1754. The government itself was not particularly stable so actions against the colonies occurred in anger and their attitude was one of a moral superiority, that they knew how to manage America better than the Americans did themselves. This of course points to a lack of sufficient knowledge of conditions and opinions in America.

The colonists had been left on their own for nearly 150 years and by the time the Revolutionary War began, they were quite adept at self-government and adequately handling the affairs of their daily lives, with no one looking over their shoulders telling them how and what to do. The Americans equated ownership of land or property with the right to vote. Property was considered the foundation of life and liberty and, in the colonial mind and tradition, these went together.

Therefore when an indirect tax on tea was made, the British felt that since it wasn't a direct tax, there should be no objection to it. The colonists viewed any tax, direct or indirect, as an attack on their property. They felt that as a representative body, the British Parliament should protect British citizens, including the colonists, from arbitrary taxation. Since they felt they were not represented, Parliament, in their eyes, gave them no protection. So, war began. August 23, 1775, George III declared that the colonies were in rebellion and warned them to stop or else.

By 1776, the colonists and their representatives in the Second Continental Congress realized that things were past the point of no return. The Declaration of Independence was drafted and declared July 4, 1776. George Washington labored against tremendous odds to wage a victorious war. The turning point in the Americans' favor occurred in 1777 with the American victory at Saratoga. This victory decided for the French to align themselves with the Americans against the British. With the aid of Admiral deGrasse and French warships blocking the entrance to Chesapeake Bay, British General Cornwallis trapped at Yorktown, Virginia, surrendered in 1781 and the war was over. The Treaty of Paris officially ending the war was signed in 1783.

During the war, and after independence was declared, the former colonies now found themselves independent states. The Second Continental Congress was conducting a war with representation by delegates from thirteen separate states. The Congress had no power to act for the states or to require them to accept and follow its wishes. A permanent united government was desperately needed. On November 15, 1777, the Articles of Confederation were adopted, creating a league of free and independent states.

The central government of the new United States of America consisted of a Congress of two to seven delegates from each state with each state having just one vote. The government under the Articles solved some of the postwar problems but had serious weaknesses. Some of its powers included: borrowing and coining money, directing foreign affairs, declaring war and making peace, building and equipping a navy, regulating weights and measures, asking the states to supply men and money for an army. The delegates to Congress had no real authority as each state carefully and jealously guarded its own interests and limited powers under the Articles.
Also, the delegates to Congress were paid by their states and had to vote as directed by their state legislatures. The serious weaknesses were the lack of power: to regulate finances, over interstate trade, over foreign trade, to enforce treaties, and military power. Something better and more efficient was needed.

In May of 1787, delegates from all states except Rhode Island began meeting in Philadelphia. At first, they met to revise the Articles of Confederation as instructed by Congress; but they soon realized that much more was needed. Abandoning the instructions, they set out to write a new Constitution, a new document, the foundation of all government in the United States and a model for representative government throughout the world.

The first order of business was the agreement among all the delegates that the convention would be kept secret. No discussion of the convention outside of the meeting room would be allowed. They wanted to be able to discuss, argue, and agree among themselves before presenting the completed document to the American people. They were afraid that if the people were aware of what was taking place before it was completed, the entire country would be plunged into argument and dissension and that it would be extremely difficult, if not impossible, to settle differences and come to an agreement. Between the official notes kept and the complete notes of future President James Madison, an accurate picture of the events of the Convention is part of the historical record.

The delegates went to Philadelphia representing different areas and different interests. They all agreed on a strong central government but not one with unlimited powers. They also agreed that no one section or part of government could control the rest. It would be a republican form of government (sometimes referred to as representative democracy) in which the supreme power was in the hands of the voters who would elect the men who would govern for them.

One of the first serious controversies involved the small states versus the large states over representation in Congress. Virginia's Governor Edmund Randolph proposed that state population determined the number of representatives sent to Congress, also known as the Virginia Plan. New Jersey delegate William Paterson countered with what is known as the New Jersey Plan, each state having equal representation.

After much argument and debate, the Great Compromise was devised, known also as the Connecticut Compromise, as proposed by Roger Sherman. It was agreed that Congress would have two houses. The Senate would have two Senators, giving equal powers in the Senate. The House of Representatives would have its members elected based on each state's population. Both houses could draft bills to debate and vote on with the exception of bills pertaining to money, which must originate in the House of Representatives.

Another major controversy involved economic differences between North and South. One concerned the counting of the African slaves for determining representation in the House of Representatives. The southern delegates wanted this but didn't want it to apply to determining taxes to be paid. The northern delegates argued the opposite: count the slaves for taxes but not for representation.

The resulting agreement was known as the "three-fifths" compromise. Three-fifths of the slaves would be counted for both taxes and determining representation in the House.

The last major compromise, also between North and South, was the Commerce Compromise. The economic interests of the northern part of the country were ones of industry and business whereas the south's economic interests were primarily in farming. The northern merchants wanted the government to regulate and control commerce with foreign nations and with the states. Of course, southern planters opposed this idea as they felt that any tariff laws passed would be unfavorable to them. The acceptable compromise to this dispute was that Congress was given the power to regulate commerce with other nations and the states, including levying tariffs on imports. However, Congress did not have the power to levy tariffs on any exports. This increased southern concern about the effect this would have on the slave trade. The delegates finally agreed that the importation of slaves would continue for 20 more years with no interference from Congress. Any import tax could not exceed 10 dollars per person. After 1808, Congress would be able to decide whether to prohibit or regulate any further importation of slaves.

Of course, when work was completed and the document was presented, nine states needed to approve for it to go into effect. There was no little amount of discussion, arguing, debating, and haranguing. The opposition had three major objections: the states seemed as if they were being asked to surrender too much power to the national government; the voters did not have enough control and influence over the men who would be elected by them to run the government; and a lack of a "bill of rights" guaranteeing hard-won individual freedoms and liberties.

Eleven states finally ratified the document and the new national government went into effect. It was no small feat that the delegates were able to produce a workable document that satisfied all opinions, feelings, and viewpoints. The separation of powers of the three branches of government and the built-in system of checks and balances to keep power balanced were a stroke of genius. It provided for the individuals and the states as well as an organized central authority to keep a new inexperienced young nation on track. They created a system of government so flexible that it had continued in its basic form to this day.

In 1789, the Electoral College unanimously elected George Washington as the first President and the new nation was on its way.

Skill 2.2.d   Understand how the new nation developed from 1791 to 1860.

Beginning with Washington's election to the Presidency in 1791 to the election of Abraham Lincoln in 1860, the United States had expanded to the boundaries of today's 48 conterminous states. During that 69-year period, four wars were fought: the War of 1812 with Great Britain, the war with the Barbary pirates in the Mediterranean, the war with Mexico, and the Seminole wars in Florida. Domestically, by 1860, the nation had had 15 presidents (Lincoln was the 16th), had greatly increased its area, established and strengthened the federal court system, saw the beginnings of and increased influence of political parties, the first and second U.S. banks, economic "panics" or depressions, the abolition movement, the controversies and turmoil leading to the Civil War. There were 33 states in the Union by 1860.

Territorial expansion began in 1783 with the signing of the Treaty of Paris ending the Revolutionary War. According to the terms of the treaty, the land gained by the Americans was all of the land between the Appalachian Mountains and the Mississippi River; from the Great Lakes to the Florida boundary. Nine additional states were formed from this area alone.

The next large territorial gain was under President Thomas Jefferson in 1803. In 1800, Napoleon Bonaparte of France secured the Louisiana Territory from Spain, who had held it since 1792. The vast area stretched westward from the Mississippi River to the Rocky Mountains as well as northward to Canada. An effort was made to keep the transaction a secret but the news reached the U.S. State Department. The U.S. didn't have any particular problem with Spanish control of the territory since Spain was weak and did not pose a threat. However, it was different with France. Though not the world power that Great Britain was, nonetheless France was still strong and, under Napoleon's leadership, was again acquiring an empire. President Jefferson had three major reasons for concern:

a.   With the French controlling New Orleans at the mouth of the Mississippi River, as well as the Gulf of Mexico, westerners would lose their "right of deposit" which would greatly affect their ability to trade. This was very important to the Americans who were living in the area between the river and the Appalachians. They were unable to get heavy products to eastern markets but had to float them on rafts down the Ohio and Mississippi Rivers to New Orleans to ships heading to Europe or the Atlantic coast ports. If France prohibited this; it would be a financial disaster.

b.   President Jefferson also worried that if the French possessed the Louisiana Territory; America would be extremely limited in its expansion into its interior.

c. Under Napoleon Bonaparte, France was becoming more powerful and aggressive and this would be a constant worry and threat to the western border of the U.S. President Jefferson was very interested in the western part of the country and firmly believed that it was both necessary and desirable to strengthen western lands. So Jefferson wrote to the American minister to Paris, Robert R. Livingston, to make an offer to Napoleon for New Orleans and West Florida, as much as $10 million for the two. Napoleon countered the offer with the question of how much the U.S. would be willing to pay for all of Louisiana. After some discussion, it was agreed to pay $15 million and the largest land transaction in history was negotiated in 1803, resulting in the eventual formation of 15 states.

In 1804, the United States engaged in the first of a series of armed conflicts with the Barbary pirates of North Africa. The Moslem rulers of Morocco, Algiers, Tunis, and Tripoli, the Barbary States of North Africa, had long been seizing ships of nations that were Christian and demanding ransoms for the crews. The Christian nations of Europe decided it was cheaper and easier to pay annually a tribute or bribe. The U.S. had been doing this since 1783 with the beginnings of trade between the Mediterranean countries and the newly independent nation. When the rulers in Tripoli demanded a ridiculously exorbitant bribe and chopped down the flagpole of the American consulate there, Jefferson had had enough. The first skirmish against Tripoli in 1804 and 1805 was successful. In 1815, the payment of bribes to the rulers ceased after the War of 1812 ended. The Americans could trade and sail freely in the Mediterranean.

United States' unintentional and accidental involvement in what was known as the War of 1812 came about due to the political and economic struggles between France and Great Britain. Napoleon's goal was complete conquest and control of Europe, including and especially Great Britain. Although British troops were temporarily driven off the mainland of Europe, the navy still controlled the seas, the seas across which France had to bring the products needed. America traded with both nations, especially with France and its colonies.

The British decided to destroy the American trade with France, mainly for two reasons: (a) Products and goods from the U.S. gave Napoleon what he needed to keep up his struggle with Britain. He and France was the enemy and it was felt that the Americans were aiding the Mother Country's enemy. (b) Britain felt threatened by the increasing strength and success of the U.S. merchant fleet. They were becoming major competitors with the ship owners and merchants in Britain.

The British issued the Orders in Council which were a series of measures prohibiting American ships from entering any French ports, not only in Europe but also in India and the West Indies. At the same time, Napoleon began efforts for a coastal blockade of the British Isles. He issued a series of Orders prohibiting all nations, including the United States, from trading with the British. And he didn't stop there. He threatened seizure of every ship entering any French ports after they stopped at any British port or British colony, even threatening to seize every ship inspected by British cruisers or that paid any duties to their government. Adding to all of this, the British were stopping American ships and seizing, or impressing, American seamen to service on British ships. Americans were outraged.

In 1807, Congress passed the Embargo Act, forbidding American ships from sailing to foreign ports. It couldn't be completely enforced and it really hurt business and trade in America so, in 1809, it was repealed. Two additional acts passed by Congress after James Madison became president attempted to regulate trade with other nations and to get Britain and France to remove all the restrictions they had put on American shipping. The catch was that whichever nation removed restrictions, the U.S. agreed not to trade with the other one. Clever Napoleon was the first to do this, prompting Madison to issue orders prohibiting trade with Britain, ignoring warnings from the British not to do so. Of course, this didn't work either and although Britain eventually rescinded the Orders in Council, war came in June of 1812 and ended Christmas Eve, 1814, with the signing of the Treaty of Ghent.

During the war, Americans were divided over not only whether or not it was necessary to even fight but also over what territories should be fought for and taken. The nation was still young and just not prepared for war. The primary American objective was to conquer Canada but it failed. Two naval and one military victories stand out for the U.S. Oliver Perry gained control of Lake Erie and Thomas Macdonough fought on Lake Champlain, both of these naval battles successfully preventing the British invasion of the United States from Canada. Nevertheless, the troops did land below Washington on the Potomac, marched into the city, and burned the public buildings, including the White House.

Andrew Jackson's victory at New Orleans was a great morale booster to Americans, giving them the impression the U.S. had won the war. The battle actually took place after Britain and the United States had reached an agreement but it had no impact on the war's outcome.

The peace treaty did little for the United States other than bringing peace, releasing prisoners of war, restoring all occupied territory, and setting up a commission to settle boundary disputes with Canada. Interestingly, the war proved to be a turning point in American history.

European events had profoundly shaped U.S. policies, especially foreign policies. After 1815, the U.S. became much more independent from European influence and began to be treated with growing respect by European nations who were impressed by the fact that the young United States showed no hesitancy in going to war with the world's greatest naval power.

The Red River cession was the next acquisition of land and came about as part of a treaty with Great Britain in 1818. It included parts of North and South Dakota and Minnesota. In 1819, Florida, both east and West, was ceded to the U.S. by Spain along with parts of Alabama, Mississippi, and Louisiana. Texas was annexed in 1845 and after the war with Mexico in 1848, the government paid $15 million for what would become the states of California, Utah, and Nevada and parts of four other states.

In 1846, the Oregon Country was ceded to the U.S., which extended the western border to the Pacific Ocean. The northern U.S. boundary was established at the 49th parallel. The states of Idaho, Oregon, and Washington were formed from this territory. In 1853, the Gadsden Purchase rounded out the present boundary of the 48 conterminous states with payment to Mexico of $10 million for land that makes up the present states of New Mexico and Arizona.

In domestic affairs of the new nation, the first problems dealt with finances-- paying for the war debts of the Revolutionary War and other financial needs. Secretary of the Treasury Alexander Hamilton wanted the government to increase tariffs and put taxes on certain products made in the U.S., for example, liquor. This money in turn would be used to pay war debts of the federal government as well as those of the states. There would be money available for expenses and needed internal improvements.

To provide for this, Hamilton favored a national bank. Secretary of State Thomas Jefferson, along with southern supporters, opposed many of Hamilton's suggested plans. Later, Jefferson relented and gave support to some proposals in return for Hamilton and his northern supporters agreeing to locate the nation's capital in the South. Jefferson continued to oppose a national bank but Congress set up the first one in 1791, chartered for the next 20 years. In 1794, Pennsylvania farmers, who made whiskey, their most important source of cash, refused to pay the liquor tax and started what came to be known as the Whiskey Rebellion. Troops sent by President Washington successfully put it down with no lives lost, thus demonstrating the growing strength of the new government.

The Judiciary Act set up the U.S. Supreme Court by providing for a Chief Justice and five associate justices. It also established federal district and circuit courts. One of the most important acts of Congress was the first 10 amendments to the Constitution called the Bill of Rights which emphasized and gave attention to the rights of individuals.

Under President John Adams, a minor diplomatic upset occurred with the government of France. By this time, the two major political parties called Federalists and Democratic-Republicans had fully developed. Hamilton and his mostly northern followers had formed the Federalist Party, which favored a strong central government and was sympathetic to Great Britain and its interests. The Democratic-Republican Party had been formed by Jefferson and his mostly Southern followers and they wanted a weak central government and stronger relations with and support of France. In 1798, the Federalists, in control of Congress, passed the Alien and Sedition Acts, written to silence vocal opposition. These acts made it a crime to voice any criticism of the President or Congress and unfairly treated all foreigners.

The legislatures of Kentucky and Virginia protested these laws, claiming they attacked freedoms and challenging their constitutionality. These Resolutions stated mainly the states had created the federal government which was considered merely as an agent for the states and was limited to certain powers and could be criticized by the states, if warranted. They went further stating that states' rights included the power to declare any act of Congress null and void if the states felt it unconstitutional. The controversy died down as the Alien and Sedition Acts expired, one by one, but the doctrine of states' rights was not finally settled until the Civil War.

Supreme Court Chief Justice John Marshall made extremely significant contributions to the American judiciary. He set or established three basic principles of law, which became the foundation of the judicial system and the federal government:

a) He started the power of judicial review; the right of the Supreme Court to determine the constitutionality of laws passed by Congress.

b) He stated that only the Supreme Court had the power to set aside laws passed by state legislatures when they contradicted the U.S. Constitution.

c) He established the right of the Supreme Court to reverse decisions of state courts.

After the U.S. purchased the Louisiana Territory, Jefferson appointed Captains Meriwether Lewis and William Clark to explore it, to find out exactly what had been bought. The expedition went all the way to the Pacific Ocean, returning two years later with maps, journals, and artifacts. This led the way for future explorers to make available more knowledge about the territory and resulted in the Westward Movement and the later belief in the doctrine of Manifest Destiny.

The election of Andrew Jackson as President signaled a swing of the political pendulum from government influence of the wealthy, aristocratic Easterners to the interests of the Western farmers and pioneers and the era of the "common man." Jacksonian democracy was a policy of equal political power for all.

After the War of 1812, Henry Clay and supporters favored economic measures that came to be known as the American System. This involved tariffs protecting American farmers and manufacturers from having to compete with foreign products, stimulating industrial growth and employment. With more people working, more farm products would be consumed, prosperous farmers would be able to buy more manufactured goods, and the additional monies from tariffs would make it possible for the government to make the needed internal improvements. To get all of this going, in 1816, Congress not only passed a high tariff, but also chartered a second Bank of the United States. Upon becoming President, Jackson fought to get rid of the bank.

One of the many duties of the bank was to regulate the supply of money for the nation. The President believed that the bank was a monopoly that favored the wealthy. Congress voted in 1832 to renew the bank's charter but Jackson vetoed the bill, withdrew the government's money, and the bank finally collapsed.

Jackson also faced the "null and void," or nullification issue from South Carolina. Congress, in 1828, passed a law placing high tariffs on goods imported into the United States. Southerners, led by South Carolina's then Vice-President of the U.S., John C. Calhoun, felt that the tariff favored the manufacturing interests of New England, denounced it as an abomination, and claimed that any state could nullify any of the federal laws it considered unconstitutional. The tariff was lowered in 1832, but not low enough to satisfy South Carolina, which promptly threatened to secede from the Union. Although Jackson agreed with the rights of states, he also believed in preservation of the Union. A year later, the tariffs were lowered and the crisis was averted.

Many social reform movements began during this period, including education, women's rights, labor, and working conditions, temperance, prisons and insane asylums. But the most intense and controversial was the abolitionists' efforts to end slavery, an effort alienating and splitting the country, hardening Southern defense of slavery, and leading to four years of bloody war. The abolitionist movement had political fallout, affecting admittance of states into the Union and the government's continued efforts to keep a balance between total numbers of free and slave states. Congressional legislation after 1820 reflected this.

The Industrial Revolution had spread from Great Britain to the United States. Before 1800, most manufacturing activities were done in small shops or in homes. However, starting in the early 1800s, factories with modern machines were built making it easier to produce goods faster. The eastern part of the country became a major industrial area although some developed in the West. At about the same time, improvements began to be made in building roads, railroads, canals, and steamboats. The increased ease of travel facilitated the westward movement as well as boosted the economy with faster and cheaper shipment of goods and products, covering larger and larger areas. Some of the innovations include the Erie Canal connecting the interior and Great Lakes with the Hudson River and the coastal port of New York. Many other natural waterways were connected by canals.

Robert Fulton's "Clermont," the first commercially successful steamboat, led the way in the fastest way to ship goods, making it the most important way to do so. Later, steam-powered railroads soon became the biggest rival of the steamboat as a means of shipping, eventually being the most important transportation method opening the West.

With expansion into the interior of the country, the United States became the leading agricultural nation in the world. The hardy pioneer farmers produced a vast surplus and emphasis went to producing products with a high-sale value. Implements such as the cotton gin and reaper aided in this. Travel and shipping were greatly assisted in areas not yet touched by railroad or, by improved or new roads, such as the National Road in the East and in the West the Oregon and Santa Fe Trails.

People were exposed to works of literature, art, newspapers, drama, live entertainment, and political rallies. With better communication and travel, more information was desired about previously unknown areas of the country, especially the West. The discovery of gold and other mineral wealth resulted in a literal surge of settlers and even more interest.

Public schools were established in many of the states with more and more children being educated. With more literacy and more participation in literature and the arts, the young nation was developing its own unique culture becoming less and less influenced by and dependent on that of Europe.

More industries and factories required more and more labor. Women, children, and, at times, entire families worked the long hours and days, until the 1830s. By that time, the factories were getting even larger and employers began hiring immigrants who were coming to America in huge numbers. Before then, efforts were made to organize a labor movement to improve working conditions and increase wages. It never really caught on until after the Civil War, but the seed had been sown.

Following is just a partial list of well-known Americans who contributed their leadership and talents in various fields and reforms:

Lucretia Mott and Elizabeth Cady Stanton for **women's rights**

Emma Hart Willard, Catharine Esther Beecher, and Mary Lyon for **education for women**

Dr. Elizabeth Blackwell, the **first woman doctor**

Antoinette Louisa Blackwell, the **first female minister**

Dorothea Lynde Dix for **reforms in prisons and insane asylums** Elihu Burritt and William Ladd for **peace movements**

Robert Owen for a **Utopian society**

Horace Mann, Henry Barmard, Calvin E. Stowe, Caleb Mills, and John Swett for **public education**

Benjamin Lundy, David Walker, William Lloyd Garrison, Isaac Hooper, Arthur and Lewis Tappan, Theodore Weld, Frederick Douglass, Harriet Tubman, James G. Birney, Henry Highland Garnet, James Forten, Robert Purvis, Harriet Beecher Stowe, Wendell Phillips, and John Brown for **abolition of slavery and the Underground Railroad**

Louisa Mae Alcott, James Fenimore Cooper, Washington Irving, Walt Whitman, Henry David Thoreau, Ralph Waldo Emerson, Herman Melville, Richard Henry Dana, Nathaniel Hawthorne, Henry Wadsworth Longfellow, John Greenleaf Whittier, Edgar Allan Poe, Oliver Wendell Holmes, **famous writers**

John C. Fremont, Zebulon Pike, Kit Carson, **explorers**

Henry Clay, Daniel Webster, Stephen Douglas, John C. Calhoun, American **statesmen**
Robert Fulton, Cyrus McCormick, Eli Whitney, **inventors**

Noah Webster, American **dictionary and spellers**

The list could go on and on but the contributions of these and many, many others greatly enhanced the unique American culture.

In between the growing economy, expansion westward of the population, and improvements in travel and mass communication, the federal government did face periodic financial depressions. Contributing to these downward spirals were land speculations, availability and soundness of money and currency, failed banks, failing businesses, and unemployment. Sometimes conditions outside the nation would help trigger it; at other times, domestic politics and presidential elections affected it. The growing strength and influence of two major political parties with opposing philosophies and methods of conducting government did not ease matters at times.

As 1860 began, the nation had extended its borders north, south, and west. Industry and agriculture were flourishing. Although the U.S. did not involve itself actively in European affairs, the relationship with Great Britain was much improved and it and other nations that dealt with the young nation accorded it more respect and admiration. Nevertheless, war was on the horizon. The country was deeply divided along political lines concerning slavery and the election of Abraham Lincoln.

Even though 13 colonies won independence, wrote a Constitution forming a union of those states under a central government, fought wars and signed treaties, purchased and explored vast areas of land, developed industry and agriculture, improved transportation, saw population expansion westward, increased each year the number of states admitted to the Union - despite all of these accomplishments, the issue of human slavery had to be settled once and for all. One historian has stated that before 1865, the nation referred to itself as "the United States are ... ," but after 1865, "the United States is ..." It took the Civil War to finally, completely unify all states into one Union.

Skill 2.2.e   Know the effects of westward expansion.

Westward expansion occurred for a number of reasons, most important being economic. Cotton had become most important to most of the people who lived in the southern states. The effects of the Industrial Revolution, which began in England, were now being felt in the United States. With the invention of power-driven machines, the demand for cotton fiber greatly increased for the yarn needed in spinning and weaving. Eli Whitney's cotton gin made the separation of the seeds from the cotton much more efficient and faster. This, in turn, increased the demand and more and more farmers became involved in the raising and selling of cotton.

The innovations and developments of better methods of long-distance transportation moved the cotton in greater quantities to textile mills in England as well as the areas of New England and Middle Atlantic States in the U.S. As prices increased along with increased demand, southern farmers began expanding by clearing increasingly more land to grow more cotton. Movement, settlement, and farming headed west to utilize the fertile soils. This, in turn, demanded increased need for a large supply of cheap labor. The system of slavery expanded, both in numbers and in the movement to lands "west" of the South.

Cotton farmers and slave owners were not the only ones heading west. Many, in other fields of economic endeavor, began the migration: trappers, miners, merchants, ranchers, and others were all seeking their fortunes. The Lewis and Clark expedition stimulated the westward push. Fur companies hired men, known as "Mountain Men", to go westward, searching for the animal pelts to supply the market and meet the demands of the East and Europe. These men in their own way explored and discovered the many passes and trails that would eventually be used by settlers in their trek to the west. The California gold rush also had a very large influence on the movement west.

There were also religious reasons for westward expansion. Increased settlement was encouraged by missionaries who traveled west with the fur traders. They sent word back east for more settlers and the results were tremendous. By the 1840s, the population increases in the Oregon country alone were at a rate of about a thousand people a year. People of many different religions and cultures as well as Southerners with black slaves made their way west which leads to a third reason: political.

It was the belief of many that the United States was destined to control all of the land between the two oceans or as one newspaper editor termed it, "Manifest Destiny." This mass migration westward put the U.S. government on a collision course with the Indians, Great Britain, Spain, and Mexico. The fur traders and missionaries ran up against the Indians in the northwest and the claims of Great Britain for the Oregon country. The U.S. and Britain had shared the Oregon country but by the 1840s, with the increases in the free and slave populations and the demand of the settlers for control and government by the U.S., the conflict had to be resolved. In a treaty, signed in 1846, by both nations, a peaceful resolution occurred with Britain giving up its claims south of the 49th parallel.

In the American southwest, the results were exactly the opposite. Spain had claimed this area since the 1540s, had spread northward from Mexico City, and, in the 1700s, had established missions, forts, villages, towns, and very large ranches. After the purchase of the Louisiana Territory in 1803, Americans began moving into Spanish territory. A few hundred American families in what is now Texas were allowed to live there but had to agree to become loyal subjects to Spain. In 1821, Mexico successfully revolted against Spanish rule, won independence, and chose to be more tolerant towards the American settlers and traders. The Mexican government encouraged and allowed extensive trade and settlement, especially in Texas. Many of the new settlers were southerners and brought with them their slaves. Slavery was outlawed in Mexico and technically illegal in Texas, although the Mexican government rather looked the other way.

With the influx of so many Americans and the liberal policies of the Mexican government, there came to be concern over the possible growth and development of an American state within Mexico. Settlement restrictions, cancellation of land grants, the forbidding of slavery and increased military activity brought everything to a head. The order of events included the fight for Texas independence, the brief Republic of Texas, eventual annexation of Texas, statehood, and finally war with Mexico. The Texas controversy was not the sole reason for war. Since American settlers had begun, pouring into the Southwest the cultural differences played a prominent part. Language, religion, law, customs, and government were totally different and opposite between the two groups. A clash was bound to occur.

The impact of the entire westward movement resulted in the completion of the borders of the present-day conterminous United States; the bloody war with Mexico; the ever-growing controversy over slave versus free states affecting the balance of power or influence in the U.S. Congress, especially the Senate; and finally to the Civil War itself.

Skill 2.2.f   Make comparisons of the political, economic, and social characteristics of both North and South from 1815 to 1860.

The drafting of the Constitution, its ratification and implementation, united 13 different, independent states into a Union under one central government. The two crucial compromises of the convention delegates concerning slaves pacified Southerners, especially the slave owners, but the issue of slavery was not settled and from then on, sectionalism became stronger and more apparent each year putting the entire country on a collision course.

Slavery in the English colonies began in 1619 when 20 Africans arrived in the colony of Virginia at Jamestown. From then on, slavery had a foothold, especially in the agricultural South, where a large amount of slave labor was needed for the extensive plantations. Free men refused to work for wages on the plantations when land was available for settling on the frontier. Therefore, slave labor was the only recourse left. If it had been profitable to use slaves in New England and the Middle Colonies, then without doubt slavery would have been more widespread. However, it came down to whether or not slavery was profitable. It was in the South, but not in the other two colonial regions.

It is interesting that the West was involved in the controversy as well as the North and South. By 1860, the country was made up of these three major regions. The people in all three sections or regions had a number of beliefs and institutions in common. Of course, there were major differences with each region having its own unique characteristics. The basic problem was their development along very different lines.

The section of the North was industrial with towns and factories growing and increasing at a very fast rate. The South had become agricultural, eventually becoming increasingly dependent on the one crop of cotton. In the West, restless pioneers moved into new frontiers seeking land, wealth, and opportunity. Many were from the South and were slave owners, bringing their slaves with them.

So between these three different parts of the country, the views on tariffs, public lands, internal improvements at federal expense, banking and currency, and the issue of slavery were decidedly, totally different. This period of U.S. history was a period of compromises, breakdowns of the compromises, desperate attempts to restore and retain harmony among the three sections, short-lived intervals of the uneasy balance of interests, and ever-increasing conflict.

At the Constitutional Convention, one of the slavery compromises concerned counting slaves for deciding the number of representatives for the House and the amount of taxes to be paid. Southerners pushed for counting the slaves for representation but not for taxes. The Northerners pushed for the opposite. The resulting compromise, sometimes referred to as the "three-fifths compromise," was that both groups agreed that three-fifths of the slaves would be counted for both taxes and representation.

The other compromise over slavery was part of the disputes over how much regulation the central government would control over commercial activities such as trade with other nations and the slave trade. It was agreed that Congress would regulate commerce with other nations including taxing imports. Southerners were worried about taxing slaves coming into the country and the possibility of Congress prohibiting the slave trade altogether. The agreement reached allowed the states to continue importation of slaves for the next 20 years until 1808, at which time Congress would make the decision as to the future of the slave trade. During the 20-year period, no more than $10 per person could be levied on slaves coming into the country.

These two "slavery' compromises were a necessary concession to have Southern support and approval for the new document and new government. Many Americans felt that the system of slavery would eventually die out in the U.S., but by 1808, cotton was becoming increasingly important in the primarily agricultural South and the institution of slavery had become firmly entrenched in Southern culture. It is also evident that as early as the Constitutional Convention, active anti-slavery feelings and opinions were very strong, leading to extremely active groups and societies.

Democracy is loosely defined as "rule by the people," either directly or through representatives. Associated with the idea of democracy are freedom, equality, and opportunity. The basic concept of democracy existed in the 13 English colonies with the practice of independent self-government. The right of qualified persons to vote, hold office and actively participate in his or her government is sometimes referred to as "political" democracy.

"Social" and "economic" democracy pertain to the idea that all have the opportunity to get an education, choose their own careers, and live as free men everyday all equal in the eyes of the law to everyone.

These three concepts of democracy were basic reasons why people came to the New World and the practices of these concepts continued on through the colonial and revolutionary periods. They were extremely influential in the shaping of the new central government under the Constitution.

As the nation extended its borders into the lands west of the Mississippi, thousands of settlers streamed into this part of the country bringing with them ideas and concepts adapting them to the development of the unique characteristics of the region. Equality for everyone, as stated in the Declaration of Independence, did not yet apply to minority groups, black Americans or American Indians. Voting rights and the right to hold public office were restricted in varying degrees in each state. All of these factors decidedly affected the political, economic, and social life of the country and all three were focused in the attitudes of the three sections of the country on slavery.

The first serious clash between North and South occurred during 1819-1820 when James Monroe was in office as President and it was concerning admitting Missouri as a state. In 1819, the U.S. consisted of 21 states: 11 free states and 10 slave states. The Missouri Territory allowed slavery and if admitted would cause an imbalance in the number of U.S. Senators. Alabama had already been admitted as a slave state and that had balanced the Senate with the North and South each having 22 senators. The first Missouri Compromise resolved the conflict by approving admission of Maine as a free state along with Missouri as a slave state, thus continuing to keep a balance of power in the Senate with the same number of free and slave states.

An additional provision of this compromise was that with the admission of Missouri, slavery would not be allowed in the rest of the Louisiana Purchase territory north of latitude 36 degrees 30'. This was acceptable to the Southern Congressmen since it was not profitable to grow cotton on land north of this latitude line anyway. It was thought that the crisis had been resolved but in the next year, it was discovered that in its state constitution, Missouri discriminated against the free blacks. Anti-slavery supporters in Congress went into an uproar, determined to exclude Missouri from the Union. Henry Clay, known as the Great Compromiser, then proposed a second Missouri Compromise which was acceptable to everyone. His proposal stated that the Constitution of the United States guaranteed protections and privileges to citizens of states and Missouri's proposed constitution could not deny these to any of its citizens. The acceptance in 1820 of this second compromise opened the way for Missouri's statehood--a temporary reprieve only.

The issue of tariffs also was a divisive factor during this period, especially between 1829 and 1833. The Embargo Act of 1807 and the War of 1812 had completely cut off the source of manufactured goods for Americans, so it was necessary to build factories to produce what was needed. After 1815 when the war had ended, Great Britain proceeded to get rid of its industrial rivals by unloading its goods in America. To protect and encourage its own industries and their products, Congress passed the Tariff of 1816, which required high duties to be levied on manufactured goods coming into the United States. Southern leaders, such as John C. Calhoun of South Carolina, supported the tariff with the assumption that the South would develop its own industries.

For a brief period after 1815, the nation enjoyed the "Era of Good Feelings." People were moving into the West; industry and agriculture were growing; a feeling of national pride united Americans in their efforts and determination to strengthen the country. However, over speculation in stocks and lands for quick profits backfired. Cotton prices were rising so many Southerners bought land for cultivation at inflated prices. Manufacturers in the industrial North purchased land to build more plants and factories as an attempt to have a part of this prosperity. Settlers in the West rushed to buy land to reap the benefits of the increasing prices of meat and grain. To have the money for all of these economic activities, all of these groups were borrowing heavily from the banks and the banks themselves encouraged this by giving loans on insubstantial security.

In late 1818, the Bank of the United States and its branches stopped renewal of personal mortgages and required state batiks to immediately pay their bank notes in gold, silver, or in national bank notes. The state banks were unable to do this so they closed their doors and were unable to do any business at all. Since mortgages could not be renewed, people lost all their properties and foreclosures were rampant throughout the country. At the same time, as all of this was occurring, cotton prices collapsed in the English market. Its high price had caused the British manufacturers to seek cheaper cotton from India for their textile mills. With the fall of cotton prices, the demand for American manufactured goods declined, revealing how fragile the economic prosperity had been.

In 1824, a higher tariff was passed by Congress, favoring the financial interests of the manufacturers in New England and the Middle Atlantic States. In addition, the 1824 tariff was closely tied to the presidential election of that year. Before becoming law, Calhoun had proposed the very high tariffs in an effort to get Eastern business interests to vote with the agricultural interests in the South (who were against it) with supporters of candidate Andrew Jackson siding with whichever side served their best interests. Jackson himself would not be involved in any of this scheming.

The bill became law, to Calhoun's surprise, due mainly to the political maneuvering of Martin van Buren and Daniel Webster. By the time the higher 1828 tariff was passed, feelings were extremely bitter in the South, who believed that the New England manufacturers greatly benefited from it. Vice-President Calhoun, also speaking for his home state of South Carolina, promptly declared that if any state felt that a federal law was unconstitutional, that state could nullify it. In 1832, Congress took the action of lowering the tariffs to a degree but not enough to please South Carolina, which promptly declared the tariff null and void, threatening to secede from the Union.

In 1833, Congress lowered the tariffs again, this time at a level acceptable to South Carolina. Although President Jackson believed in states' rights, he also firmly believed in and determined to keep the preservation of the Union. A constitutional crisis had been averted but sectional divisions were getting deeper and more pronounced. The abolition movement was growing rapidly, becoming an important issue in the North.

The slavery issue was at the root of every problem, crisis, event, decision, and struggle from then on. The next crisis involved the issue concerning Texas. By 1836, Texas was an independent republic with its own constitution. During its fight for independence, Americans were sympathetic to and supportive of the Texans and some recruited volunteers who crossed into Texas to help the struggle. Problems arose when the state petitioned Congress for statehood. Texas wanted to allow slavery but Northerners in Congress opposed admission to the Union because it would disrupt the balance between free and slave states and give Southerners in Congress increased influence. There were others who believed that granting statehood to Texas would lead to a war with Mexico, which had refused to recognize Texas independence. For the time being, statehood was put on hold.

Friction increased between land-hungry Americans swarming into western lands and the Mexican government, which controlled these lands. The clash was not only political but also cultural and economic. The Spanish influence permeated all parts of southwestern life: law, language, architecture, and customs. By this time, the doctrine of Manifest Destiny was in the hearts and on the lips of those seeking new areas of settlement and a new life. Americans were demanding U.S. control of not only the Mexican Territory but also Oregon. Peaceful negotiations with Great Britain secured Oregon but it took two years of war to gain control of the southwestern U.S.

In addition, the Mexican government owed debts to U.S. citizens whose property was damaged or destroyed during its struggle for independence from Spain. By the time war broke out in 1845, Mexico had not paid its war debts. The government was weak, corrupt, irresponsible, torn by revolutions, and not in decent financial shape. Mexico was also bitter over American expansion into Texas and the 1836 revolution, which resulted in Texas independence. In the 1844 Presidential election, the Democrats pushed for annexation of Texas and Oregon and after winning, they started the procedure to admit Texas to the Union.

When statehood occurred, diplomatic relations between the U.S. and Mexico was ended. President Polk wanted U.S. control of the entire southwest, from Texas to the Pacific Ocean. He sent a diplomatic mission with an offer to purchase New Mexico and Upper California but the Mexican government refused to even receive the diplomat. Consequently, in 1846, each nation claimed aggression on the part of the other and war was declared. The treaty signed in 1848 and a subsequent one in 1853 completed the southwestern boundary of the United States, reaching to the Pacific Ocean, as President Polk wished.

The slavery issue flared again not to be done away with until the end of the Civil War. It was obvious that the newly acquired territory would be divided up into territories and later become states. In addition to the two factions of Northerners who advocated prohibition of slavery and of Southerners who favored slavery existing there, a third faction arose supporting the doctrine of "popular sovereignty" which stated that people living in territories and states should be allowed to decide for themselves whether or not slavery should be permitted. In 1849, California applied for admittance to the Union and the furor began.

The result was the Compromise of 1850, a series of laws designed as a final solution to the issue. Concessions made to the North included the admission of California as a free state and the abolition of slave trading in Washington, D.C. The laws also provided for the creation of the New Mexico and Utah territories. As a concession to Southerners, the residents there would decide whether to permit slavery when these two territories became states. In addition, Congress authorized implementation of stricter measures to capture runaway slaves.

A few years later, Congress took up consideration of new territories between Missouri and present-day Idaho. Again, heated debate over permitting slavery in these areas flared up. Those opposed to slavery used the Missouri Compromise to prove their point showing that the land being considered for territories was part of the area the Compromise had designated as banned to slavery.
But on May 25, 1854, Congress passed the infamous Kansas-Nebraska Act which nullified this provision, created the territories of Kansas and Nebraska, and provided for the people of these two territories to decide for themselves whether or not to permit slavery to exist there. Feelings were so deep and divided that any further attempts to compromise would meet with little, if any, success. Political and social turmoil swirled everywhere. Kansas was called "Bleeding Kansas" because of the extreme violence and bloodshed throughout the territory because two governments existed there, one pro-slavery and the other anti-slavery.

The Supreme Court in 1857 handed down a decision guaranteed to cause explosions throughout the country. Dred Scott was a slave whose owner had taken him from slave state Missouri, then to free state Illinois, into Minnesota Territory, free under the provisions of the Missouri Compromise, then finally back to slave state Missouri. Abolitionists pursued the dilemma by presenting a court case, stating that since Scott had lived in a free state and free territory, he was in actuality a free man. Two lower courts had ruled before the Supreme Court became involved, one ruling in favor and one against. The Supreme Court decided that residing in a free state and free territory did not make Scott a free man because Scott (and all other slaves) was not U.S. citizens or state citizens of Missouri. Therefore, he did not have the right to sue in state or federal courts. The Court went a step further and ruled that the old Missouri Compromise was now unconstitutional because Congress did not have the power to prohibit slavery in the Territories.

Anti-slavery supporters were stunned. They had just recently formed the new Republican Party and one of its platforms was keeping slavery out of the Territories. Now, according to the decision in the Dred Scott case, this basic party principle was unconstitutional. The only way to ban slavery in new areas was by a Constitutional amendment, requiring ratification by three-fourths of all states. At this time, this was out of the question because the supporters would be unable to get a majority due to Southern opposition.

In 1858, Abraham Lincoln and Stephen A. Douglas were running for the office of U.S. Senator from Illinois and participated in a series of debates, which directly affected the outcome of the 1860 Presidential election. Douglas, a Democrat, was up for re-election and knew that if he won this race, he had a good chance of becoming President in 1860. Lincoln, a Republican, was not an abolitionist but he believed that slavery was wrong morally and he firmly believed in and supported the Republican Party principle that slavery must not be allowed to extend any further.

Douglas, on the other hand, originated the doctrine of "popular sovereignty" and was responsible for supporting and getting through Congress the inflammatory Kansas-Nebraska Act. In the course of the debates, Lincoln challenged Douglas to show that popular sovereignty reconciled with the Dred Scott decision. Either way he answered Lincoln, Douglas would lose crucial support from one group or the other. If he supported the Dred Scott decision, Southerners would support him but he would lose Northern support. If he stayed with popular sovereignty, Northern support would be his but Southern support would be lost. His reply to Lincoln, stating that Territorial legislatures could exclude slavery by refusing to pass laws supporting it, gave him enough support and approval to be re-elected to the Senate. But it cost him the Democratic nomination for President in 1860.

Southerners came to the realization that Douglas supported and devoted to popular sovereignty but not necessarily to the expansion of slavery. On the other hand, two years later, Lincoln received the nomination of the Republican Party for President.

In 1859, abolitionist John Brown and his followers seized the federal arsenal at Harper's Ferry in what is now West Virginia. His purpose was to take the guns stored in the arsenal, give them to slaves nearby, and lead them in a widespread rebellion. He and his men were captured by Colonel Robert E. Lee of the United States Army and after a trial with a guilty verdict, he was hanged. Most Southerners felt that the majority of Northerners approved of Brown's actions but in actuality, most of them were stunned and shocked. Southern newspapers took great pains to quote a small but well-known minority of abolitionists who applauded and supported Brown's actions. This merely served to widen the gap between the two sections.

The final straw came with the election of Lincoln to the Presidency the next year. Due to a split in the Democratic Party, there were four candidates from four political parties. With Lincoln receiving a minority of the popular vote and a majority of electoral votes, the Southern states, one by one, voted to secede from the Union as they had promised they would do if Lincoln and the Republicans were victorious. The die was cast.

Skill 2.2.g Be knowledgeable about the Civil War and Reconstruction from 1860 to 1877.

It is ironic that South Carolina was the first state to secede from the Union and the first shots of the war were fired on Fort Sumter in Charleston Harbor. Both sides quickly prepared for war. The North had more in its favor: a larger population; superiority in finances and transportation facilities; manufacturing, agricultural, and natural resources. The North possessed most of the nation's gold, had about 92% of all industries, and almost all known supplies of copper, coal, iron, and various other minerals. Since most of the nation's railroads were in the North and mid-West, men and supplies could be moved wherever needed; food could be transported from the farms of the mid-West to workers in the East and to soldiers on the battlefields. Trade with nations overseas could go on as usual due to control of the navy and the merchant fleet. The Northern states numbered 24 and included western (California and Oregon) and border (Maryland, Delaware, Kentucky, Missouri, and West Virginia) states.

The Southern states numbered 11 and included South Carolina, Georgia, Florida, Alabama, Mississippi, Louisiana, Texas, Virginia, North Carolina, Tennessee, and Arkansas, making up the Confederacy. Although outnumbered in population, the South was completely confident of victory. They knew that all they had to do was fight a defensive war, protecting their own territory until the North, who had to invade and defeat an area almost the size of Western Europe, tired of the struggle and gave up. Another advantage of the South was that a number of its best officers had graduated from the U.S. Military Academy at West Point and had had long years of army experience, some even exercising varying degrees of command in the Indian wars and the war with Mexico. Men from the South were conditioned to living outdoors and were more familiar with horses and firearms than many men from northeastern cities. Since cotton was such an important crop, Southerners felt that British and French textile mills were so dependent on raw cotton that they would be forced to help the Confederacy in the war.

The South had specific reasons and goals for fighting the war, more so than the North. The major aim of the Confederacy never wavered: to win independence, the right to govern themselves as they wished, and to preserve slavery. The Northerners were not as clear in their reasons for conducting war. At the beginning, most believed, along with Lincoln, that preservation of the Union was paramount. Only a few extremely fanatical abolitionists looked on the war as a way to end slavery. However, by war's end, more and more northerners had come to believe that freeing the slaves was just as important as restoring the Union.

The war strategies for both sides were relatively clear and simple. The South planned a defensive war, wearing down the North until it agreed to peace on Southern terms. The exception was to gain control of Washington, D.C., go North through the Shenandoah Valley into Maryland and Pennsylvania in order to drive a wedge between the Northeast and mid-West, interrupt the lines of communication, and end the war quickly. The North had three basic strategies:

a blockade the Confederate coastline in order to cripple the South;

a seize control of the Mississippi River and interior railroad lines to split the Confederacy in two;

c. seize the Confederate capital of Richmond, Virginia, driving southward joining up with Union forces coming east from the Mississippi Valley.

The South won decisively until the Battle of Gettysburg, July 1 - 3, 1863. Until Gettysburg, Lincoln's commanders, McDowell and McClellan, were less than desirable, Burnside and Hooker, not what was needed. Lee, on the other hand, had many able officers, Jackson and Stuart depended on heavily by him. Jackson died at Chancellorsville and was replaced by Longstreet. Lee decided to invade the North and depended on J.E.B. Stuart and his cavalry to keep him informed of the location of Union troops and their strengths. Four things worked against Lee at Gettysburg:

1) The Union troops gained the best positions and the best ground first, making it easier to make a stand there.

2) Lee's move into Northern territory put him and his army a long way from food and supply lines. They were more or less on their own.

3) Lee thought that his Army of Northern Virginia was invincible and could fight and win under any conditions or circumstances.

4) Stuart and his men did not arrive at Gettysburg until the end of the second day of fighting and by then, it was too little too late. He and the men had had to detour around Union soldiers and he was delayed getting the information Lee needed.

Consequently, he made the mistake of failing to listen to Longstreet and following the strategy of regrouping back into Southern territory to the supply lines. Lee felt that regrouping was retreating and almost an admission of defeat.

He was convinced the army would be victorious. Longstreet was concerned about the Union troops occupying the best positions and felt that regrouping to a better position would be an advantage. He was also very concerned about the distance from supply lines.

It was not the intention of either side to fight there but the fighting began when a Confederate brigade stumbled into a unit of Union cavalry while looking for shoes. The third and last day Lee launched the final attempt to break Union lines. General George Pickett sent his division of three brigades under Generals Garnet, Kemper, and Armistead against Union troops on Cemetery Ridge under command of General Winfield Scott Hancock. Union lines held and Lee and the defeated Army of Northern Virginia made their way back to Virginia. Although Lincoln's commander George Meade successfully turned back a Confederate charge, he and the Union troops failed to pursue Lee and the Confederates. This battle was the turning point for the North. After this, Lee never again had the troop strength to launch a major offensive.

The day after Gettysburg, on July 4, Vicksburg, Mississippi surrendered to Union General Ulysses Grant, thus severing the western Confederacy from the eastern part. In September 1863, the Confederacy won its last important victory at Chickamauga. In November, the Union victory at Chattanooga made it possible for Union troops to go into Alabama and Georgia, splitting the eastern Confederacy in two. Lincoln gave Grant command of all Northern armies in March of 1864. Grant led his armies into battles in Virginia while Phil Sheridan and his cavalry did as much damage as possible. In a skirmish at a place called Yellow Tavern, Virginia, Sheridan's and Stuart's forces met, with Stuart being fatally wounded. The Union won the Battle of Mobile Bay and in May 1864, William Tecumseh Sherman began his march to successfully demolish Atlanta, then on to Savannah. He and his troops turned northward through the Carolinas to Grant in Virginia. On April 9, 1865, Lee formally surrendered to Grant at Appamattox Courthouse, Virginia.

The Civil War took more American lives than any other war in history, the South losing one-third of its soldiers in battle compared to about one-sixth for the North. More than half of the total deaths were caused by disease and the horrendous conditions of field hospitals. Both sections paid a tremendous economic price but the South suffered more severely from direct damages. Destruction was pervasive with towns, farms, trade, industry, lives and homes of men, women, children all destroyed and an entire Southern way of life was lost. The deep resentment, bitterness, and hatred that remained for generations gradually lessened as the years went by but legacies of it surface and remain to this day.

The South had no voice in the political, social, and cultural affairs of the nation, lessening to a great degree the influence of the more traditional Southern ideals. The Northern Yankee Protestant ideals of hard work, education, and economic freedom became the standard of the United States and helped influence the development of the nation into a modem, industrial power.

The effects of the Civil War were tremendous. It changed the methods of waging war and has been called the first modern war. It introduced weapons and tactics that, when improved later, were used extensively in wars of the late 1800s and 1900s. Civil War soldiers were the first to fight in trenches, first to fight under a unified command, first to wage a defense called "major cordon defense", a strategy of advance on all fronts. They were also the first to use repeating and breech loading weapons. Observation balloons were first used during the war along with submarines, ironclad ships, and mines. Telegraphy and railroads were put to use first in the Civil War. It was considered a modern war because of the vast destruction and was "total war", involving the use of all resources of the opposing sides. There was probably no *way* it could have ended other than total defeat and unconditional surrender of one side or the other.

By executive proclamation and constitutional amendment, slavery was officially and finally ended, although there remained deep prejudice and racism, still raising its ugly head today. Also, the Union was preserved and the states were finally truly united. Sectionalism, especially in the area of politics, remained strong for another 100 years but not to the degree and with the violence as existed before 1861. It has been noted that the Civil War may have been American democracy's greatest failure for, from 1861 to 1865, calm reason, basic to democracy, fell to human passion. Yet, democracy did survive.

The victory of the North established that no state has the right to end or leave the Union. Because of unity, the U.S. became a major global power. Lincoln never proposed to punish the South. He was most concerned with restoring the South to the Union in a program that was flexible and practical rather than rigid and unbending. In fact he never really felt that the states had succeeded in leaving the Union but that they had left the 'family circle" for a short time. His plans consisted of two major steps:

All Southerners taking an oath of allegiance to the Union promising to accept all federal laws and proclamations dealing with slavery would receive a full pardon. The only ones excluded from this were men who had resigned from civil and military positions in the federal government to serve in the Confederacy, those who were part of the Confederate government, those in the Confederate army above the rank of lieutenant, and Confederates who were guilty of mistreating prisoners of war and blacks.

A state would be able to write a new constitution, elect new officials, and return to the Union fully equal to all other states on certain conditions: a minimum number of persons (at least 10% of those who were qualified voters in their states before secession from the Union who had voted in the 1860 election) must take an oath of allegiance.

As the war dragged on to its bloody, destructive conclusion, Lincoln was very concerned and anxious to get the states restored to the Union and showed flexibility in his thinking as he made changes to his Reconstruction program to make it as easy and painless as possible. Of course, Congress had final approval of many actions and it would be interesting to know how differently things might have turned out if Lincoln had lived to see some or all of his kind policies, supported by fellow moderates, put into action. Unfortunately, it didn't turn out that way. After Andrew Johnson became President and the radical Republicans gained control of Congress, the harsh measures of radical Reconstruction were implemented.

The economic and social chaos in the South after the war was unbelievable with starvation and disease rampant, especially in the cities. The U.S. Army provided some relief of food and clothing for both white and blacks but the major responsibility fell to the Freedmen's Bureau. Though the bureau agents to a certain extent helped southern whites, their main responsibility was to the freed slaves. They were to assist the freedmen to become self-supporting and protect them from being taken advantage of by others. Northerners looked on it as a real, honest effort to help the South out of the chaos it was in. Most white Southerners charged the bureau with causing racial friction, deliberately encouraging the freedmen to consider former owners as enemies.

As a result, as southern leaders began to be able to restore life as it had once been, they adopted a set of laws known as "black codes", containing many of the provisions of the prewar "slave codes." There were certain improvements in the lives of freedmen, but the codes denied the freedmen their basic civil rights. In short, except for the condition of freedom and a few civil rights, white Southerners made every effort to keep the freedmen in a way of life subordinate to theirs. Radicals in Congress pointed out these illegal actions by white Southerners as evidence that they were unwilling to recognize, accept, and support the complete freedom of black Americans and could not be trusted. Therefore, Congress drafted its own program of Reconstruction, including laws that would protect and further the rights of blacks. Three amendments were added to the Constitution: the 13th Amendment of 1865 outlawed slavery throughout the entire United States. The 14th Amendment of 1868 made blacks American citizens. The 15th Amendment of 1870 gave black Americans the right to vote and made it illegal to deny anyone the right to vote based on race.

Federal troops were stationed throughout the South and protected Republicans who took control of Southern governments. Bitterly resentful, white Southerners fought the new political system by joining a secret society called the Ku Klux Klan, using violence to keep black Americans from voting and getting equality. However, before being allowed to rejoin the Union, the Confederate states were required to agree to all federal laws. Between 1866 and 1870, all of them had returned to the Union, but Northern interest in Reconstruction was fading. Reconstruction officially ended when the last Federal troops left the South in 1877. It can be said that Reconstruction had a limited success as it set up public school systems and expanded legal rights of black Americans. Nevertheless, white supremacy came to be in control again and its bitter fruitage is still with us today.

Lincoln and Johnson had considered the conflict of Civil War as a "rebellion of individuals," but Congressional Radicals, such as Charles Sumner in the Senate, considered the Southern states as complete political organizations and were now in the same position as any unorganized Territory and should be treated as such. Radical House leader Thaddeus Stevens considered the Confederate States, not as Territories, but as conquered provinces and felt they should be treated that way. President Johnson refused to work with Congressional moderates, insisting on having his own way. As a result the Radicals gained control of both houses of Congress and when Johnson opposed their harsh measures they came within one vote of impeaching him.

General Grant was elected President in 1868, serving two scandal-ridden terms. He was himself an honest, upright person but he greatly lacked political experience and his greatest weakness was a blind loyalty to his friends. He absolutely refused to believe that his friends were not honest and stubbornly would not admit to their using him to further their own interests. One of the sad results of the war was the rapid growth of business and industry with large corporations controlled by unscrupulous men. However, after 1877, some degree of normalcy returned and there was time for rebuilding, expansion, and growth.

Skill 2.2.h   Understand the significance of post-Reconstruction industrialization and reform.

There was a marked degree of industrialization before and during the Civil War, but at war's end, industry in America was small. After the war, dramatic changes took place: machines replacing hand labor, extensive nationwide railroad service making possible the wider distribution of goods, invention of new products made available in large quantities, large amounts of money from bankers and investors for expansion of business operations. American life was definitely affected by this phenomenal industrial growth. Cities became the centers of this new business activity resulting in mass population movements there and tremendous growth. This new boom in business resulted in huge fortunes for some Americans and extreme poverty for many others. The discontent this caused resulted in a number of new reform movements from which came measures controlling the power and size of big business and helping the poor.

Of course, industry before, during, and after the Civil War was centered mainly in the North, especially the tremendous industrial growth after. The late 1800s and early 1900s saw the increasing buildup of military strength and the U.S. becoming a world power.

The use of machines in industry enabled workers to produce a large quantity of goods much faster than by hand. With the increase in business, hundreds of workers were hired, assigned to perform a certain job in the production process. This was a method of organization called "division of labor" and by its increasing the rate of production, businesses lowered prices for their products making the products affordable for more people. As a result, sales and businesses were increasingly successful and profitable.

A great variety of new products or inventions became available such as: the typewriter, the telephone, barbed wire, the electric light, the phonograph, and the gasoline automobile. From this list, the one that had the greatest effect on America's economy was the automobile.

The increase in business and industry was greatly affected by the many rich natural resources that were found throughout the nation. The industrial machines were powered by the abundant water supply. The construction industry as well as products made from wood depended heavily on lumber from the forests. Coal and iron ore in abundance were needed for the steel industry, which profited and increased from the use of steel in such things as skyscrapers, automobiles, bridges, railroad tracks, and machines. Other minerals such as silver, copper, and petroleum played a large role in industrial growth, especially petroleum, from which gasoline was refined as fuel for the increasingly popular automobile.

Between 1870 and 1916, more than 25 million immigrants came into the United States adding to the phenomenal population growth taking place. This tremendous growth aided business and industry in two ways: (1) The number of consumers increased creating a greater demand for products thus enlarging the markets for the products. And (2) with increased production and expanding business, more workers were available for newly created jobs. The completion of the nation's transcontinental railroad in 1869 contributed greatly to the nation's economic and industrial growth. Some examples of the benefits of using the railroads include: raw materials were shipped quickly by the mining companies and finished products were sent to all parts of the country. Many wealthy industrialists and railroad owners saw tremendous profits steadily increasing due to this improved method of transportation.

As business grew, methods of sales and promotion were developed. Salespersons went to all parts of the country, promoting the varied products, opening large department stores in the growing cities, offering the varied products at reasonable affordable prices. People who lived too far from the cities, making it impossible to shop there, had the advantage of using a mail order service, buying what they needed from catalogs furnished by the companies. The developments in communication, such as the telephone and telegraph, increased the efficiency and prosperity of big business.

Investments in corporate stocks and bonds resulted from business prosperity. Individuals began investing heavily in an eager desire to share in the profits, and their investments made available the needed capital for companies to expand their operations. From this, banks increased in number throughout the country, making loans to businesses and significant contributions to economic growth. At the same time, during the 1880s, government made little effort to regulate businesses. This gave rise to monopolies where larger businesses were rid of their smaller competitors and assumed complete control of their industries. Some owners in the same business would join or merge to form one company. Others formed what were called "trusts," a type of monopoly in which rival businesses were controlled but not formally owned. Monopolies had some good effects on the economy. Out of them grew the large, efficient corporations, which made important contributions to the growth of the nation's economy. Also, the monopolies enabled businesses to keep their sales steady and avoid sharp fluctuations in price and production. At the same time, the downside of monopolies was the unfair business practices of the business leaders. Some acquired so much power that they took unfair advantage of others. Those who had little or no competition would require their suppliers to supply goods at a low cost, sell the finished products at high prices, and reduce the quality of the product to save money.

The late 1800s and early 1900s were a period of the efforts of many to make significant reforms and changes in the areas of politics, society, and the economy. There was a need to reduce the levels of poverty and to improve the living conditions of those affected by it. Regulations of big business, getting rid of governmental corruption and making it more responsive to the needs of the people were also on the list of reforms to be accomplished. Until 1890, there was very little success, but from 1890 on, the reformers gained increased public support and were able to achieve some influence in government. Since some of these individuals referred to themselves as "progressives," the period of 1890 to 1917 is referred to by historians as the Progressive Era.

Skilled laborers were organized into a labor union called the American Federation of Labor, in an effort to gain better working conditions and wages for its members. Farmers joined organizations such as the National Grange and Farmers Alliances. Farmers were producing more food than people could afford to buy, the result of (1) new farm lands rapidly opening up on the plains and prairies, and (2) development and availability of new farm machinery and newer and better methods of farming. They tried selling their surplus abroad but faced stiff competition from other nations selling the same farm products.

Other problems contributed significantly to their situation. Items they needed for daily life were priced exorbitantly high. Having to borrow money to carry on fanning activities kept them constantly in debt. Higher interest rates, shortage of money, falling farm prices, having to deal with the so-called middlemen, and the increasingly high charges by the railroads to haul farm products to large markets all contributed to the desperate need for reform to relieve the plight of American farmers.

American women began actively campaigning for the right to vote. Elizabeth Cady Stanton and Susan B. Anthony in 1869 founded the organization called National Women Suffrage Association, the same year the Wyoming Territory gave women the right to vote. Soon after, a few states followed by giving women the right to vote, limited to local elections only.

Governmental reform began with the passage of the Civil Service Act, also known as the Pendleton Act. It provided for the Civil Service Commission, a federal agency responsible for giving jobs based on merit rather than as political rewards or favors. Another successful reform was the adoption of the secret ballot in voting, as were such measures as the direct primary, referendum, recall, and direct election of U.S. Senators by the people rather than by their state legislatures. Following the success of reforms made at the national level, the progressives were successful in gaining reforms in government at state and local levels.

After 1890, more and more attention was called to needs and problems through the efforts of social workers and clergy and the writings of people such as Lincoln Steffans, Ida M. Tarbell, and Upton Sinclair.

Presidents Theodore Roosevelt, William Howard Taft, and Woodrow Wilson supported many of the reform laws after 1890 and in 1884, President Grover Cleveland did much to see that the Civil Service Act was enforced. After 1880, a number of political or "third" parties were formed and although unsuccessful in getting their Presidential candidates elected, significant reform legislation, including Constitutional amendments, were passed by Congress and became law due to their efforts. Such legislative acts included the Sherman Antitrust Act of 1890, the Clayton Antitrust Act of 1914, the Underwood Tariff of 1913, and the establishment of the Federal Trade Commission in 1914. By the 1890s and early 1900s, the United States had become a world power and began a leading role in international affairs. War loomed on the horizon once again and the stage was set for increased activity in world affairs, which had been avoided since the end of the Civil War.

Skill 2.2.i   Understand the importance and impact of events, issues, and effects of the period of World War I.

During the period of 1823 to the 1890s, the major interests and efforts of the American people were concentrated on expansion, settlement, and development of the continental United States. The Civil War, 1861-1865, preserved the Union and eliminated the system of slavery and from 1865 onward, the focus was on taming the West and developing industry. During this period of time, travel and trade between the United States and Europe were continuous. By the 1890s, American interests turned to areas outside the boundaries of the United States. The West was developing into a major industrial area and people in the United States became very interested in selling their factory and farm surplus to overseas markets. In fact, some Americans desired getting and controlling land outside the U.S. boundaries.

Before the 1890s, the U.S. had little to do with foreign affairs, was not a strong nation militarily, and had inconsequential influence on international political affairs. In fact, the Europeans looked on the American diplomats as inept and bungling in their diplomatic efforts and activities. However, all of this changed and the Spanish-American War of 1898 saw the entry of the United States as a world power.

During the 1890s, Spain controlled such overseas possessions as Puerto Rico, the Philippines, and Cuba. Cubans rebelled against Spanish rule and the U.S. government found itself besieged by demands from Americans to assist the Cubans in their revolt. When the U.S. battleship Maine blew up off the coast of Havana, Cuba, Americans blamed the Spaniards for it and demanded American action against Spain. Two months later, Congress declared war on Spain and the U.S. quickly defeated them. The peace treaty gave the U.S. possession of Puerto Rico, the Philippines, Guam and Hawaii, which was annexed during the war.

This success enlarged and expanded the U.S. role in foreign affairs. Under the administration of Theodore Roosevelt, the U.S. armed forces were built up, greatly increasing its strength. Roosevelt's foreign policy was summed up in the slogan of "Speak softly and carry a big stick," backing up the efforts in diplomacy with a strong military. During the years before the outbreak of World War I, evidence of U.S. emergence as a world power could be seen in a number of actions. Using the Monroe Doctrine of non-involvement of Europe in the affairs of the Western Hemisphere, President Roosevelt forced Italy, Germany, and Great Britain to remove their blockade of Venezuela; gained the rights to construct the Panama Canal by threatening force; assumed the finances of the Dominican Republic to stabilize it and prevent any intervention by Europeans; and in 1916 under President Woodrow Wilson, to keep order, U.S. troops were sent to the Dominican Republic.

In Europe, war broke out in 1914, involved nearly 30 nations, and ended in 1918. One of the major causes of the war was the tremendous surge of nationalism during the 1800s and early 1900s. People of the same nationality or ethnic group sharing a common history, language or culture began uniting or demanding the right of unification, especially in the empires of Eastern Europe, such as Russian Ottoman and Austrian-Hungarian Empires. Getting stronger and more intense were the beliefs of these peoples in loyalty to common political, social, and economic goals considered to be before any loyalty to the controlling nation or empire.

Emotions ran high and minor disputes magnified into major ones and sometimes quickly led to threats of war. Especially sensitive to these conditions was the area of the states on the Balkan Peninsula. Along with the imperialistic colonization for industrial raw materials, military build-up (especially by Germany), and diplomatic and military alliances, the conditions for one tiny spark to set off the explosion were in place. In July 1914, a Serbian national assassinated the Austrian heir to the throne and his wife and war began a few weeks later. There were a few attempts to keep war from starting, but these efforts were futile.

World War I saw the introduction of such warfare as use of tanks, airplanes, machine guns, submarines, poison gas, and flame throwers. Fighting on the Western front was characterized by a series of trenches that were used throughout the war until 1918. U.S. involvement in the war did not occur until 1916. When it began in 1914, President Woodrow Wilson declared that the U.S. was neutral and most Americans were opposed to any involvement anyway. In 1916, Wilson was reelected to a second term based on the slogan proclaiming his efforts at keeping America out of the war. For a few months after, he put forth most of his efforts to stopping the war but German submarines began unlimited warfare against American merchant shipping.

At the same time, Great Britain intercepted and decoded a secret message from Germany to Mexico urging Mexico to go to war against the U.S. The publishing of this information along with continued German destruction of American ships resulted in the eventual entry of the U.S. into the conflict, the first time the country prepared to fight in a conflict not on American soil. Though unprepared for war, governmental efforts and activities resulted in massive defense mobilization with America's economy directed to the war effort. Though America made important contributions of war materials, its greatest contribution to the war was manpower, soldiers desperately needed by the Allies.

Some ten months before the war ended, President Wilson had proposed a program called the Fourteen Points as a method of bringing the war to an end with an equitable peace settlement. In these Points he had five points setting out general ideals; there were eight pertaining to immediately working to resolve territorial and political problems; and the fourteenth point counseled establishing an organization of nations to help keep world peace.

When Germany agreed in 1918 to an armistice, it assumed that the peace settlement would be drawn up on the basis of these Fourteen Points. However, the peace conference in Paris ignored these points and Wilson had to be content with efforts at establishing the League of Nations. Italy, France, and Great Britain, having suffered and sacrificed far more in the war than America, wanted retribution. The treaties punished severely the Central Powers, taking away arms and territories and requiring payment of reparations. Germany was punished more than the others and, according to one clause in the treaty, was forced to assume the responsibility for causing the war.

Pre-war empires lost tremendous amounts of territories as well as the wealth of natural resources in them. New, independent nations were formed and some predominately ethnic areas came under control of nations of different cultural backgrounds. Some national boundary changes overlapped and created tensions and hard feelings as well as political and economic confusion. The wishes and desires of every national or cultural group could not possibly be realized and satisfied, resulting in disappointments for both; those who were victorious and those who were defeated. Germany received harsher terms than expected from the treaty which weakened its post-war government and, along with the world-wide depression of the 1930s, set the stage for the rise of Adolf Hitler and his Nationalist Socialist Party and World War II.

President Wilson lost in his efforts to get the U.S. Senate to approve the peace treaty. The Senate at the time was a reflection of American public opinion and its rejection of the treaty was a rejection of Wilson. The approval of the treaty would have made the U.S. a member of the League of Nations but Americans had just come off a bloody war to ensure that democracy would exist throughout the world. Americans just did not want to accept any responsibility that resulted from its new position of power and were afraid that membership in the League of Nations would embroil the U.S. in future disputes in Europe.

Skill 2.2.j Understand the importance and impact of events, issues, and effects of the period of World War II.

The end of World War I and the decade of the 1920s saw tremendous changes in the United States, signifying the beginning of its development into its modern society today. The shift from farm to city life was occurring in tremendous numbers. Social changes and problems were occurring at such a fast pace that it was extremely difficult and perplexing for many Americans to adjust to them. Politically the 18th Amendment to the Constitution, the so-called prohibition amendment, prohibited selling alcoholic beverages throughout the U.S. resulting in problems affecting all aspects of society. The passage of the 19th Amendment gave to women the right to vote in all elections. The decade of the 1920s also showed a marked change in roles and opportunities for women with more and more of them seeking and finding careers outside the home. They began to think of themselves as the equal of men and not as much as housewives and mothers.

The influence of the automobile, the entertainment industry, and the rejection of the morals and values of pre-World War I life, resulted in the fast-paced "Roaring Twenties", and had significant effects on events leading to the depression-era 1930s and another world war. Many Americans greatly desired the pre-war life and supported political policies and candidates in favor of the return to what was considered normal. It was desired to end government's strong role and adopt a policy of isolating the country from world affairs, a result of the war.

Prohibition of the sale of alcohol had caused the increased activities of bootlegging and the rise of underworld gangs and the illegal speakeasies, the jazz music and dances they promoted. The customers of these clubs were considered "modern," reflected by extremes in clothing, hairstyles, and attitudes towards authority and life. Movies and, to a certain degree, other types of entertainment, along with increased interest in sports figures and the accomplishments of national heroes, such as Lindbergh, influenced Americans to admire, emulate, and support individual accomplishments.

As wild and uninhibited modern behavior became, this decade witnessed an increase in a religious tradition known as "revivalism," emotional preaching. Although law and order were demanded by many Americans, the administration of President Warren G. Harding was marked by widespread corruption and scandal, not unlike the administration of Ulysses S. Grant, except Grant was honest and innocent. The decade of the 20s also saw the resurgence of such racist organizations as the Ku Klux Klan.

The U.S. economy experienced a tremendous period of boom. Restrictions on business because of war no longer existed and the conservatives in control adopted policies that helped and encouraged big business. To keep foreign goods from competing with American goods, tariffs were raised to the highest level. New products were developed by American manufacturers and many different items became readily available to the people. These included refrigerators, radios, washing machines, and, most importantly, the automobile.

Americans in the 1920s heavily invested in corporation stocks, providing companies a large amount of capital for expanding their businesses. The more money investors put into the stock market, the more the value of the stocks increased. This, in turn, led to widespread speculation that increased stock value to a point beyond the level that was justified by earnings and dividends.

Much of the stock speculation involved paying a small part of the cost and borrowing the rest. This led eventually to the stock market crash of 1929, financial ruin for many investors, a weakening of the nation's economy, and the Great Depression of the 1930s. The depression hit the United States tremendously hard resulting in bank failures, loss of jobs due to cut-backs in production and a lack of money leading to a sharp decline in spending which in turn affected businesses, factories and stores, and higher unemployment. Farm products were not affordable so the farmers suffered even more. Foreign trade sharply decreased and in the early 1930s, the U.S. economy was effectively paralyzed. Europe was affected even more so.

The war had seriously damaged the economies of the European countries, both the victors and the defeated, leaving them deeply in debt. There was difficulty on both sides paying off war debts and loans. It was difficult to find jobs and some countries like Japan and Italy found themselves without enough resources and more than enough people. Solving these problems by expanding the territory merely set up conditions for war later. Germany suffered horribly with runaway inflation ruining the value of its money and wiping out the savings of millions. Even though the U.S. made loans to Germany, which helped the government to restore some order and which provided a short existence of some economic stability in Europe, the Great Depression only served to undo any good that had been done. Mass unemployment, poverty, and despair greatly weakened the democratic governments that had been formed and greatly strengthened the increasing power and influence of extreme political movements, such as communism, fascism, and national-socialism. These ideologies promised to put an end to the economic problems.

The extreme form of patriotism called nationalism that had been the chief cause of World War I grew even stronger after the war ended in 1918. The political, social, and economic unrest fueled nationalism and it became an effective tool enabling dictators to gain and maintain power from the 1930s to the end of World War II in 1945. In the Soviet Union, Joseph Stalin succeeded in gaining political control and establishing a strong harsh dictatorship. Benito Mussolini and the Fascist party, promising prosperity and order in Italy, gained national support and set up a strong government. In Japan, although the ruler was considered Emperor **Hirohito,** actual control and administration of government came under military officers. In Germany, the results of war, harsh treaty terms, loss of territory, great economic chaos and collapse all enabled **Adolf Hitler** and his Nazi party to gain complete power and control.

Germany, Italy, and Japan initiated a policy of aggressive territorial expansion with Japan being the first to conquer. In 1931, the Japanese forces seized control of Manchuria, a part of China containing rich natural resources, and in 1937 began an attack on China, occupying most of its eastern part by 1938. Italy invaded Ethiopia in Africa in 1935, having it totally under its control by 1936. The Soviet Union did not invade or take over any territory but along with Italy and Germany, actively participated in the Spanish Civil War, using it as a proving ground to test tactics and weapons setting the stage for World War II.

In Germany, almost immediately after taking power, in direct violation of the World War I peace treaty, Hitler began the buildup of the armed forces. He sent troops into the Rhineland in 1936, invaded Austria in 1938 and united it with Germany, seized control of the Sudetenland in 1938 (part of western Czechoslovakia and containing mostly Germans), the rest of Czechoslovakia in March 1939, and, on September 1, 1939, began World War II in Europe by invading Poland. In 1940, Germany invaded and controlled Norway, Denmark, Belgium, Luxembourg, the Netherlands, and France.

After the war began in Europe, U.S. **President Franklin D. Roosevelt** announced that the United States was neutral. Most Americans, although hoping for an Allied victory, wanted the U.S. to stay out of the war. President Roosevelt and his supporters, called "interventionists," favored all aid except war to the Allied nations fighting Axis aggression. They were fearful that an Axis victory would seriously threaten and endanger all democracies. On the other hand, the "isolationists" were against any U.S. aid being given to the warring nations, accusing President Roosevelt of leading the U.S. into a war very much unprepared to fight. Roosevelt's plan was to defeat the Axis nations by sending the Allied nations the equipment needed to fight; ships, aircraft, tanks, and other war materials.

In Asia, the U.S. had opposed Japan's invasion of Southeast Asia, an effort to gain Japanese control of that region's rich resources. Consequently, the U.S. stopped all important exports to Japan, whose industries depended heavily on petroleum, scrap metal, and other raw materials. Later Roosevelt refused the Japanese withdrawal of its funds from American banks. General Tojo became the Japanese premier in October 1941 and quickly realized that the U.S. Navy was powerful enough to block Japanese expansion into Asia. Deciding to cripple the Pacific Fleet, the Japanese aircraft, without warning, bombed the Fleet December 7, 1941, while at anchor in **Pearl Harbor** in Hawaii. Temporarily it was a success. It destroyed many aircraft and disabled much of the U.S. Pacific Fleet. In the end, it was a costly mistake as it quickly motivated the Americans to prepare for and wage war.

Military strategy in the European theater of war as developed by **Roosevelt, Churchill, and Stalin** was to concentrate on Germany's defeat first, then Japan's. The start was made in North Africa, pushing Germans and Italians off the continent, beginning in the summer of 1942 and ending successfully in May, 1943. Before the war, Hitler and Stalin had signed a non-aggression pact in 1939, which Hitler violated in 1941 by invading the Soviet Union. The German defeat at Stalingrad, marked a turning point in the war, was brought about by a combination of entrapment by Soviet troops and death of German troops by starvation and freezing due to the horrendous winter conditions. All of this occurred at the same time the Allies were driving them out of North Africa. The liberation of Italy began in July 1943 and ended May 2, 1945. The third part of the strategy was **D-Day, June 6, 1944,** with the Allied invasion of France at Normandy. At the same time, starting in January, 1943, the Soviets began pushing the German troops back into Europe and they were greatly assisted by supplies from Britain and the United States. By April, 1945, Allies occupied positions beyond the Rhine and the Soviets moved on to Berlin, surrounding it by April 25. Germany surrendered May 7 and the war in Europe was finally over.

Meanwhile, in the Pacific, in the six months after the attack on Pearl Harbor, Japanese forces moved across Southeast Asia and the western Pacific Ocean. By August, 1942, the Japanese Empire was at its largest size and stretched northeast to Alaska's Aleutian Islands, west to Burma, south to what is now Indonesia. Invaded and controlled areas included Hong Kong, Guam, Wake Island, Thailand, part of Malaysia, Singapore, the Philippines, and bombed Darwin on the north coast of Australia.

The raid of General Doolittle's bombers on Japanese cities and the American naval victory at Midway along with the fighting in the Battle of the Coral Sea helped turn the tide against Japan. Island-hopping by U.S. Seabees and Marines and the grueling bloody battles fought resulted in gradually pushing the Japanese back towards Japan.

After victory was attained in Europe, concentrated efforts were made to secure Japan's surrender, but it took dropping two atomic bombs on the cities of Hiroshima and Nagasaki to finally end the war in the Pacific. Japan formally surrendered on September 2, 1945, aboard the U.S. battleship Missouri, anchored in Tokyo Bay. The war was finally ended.

Before war in Europe had ended, the Allies had agreed on a military occupation of Germany, with it being divided into four zones each one occupied by Great Britain, France, the Soviet Union, and the United States and the four powers jointly administering Berlin. After the war, the Allies agreed that Germany's armed forces would be abolished, the Nazi Party outlawed, and the territory east of the Oder and Neisse Rivers taken away. Nazi leaders were accused of war crimes and brought to trial. After Japan's defeat, the Allies began a military occupation directed by American General Douglas MacArthur, who introduced a number of reforms eventually ridding Japan of its military institutions transforming it into a democracy. A constitution was drawn up in 1947 transferring all political rights from the emperor to the people, granting women the right to vote, and denying Japan the right to declare war. War crimes trials of 25 war leaders and government officials were also conducted. The U.S. did not sign a peace treaty until 1951. The treaty permitted Japan to rearm but took away its overseas empire.

Again, after a major world war came efforts to prevent war from occurring again throughout the world. Preliminary work began in 1943 when the U.S., Great Britain, the Soviet Union, and China sent representatives to Moscow where they agreed to set up an international organization that would work to promote peace around the earth. In 1944, the four Allied powers met again and made the decision to name the organization the United Nations. In 1945, a charter for the U. N. was drawn up and signed, taking effect in October of that year.

Major consequences of the war included horrendous death and destruction, millions of displaced persons, the gaining of strength and spread of Communism and Cold War tensions as a result of the beginning of the nuclear age. World War II ended more lives and caused more devastation than any other war.

Besides the losses of millions of military personnel, the devastation and destruction directly affected civilians, reducing cities, houses, and factories to ruin and rubble and totally wrecking communication and transportation systems. Millions of civilian deaths, especially in China and the Soviet Union, were the results of famine.

More than 12 million people were uprooted by wars end having no place to live. Included were prisoners of war, those that survived Nazi concentration camps and slave labor camps, orphans, and people who escaped war-torn areas and invading armies. Changing national boundary lines also caused the mass movement of displaced persons.

Germany and Japan were completely defeated; Great Britain and France were seriously weakened; and the Soviet Union and the United States became the world's leading powers. Although allied during the war, the alliance fell apart as the Soviets pushed Communism in Europe and Asia. In spite of the tremendous destruction it suffered, the Soviet Union was stronger than ever. During the war, it took control of Lithuania, Estonia, and Latvia and by mid-1945 parts of Poland, Czechoslovakia, Finland, and Romania. It helped Communist governments gain power in Bulgaria, Romania, Hungary, Czechoslovakia, Poland, and North Korea. China fell to **Mao Zedong's** Communist forces in 1949. Until the fall of the Berlin Wall in 1989 and the dissolution of Communist governments in Eastern Europe and the Soviet Union, the United States and the Soviet Union faced off in what was called a Cold War. The possibility of the terrifying destruction by nuclear weapons loomed over both countries.

Skill 2.2.k   Know and understand the key events and issues pertaining to foreign affairs from post World War II to the present.

The major thrust of U.S. foreign policy from the end of World War II to 1990 was the post-war struggle between non-Communist nations, led by the United States, and the Soviet Union and the Communist nations who were its allies. It was referred to as a "Cold War" because its conflicts did not lead to a major war of fighting, or a "hot war." Both the Soviet Union and the United States embarked on an arsenal buildup of atomic and hydrogen bombs as well as other nuclear weapons. Both nations had the capability of destroying each other but because of the continuous threat of nuclear war and accidents, extreme caution was practiced on both sides. The efforts of both sides to serve and protect their political philosophies and to support and assist their allies resulted in a number of events during this 45-year period.

In 1946, Josef Stalin stated publicly that the presence of capitalism and its development of the world's economy made international peace impossible. This resulted in an American diplomat in Moscow named George F. Kennan to propose, as a response to Stalin and as a statement of U.S. foreign policy, the idea and goal of the U.S. to be to contain or limit the extension or expansion of Soviet Communist policies and activities. After Soviet efforts to make trouble in Iran, Greece, and Turkey, U.S. President Harry Truman stated what is known as the Truman Doctrine which committed the U.S. to a policy of intervention in order to contain or stop the spread of communism throughout the world.

After 1945, social and economic chaos continued in Western Europe, especially in Germany. Secretary of State George C. Marshall came to realize that the U.S. had greatly serious problems and to assist in the recovery, he proposed a program known as the European Recovery Program or the Marshall Plan. Although the Soviet Union withdrew from any participation, the U.S. continued the work of assisting Europe in regaining economic stability. In Germany, the situation was critical with the American Army shouldering the staggering burden of relieving the serious problems of the German economy. In February 1948, Britain and the U.S. combined their two zones, with France joining in June.

The Soviets were opposed to German unification and in April 1948 took serious action to either stop it or to force the Allies to give up control of West Berlin to the Soviets. The Soviets blocked all road traffic access to West Berlin from West Germany. To avoid any armed conflict, it was decided to airlift into West Berlin the needed food and supplies. From June 1948 to mid-May 1949 Allied air forces flew in all that was needed for the West Berliners, forcing the Soviets to lift the blockade and permit vehicular traffic access to the city.

The first "hot war" in the post-World War 11 era was the Korean War, begun June 25, 1950 and ending July 27, 1953. Troops from Communist North Korea invaded democratic South Korea in an effort to unite both sections under Communist control. The United Nations organization asked its member nations to furnish troops to help restore peace. Many nations responded and President Truman sent American troops to help the South Koreans. The war dragged on for three years and ended with a truce, not a peace treaty. Like Germany then, Korea remained divided and does so to this day.

In 1954, the French were forced to give up their colonial claims in Indochina, the present-day countries of Vietnam, Laos, and Cambodia. Afterwards, the Communist northern part of Vietnam began battling with the democratic southern part over control of the entire country. In the late 1950s and early 1960s, U.S. Presidents Eisenhower and Kennedy sent to Vietnam a number of military advisers and military aid to assist and support South Vietnam's non-Communist government. During Lyndon Johnson's presidency, the war escalated with thousands of American troops being sent to participate in combat with the South Vietnamese. The war was extremely unpopular in America and caused such serious divisiveness among its citizens that Johnson decided not to seek reelection in 1968. It was in President Richard Nixon's second term in office that the U.S. signed an agreement ending war in Vietnam and restoring peace. This was done January 27, 1973, and by March 29, the last American combat troops and American prisoners of war left Vietnam for home. It was the longest war in U.S. history and to this day carries the perception that it was a "lost war."

In 1962, during the administration of President John F. Kennedy, Premier Khrushchev and the Soviets decided, as a protective measure for Cuba against an American invasion, to install nuclear missiles on the island. In October, American U-2 spy planes photographed over Cuba what were identified as missile bases under construction. The decision in the White House was how to handle the situation without starting a war. The only recourse was removal of the missile sites and preventing more being set up. Kennedy announced that the U.S. had set up a "quarantine" of Soviet ships heading to Cuba. It was in reality a blockade but the word itself could not be used publicly as a blockade was actually considered an act of war.

A week of incredible tension and anxiety gripped the entire world until Khrushchev capitulated. Soviet ships carrying missiles for the Cuban bases turned back and the crisis eased. What precipitated the crisis was Khrushchev's underestimation of Kennedy. The President made no effort to prevent the erection of the Berlin Wall and was reluctant to commit American troops to invade Cuba and overthrow Fidel Castro. The Soviets assumed this was a weakness and decided they could install the missiles without any interference.

The Soviets were concerned about American missiles installed in Turkey aimed at the Soviet Union and about a possible invasion of Cuba. If successful, Khrushchev would demonstrate to the Russian and Chinese critics of his policy of peaceful coexistence that he was tough and not to be intimidated. At the same time, the Americans feared that if Russian missiles were put in place and launched from Cuba to the U.S., the short distance of 90 miles would not allow enough time for adequate warning and originate from a direction that radar systems could not detect. Also, it was felt that if America gave in and allowed a Soviet presence practically at the back door that the effect on American security and morale would be devastating.

As tensions eased in the aftermath of the crisis, several agreements were made. The missiles in Turkey were removed, as they were obsolete. A telephone "hot line" was set up between Moscow and Washington to make it possible for the two heads of government to have instant contact with each other. The U.S. agreed to sell its surplus wheat to the Soviets.

Probably the highlight of the foreign policy of President Richard Nixon, after the end of the Vietnam War and withdrawal of troops, was his 1972 trip to China. Since 1949, when the Communists gained control of China, the policy of the U.S. government refused to recognize the Communist government but regarded the legitimate government of China to be that of Chiang Kai-shek, exiled on the island of Taiwan.

In 1971, Nixon sent Henry Kissinger on a secret trip to Peking to investigate whether or not it would be possible for America to give recognition to China. In February 1972, President and Mrs. Nixon spent a number of days in the country visiting well-known Chinese landmarks, dining with the two leaders, Mao Tse-tung and Chou En-lai. Agreements were made for cultural and scientific exchanges, eventual resumption of trade, and future unification of the mainland with Taiwan. In 1979, formal diplomatic recognition was achieved. With this one visit, the pattern of the Cold War was essentially shifted.

In the administration of President Jimmy Carter, Egyptian President Anwar el-Sadat and Israeli Prime Minister Menachem Begin met at presidential retreat Camp David and agreed, after a series of meetings, to sign a formal treaty of peace between the two countries. In 1979, the Soviet invasion of Afghanistan was perceived by Carter and his advisers as a threat to the rich oil fields in the Persian Gulf but at the time, U.S. military capability to prevent further Soviet aggression in the Middle East was weak. The last year of Carter's presidential term was taken up with the 53 American hostages held in Iran. The shah had been deposed and control of the government and the country was in the hands of Muslim leader, Ayatollah Ruhollah Khomeini.

Khomeini's extreme hatred for the U.S. was the result of the 1953 overthrow of Iran's Mossadegh government, sponsored by the CIA. To make matters worse, the CIA proceeded to train the shah's ruthless secret police force. So when the terminally ill exiled shah was allowed into the U.S. for medical treatment, a fanatical mob stormed into the American embassy taking the 53 Americans as prisoners, supported and encouraged by Khomeini.

President Carter froze all Iranian assets in the U.S., set up trade restrictions, and approved a risky rescue attempt, which failed. He had appealed to the UN for aid in gaining release for the hostages and to European allies to join the trade embargo on Iran. Khomeini ignored UN requests for releasing the Americans and Europeans refused to support the embargo so as not to risk losing access to Iran's oil. American prestige was damaged and Carter's chances for reelection were doomed. The hostages were released on the day of Ronald Reagan's inauguration as President when Carter released Iranian assets as ransom.

The foreign policy of President Ronald Reagan was, in his first term, focused primarily on the Western Hemisphere, particularly in Central America and the West Indies. U.S. involvement in the domestic revolutions of El Salvador and Nicaragua continued into Reagan's second term when Congress held televised hearings on what came to be known as the Iran-Contra Affair. A cover-up was exposed showing that profits from secretly selling military hardware to Iran had been used to give support to rebels, called Contras, who were fighting in Nicaragua.

In 1983 in Lebanon, 241 American Marines were killed when an Islamic suicide bomber drove an explosive-laden truck into U.S. Marines headquarters located at the airport in Beirut. This tragic event came as part of the unrest and violence between the Israelis and the Palestinian Liberation Organization (PLO) forces in southern Lebanon.

In the same month, 1,900 U.S. Marines landed on the island of Grenada to rescue a small group of American medical students at the medical school and depose the leftist government. Perhaps the most intriguing and far-reaching event towards the end of Reagan's second term was the arms-reduction agreement Reagan reached with Soviet General Secretary Mikhail Gorbachev. Gorbachev began easing East-West tensions by stressing the importance of cooperation with the West and easing the harsh and restrictive life of the people in the Soviet Union. In retrospect, it was clearly a prelude to the events occurring during the administration of President George Bush.

After Bush took office, it appeared for a brief period that democracy would gain a hold and influence in China but the brief movement was quickly and decisively crushed. The biggest surprise was the fall of the Berlin Wall, resulting in the unification of all of Germany, the loss of power of the Communists in other Eastern European countries, and the fall of Communism in the Soviet Union and the breakup of its republics into independent nations. The countries of Poland, Hungary, Romania, Czechoslovakia, Albania, and Bulgaria replaced Communist rule for a democratic one.

The former Yugoslavia broke apart into individual ethnic enclaves with the republics of Serbia, Croatia, and Bosnia-Herzegovina embarking on wars of ethnic cleansing between Catholics, Orthodox, and Muslims. In Russia, as in the other former republics and satellites, democratic governments were put into operation and the difficult task of changing communist economies into ones of capitalistic free enterprise began. For all practical purposes, it appeared that the tensions and dangers of the post-World War II "Cold War" between the U.S. and Soviet-led Communism were over.

President Bush, in December of 1989, sent U.S. troops to invade Panama and arrest the Panamanian dictator Manuel Noriega. Although he had periodically assisted CIA operations with intelligence information, at the same time, Noriega laundered money from drug smuggling and gunrunning through Panama's banks. Though ignored for a short time, it became too embarrassing for the American intelligence community. When a political associate tried unsuccessfully to depose him and an off-duty U.S. Marine was shot and killed at a roadblock, Bush acted. Noriega was brought to the U.S. where he stood trial on charges of drug distribution and racketeering.

During the time of the American hostage crisis, Iraq and Iran fought a war in which the U.S. and most of Iraq's neighbors supported Iraq. In a five-year period, **Saddam Hussein** received from the U.S. $500 million worth of American technology, including lasers, advanced computers, and special machine tools used in missile development. The Iraq-Iran war was a bloody one resulting in a stalemate with a UN truce ending it. Neighboring Kuwait, in direct opposition to OPEC agreements, increased oil production.

This caused oil prices to drop, which upset Hussein, who was deeply in debt from the war and totally dependent on oil revenues. After a short period of time, Saddam invaded and occupied Kuwait. The U.S. made extensive plans to put into operation strategy to successfully carry out Operation Desert Storm, the liberation of Kuwait. In four days, February 24-28, 1991, the war was over and Iraq had been defeated, its troops driven back into their country. Saddam remained in power although Iraq's economy was seriously damaged.

President Bill Clinton sent U.S. troops to Haiti to protect the efforts of Jean-Bertrand Aristide to gain democratic power and to Bosnia to assist UN peacekeeping forces. He also inherited from the Bush administration the problem of Somalia in East Africa, where U.S. troops had been sent in December 1992 to support UN efforts to end the starvation of the Somalis and restore peace. The efforts were successful at first, but eventually failed due to the severity of the intricate political problems within the country. After U.S. soldiers were killed in an ambush along with 300 Somalis, American troops were withdrawn and returned home.

Skill 2.2.I   Recognize and be able to discuss the political, economic, and social issues of the 20th Century.

During the late 1800s and early 1900s, many Americans were concerned about and began actively campaigning for significant changes and reforms in the social, economic, and political systems in the country. Among their goals was ridding government corruption, regulating big businesses, reducing poverty, improving the lives of the poor and their living conditions, and ensuring more government response to the needs of the people.

Early efforts at reform began with movements to organize farmers and laborers, the push to give women the right to vote, and the successful passage of Congressional legislation establishing merit as the basis for federal jobs rather than political favoritism. Other efforts were directed towards improvements in education, living conditions in city slums, breaking up trusts, and monopolies in big businesses.

After World War I ended, the 18th Amendment to the U.S. Constitution was passed, forbidding the sale of alcoholic beverages. The violence and upheaval it caused was a major characteristic of the wild decade of the 1920s. The wild financial speculations came to an abrupt end with the stock market crash of October 1929, plunging the U.S. into the Great Depression.

The election of Franklin Roosevelt to the office of President in 1932 was the start of the social and economic recovery and reform legislative acts designed to gradually ease the country back to more prosperity. These acts included relief for the nation's farmers, regulation of banks, public works providing jobs for the unemployed, and giving aid to manufacturers. Some of the agencies set up to implement these measures included the Works Progress Administration (WPA), Civilian Conservation Camps (CCC), the Farm Credit Administration (FCA), and the Social Security Board. These last two agencies gave credit to farmers and set up the nation's social security system.

After World War II and the Korean War, efforts began to relieve the problems of millions of African-Americans, including ending discrimination in education, housing, and jobs and the grinding widespread poverty. The efforts of civil rights leaders found success in a number of Supreme Court decisions, the best-known case, "Brown vs Board of Education of Topeka (1954)" ending compulsory segregation in public schools. In the 1960s, the civil rights movement under the leadership of **Dr. Martin Luther King, Jr.,** really gained momentum and under **President Lyndon B. Johnson,** the **Civil Rights Acts of 1964 and 1968** prohibited discrimination in housing sales and rentals, employment, public accommodations, and voter registration.

Poverty remained a serious problem in the central sections of large cities resulting in riots and soaring crime rates, which ultimately found its way to the suburbs. The escalation of the war in Vietnam and the social conflict and upheaval of support vs opposition to U.S. involvement led to antiwar demonstrations, escalation of drug abuse, weakening of the family unit, homelessness, poverty, mental illness, along with increasing social, mental, and physical problems experienced by the Vietnam veterans returning to families, marriages, and a country all divided and torn apart.

The Watergate scandal resulting in the first-ever resignation of a sitting American president was the most crucial domestic crisis of the 1970s. The population of the U.S. had greatly increased and along with it the nation's industries and the resulting harmful pollution of the environment. Factory smoke, automobile exhaust, waste from factories and other sources all combined to create hazardous air, water, and ground pollution which, if not brought under control and significantly diminished, would severely endanger all life on earth.

The 1980s was the decade of the horrible Exxon Valdez oil spill off the Alaskan coast and the nuclear accident and melt-down at the Ukrainian nuclear power plant at Chernobyl. The U.S. had a narrow escape with the near disaster at Three Mile Island Nuclear Plant in Pennsylvania.

Inflation increased in the late 1960s, and the 1970s witnessed a period of high unemployment, the result of a severe recession. The decision of the OPEC (Organization of Petroleum Exporting Countries) ministers to cut back on oil production thus raising the price of a barrel of oil created a fuel shortage. This made it clear that energy and fuel conservation was necessary in the American economy, especially since fuel shortages created two energy crises during the decade of the 1970s. Americans experienced shortages of fuel oil for heating and gasoline for cars and other vehicles.

The 1980s saw the difficulties of rising inflation, recession, recovery, and the insecurity of long-term employment. Foreign competition and imports, the use of robots and other advanced technology in industries, the opening and operation of American companies and factories in other countries to lower labor costs all contributed to the economic and employment problems.

The nation's farmers experienced economic hardships and October, 1987 saw another one-day significant drop in the Dow Jones on the New York Stock Exchange. January 28, 1986 was the day of the loss of the seven crew members of the NASA space shuttle "Challenger". The reliability and soundness of numerous savings and loans institutions were in serious jeopardy when hundreds of these failed and others went into bankruptcy due to customer default on loans and mismanagement. Congressional legislation helped rebuild the industry.

Skill 2.2. m   Recognize the significant accomplishments made by immigrants, racial, ethnic, and gender groups.

Most students of American history are aware of the tremendous influx of immigrants to America during the 19th century. It is also a known fact that the majority settled in the ethnic neighborhoods and communities of the large cities, close to friends, relatives, and the work they were able to find. After the Civil War ended, the U.S. Congress passed the 1862 Homestead Act and the West began to open up for settlement. There is one interesting fact some are not aware of. More than half of the hardy pioneers who went to homestead and farm western lands were European immigrants: Swedes, Norwegians, Czechs, Germans, Danes, Finns, and Russians.

By far, the nation's immigrants were an important reason for America's phenomenal industrial growth from 1865 to 1900. They came seeking work and better opportunities for themselves and their families than what life in their native country could give them. What they found in America was suspicion and distrust because they were competitors with Americans for jobs, housing, and decent wages. Their languages, customs, and ways of living were different, especially between the different national and ethnic groups. Until the early 1880s, most immigrants were from the parts of northwestern Europe such as Germany, Scandinavia, the Netherlands, Ireland, and Great Britain.

After 1890, the new arrivals increasingly came from eastern and southern Europe. Chinese immigrants on the Pacific coast, so crucial to the construction of the western part of the first transcontinental railroad, were the first to experience this increasing distrust which eventually erupted into violence and bloodshed. From about 1879 to the present time, the U.S. Congress made, repealed, and amended numerous pieces of legislation concerning quotas, restrictions, and other requirements pertaining to immigrants. The immigrant laborers, both skilled and unskilled, were the foundation of the modern labor union movement as a means of gaining recognition, support, respect, rights, fair wages, and better working conditions.

The historical record of African-Americans is known to all. Sold into slavery by rival tribes, they were brought against their will to the West Indies and southern America to slave on the plantations in a life-long condition of servitude and bondage. The 13th Constitutional Amendment abolished slavery; the 14th gave them U.S. citizenship; and the 15th gave them the right to vote. Efforts of well-known African-Americans resulted in some improvements although the struggle was continuous without let-up. Many were outspoken and urged and led protests against the continued onslaught of discrimination and inequality.

The leading black spokesman from 1890 to 1915 was educator Booker T. Washington. He recognized the need of vocational education for African-Americans, educating them for skills and training for such areas as domestic service, farming, the skilled trades, and small business enterprises. He founded and built in Alabama the famous Tuskegee Institute.

W.E.B. DuBois, another outstanding African-American leader and spokesman, believed that only continuous and vigorous protests against injustices and inequalities coupled with appeals to black pride would effect changes. The results of his efforts was the formation of the Urban League and the NAACP (the National Association for the Advancement of Colored People) which today continue to eliminate discriminations and secure equality and equal rights.

Others who made significant contributions were **Dr. George Washington Carver's** work improving agricultural techniques for both black and white farmers; the writers William Wells Brown, Paul L. Dunbar, Langston Hughes, and Charles W. Chesnutt; the music of Duke Ellington, W.C. Handy, Marion Anderson, Louis Armstrong, Leontyne Price, Jessye Norman, Ella Fitzgerald, and many, many others.

Students of American history are greatly familiar with the accomplishments and contributions of American women. Previous mention has been made of the accomplishments of such 19th century women as: writer Louisa Mae Alcott; abolitionist Harriet Beecher Stowe; women's rights activists Elizabeth Cady Stanton and Lucretia Mott; physician Dr. Elizabeth Blackwell; women's education activists Mary Lyon, Catharine Esther Beecher, and Emma Hart Willard; prison and asylum reform activist Dorothea Dix; social reformer, humanitarian, pursuer of peace Jane Addams; aviatrix Amelia Earhart; women's suffrage activists Susan B. Anthony, Carrie Chapman Catt, and Anna Howard Shaw; Supreme Court Associate Justices Sandra Day O'Connor and Ruth Bader Ginsberg; and many, many more who have made tremendous contributions in science, politics and government, music and the arts (such as Jane Alexander who is National Chairperson of the National Endowment for the Arts), education, athletics, law, etc.

Skill 2.2.n   Be able to demonstrate a knowledge of Illinois history.

See Competency 4.5

Competency 2.3   Understand major trends, key turning points, and the roles of influential individuals and groups in world history.

Prehistory is defined as the period of man's achievements before the development of writing. In the Stone Age cultures, there were three different periods. They are the **Lower Paleolithic Period** with the use of crude tools. The **Upper Paleolithic Period** exhibiting a greater variety of better-made tools and implements, the wearing of clothing, highly organized group life, and skills in art. And finally the **Neolithic Period** which showed domesticated animals, food production, the arts of knitting, spinning and weaving cloth, starting fires through friction, building houses rather than living in caves, the development of institutions including the family, religion, and a form of government or the origin of the state.

Ancient civilizations were those cultures which developed to a greater degree and were considered advanced. These included the following eleven with their major accomplishments.

Egypt made numerous significant contributions including construction of the great pyramids; development of hieroglyphic writing; preservation of bodies after death; making paper from papyrus; contributing to developments in arithmetic and geometry; the invention of the method of counting in groups of 1-10 (the decimal system); completion of a solar calendar; and laying the foundation for science and astronomy.

The ancient civilization of the **Sumerians** invented the wheel; developed irrigation through use of canals, dikes, and devices for raising water; devised the system of cuneiform writing; learned to divide time; and built large boats for trade. The Babylonians devised the famous **Code of Hammurabi**, a code of laws.

The ancient **Assyrians** were warlike and aggressive due to a highly organized military and used horse drawn chariots.

The **Hebrews**, also known as the ancient Israelites instituted "monotheism," which is the worship of one God, Yahweh, and combined the 66 books of the Hebrew and Christian Greek scriptures into the Bible we have today.

The **Minoans** had a system of writing using symbols to represent syllables in words. They built palaces with multiple levels containing many rooms, water and sewage systems with flush toilets, bathtubs, hot and cold running water, and bright paintings on the walls.

The **Mycenaeans** changed the Minoan writing system to aid their own language and used symbols to represent syllables.

The **Phoenicians** were sea traders well known for their manufacturing skills in glass and metals and the development of their famous purple dye. They became so very proficient in the skill of navigation that they were able to sail by the stars at night. Further, they devised an alphabet using symbols to represent single sounds, which was an improved extension of the Egyptian principle and writing system.

In **India**, the caste system was developed, the principle of zero in mathematics was discovered, and the major religion of Hinduism was begun.

China began building the Great Wall; practiced crop rotation and terrace farming; increased the importance of the silk industry, and developed caravan routes across Central Asia for extensive trade. Also, they increased proficiency in rice cultivation and developed a written language based on drawings or pictographs (no alphabet symbolizing sounds as each word or character had a form different from all others).

The ancient **Persians** developed an alphabet; contributed the religions/philosophies of **Zoroastrianism**, **Mithraism**, and **Gnosticism**; and allowed conquered peoples to retain their own customs, laws, and religions.

The classical civilization of **Greece** reached the highest levels in man's achievements based on the foundations already laid by such ancient groups as the Egyptians, Phoenicians, Minoans, and Mycenaeans.

Among the more important contributions of Greece were the Greek alphabet derived from the Phoenician letters which formed the basis for the Roman alphabet and our present-day alphabet. Extensive trading and colonization resulted in the spread of the Greek civilization. The love of sports, with emphasis on a sound body, led to the tradition of the Olympic Games. Greece was responsible for the rise of independent, strong city-states. Note the complete contrast between independent, freedom-loving Athens with its practice of pure democracy i.e. direct, personal, active participation in government by qualified citizens and the rigid, totalitarian, militaristic Sparta. Other important areas that the Greeks are credited with influencing include drama, epic and lyric poetry, fables, myths centered on the many gods and goddesses, science, astronomy, medicine, mathematics, philosophy, art, architecture, and recording historical events. The conquests of Alexander the Great spread Greek ideas to the areas he conquered and brought to the Greek world many ideas from Asia including the value of ideas, wisdom, curiosity, and the desire to learn as much about the world as possible.

A most interesting and significant characteristic of the Greek, Hellenic, and Roman civilizations was "secularism" where emphasis shifted away from religion to the state. Men were not absorbed in or dominated by religion as had been the case in Egypt and the nations located in Mesopotamia. Religion and its leaders did not dominate the state and its authority was greatly diminished.

In **India**, Hinduism was a continuing influence along with the rise of Buddhism. Industry and commerce developed along with extensive trading with the Near East. Outstanding advances in the fields of science and medicine were made along with being one of the first to be active in navigation and maritime enterprises during this time.

China is considered by some historians to be the oldest, uninterrupted civilization in the world and was in existence around the same time as the ancient civilizations founded in **Egypt**, **Mesopotamia**, and the **Indus Valley**. The Chinese studied nature and weather; stressed the importance of education, family, and a strong central government; followed the religions of Buddhism, Confucianism, and Taoism; and invented such things as gunpowder, paper, printing, and the magnetic compass.

The civilization in **Japan** appeared during this time having borrowed much of their culture from China. It was the last of these classical civilizations to develop. Although they used, accepted, and copied Chinese art, law, architecture, dress, and writing, the Japanese refined these into their own unique way of life, including incorporating the religion of Buddhism into their culture.

The civilizations in **Africa** south of the Sahara were developing the refining and use of iron, especially for farm implements and later for weapons. Trading was overland using camels and at important seaports. The Arab influence was extremely important, as was their later contact with Indians, Christian Nubians, and Persians. In fact, their trading activities were probably the most important factor in the spread of and assimilation of different ideas and stimulation of cultural growth.

The **Vikings** had a lot of influence at this time with spreading their ideas and knowledge of trade routes and sailing, accomplished first through their conquests and later through trade.

In other parts of the world were the **Byzantine** and **Saracenic** (or Islamic) civilizations, both dominated by religion. The major contributions of the Saracens were in the areas of science and philosophy. Included were accomplishments in astronomy, mathematics, physics, chemistry, medicine, literature, art, trade and manufacturing, agriculture, and a marked influence on the Renaissance period of history.

The **Byzantines** (Christians) made important contributions in art and the preservation of Greek and Roman achievements including architecture (especially in Eastern Europe and Russia), the Code of Justinian and Roman law.

The ancient empire of **Ghana** occupied an area that is now known as Northern Senegal and Southern Mauritania. There is no absolute certainty regarding the origin of this empire. Oral history dates the rise of the empire to the 7th century BCE. Most believe, however, that the date should be placed much later. Many believe the nomads who were herding animals on the fringes of the desert posed a threat to the early Soninke people, who were an agricultural community. In times of drought, it is believed the nomads raided the agricultural villages for water and places to pasture their herds. To protect their selves, it is believed that these farming communities formed a loose confederation that eventually became the empire of ancient Ghana.

The word "Ghana" means king or war chief. It is believed that the Arabs and Europeans took this reference to the king to be the name of the society. These rulers conquered neighboring communities and thus extended the boundaries of the growing empire. The purpose of expansion was to gain control of trade routes. By the fifth century (some say the seventh century) a kingdom had been established. This kingship was significantly different from most other kingships of the time. First, kingship was matrilineal. The sister of the king provided the heir to the throne. Second, the king ruled in conjunction with a People's Council chosen from all social strata.

The empire's economic vitality was determined by geographical location. It was situated midway between the desert, which was the major source of salt and the gold fields. This location along the trade routes of the camel caravans provided exceptional opportunity for economic development. The caravans brought copper, salt, dried fruit, clothing, manufactured goods, etc. For these goods, the people of Ghana traded kola nuts, leather goods, gold, hides, ivory and slaves. In addition, the empire collected taxes on every trade item that entered the boundaries of the empire.

With the revenue from the trade goods tax, the empire supported a government, an army that protected the trade routes and the borders, the maintenance of the capital, and primary market centers. But it was control of the gold fields that gave the empire political power and economic prosperity. The location of the gold fields was a carefully guarded secret. By the 10th century, Ghana was very rich and controlled an area about the size of the state of Texas. Demand for this gold sharply increased in the 9th and 10th centuries as the Islamic states of Northern Africa began to mint coins. As the gold trade expanded, so did the empire.

The availability of local iron ore enabled the early people of the Ghana kingdom to make more efficient farm implements and effective weapons. But in the 11th century the Berbers attacked the empire in an attempt to gain control of the gold fields and to purify Islam as it was practiced in Ghana. They eventually withdrew, but they left behind a greatly weakened empire. Later invasions and internal rebellions further weakened the empire and made the trade routes quite dangerous. The merchants moved east and the empire began to crumble. A serious drought compounded the disintegration of the empire through deterioration of the environment and overgrazing. By the middle of the 13th century, the empire was just a memory.

The **Tang Dynasty** extended from 618 to 907. Its capital was the most heavily populated of any city in the world at the time. Buddhism was adopted by the imperial family (Li) and became an integral part of Chinese culture. The emperor, however, feared the monasteries and began to take action against them in the 10th century. Confucianism experienced a rebirth during the time of this dynasty as an instrument of state administration. Following a civil war, the central government lost control of local areas. Warlords arose in 907, and China was divided into north and south. These areas came to be ruled by short-lived minor dynasties. A major political accomplishment of this period was the creation of a class of career government officials, who functioned between the populace and the government. This class of "scholar-officials" continued to fulfill this function in government and society until 1911.

The period of the Tang Dynasty is generally considered a pinnacle of Chinese civilization. Through contact with the Middle East and India, the period of the Tang Dynasty was marked by great creativity in many areas. Block printing was invented, and made much information and literature available to wide audiences.

In science, astronomers calculated the paths of the sun and the moon and the movements of the constellations. This facilitated the development of the calendar. In agriculture, such technologies as cultivating the land by setting it on fire, the curved-shaft plow, separate cultivation of seedlings, and sophisticated irrigation system increased productivity. Hybrid breeds of horses and mules were created to strengthen the labor supply. In medicine, there were achievements like the understanding of the circulatory system and the digestive system and great advances in pharmacology. Ceramics was another area in which great advances were made. A new type of glazing was invented that gave Tang Dynasty porcelain and earthenware its unique appearance through three-colored glazing.

In literature, the poetry of the period is generally considered the best in the entire history of Chinese literature. The rebirth of Confucianism led to the publication of many commentaries on the classical writings. Encyclopedias on several subjects were produced, as well as histories and philosophical works.

SUBAREA III: HISTORICAL CONCEPTS AND WORLD HISTORY

Competency 3.1 Understand the prehistory of human civilization and the development of world civilizations from 1000 B.C.E. to 1500 C.E.

Skill 3.1.a Establish an understanding of prehistory and the ancient civilizations, including the non-Western world.

Prehistory is defined as the period of man's achievements before the development of writing. In the Stone Age cultures, there were three different periods. They are the Lower Paleolithic period with the use of crude tools; the Upper Paleolithic period exhibiting a greater variety of better-made tools and implements, the wearing of clothing, highly organized group life, and skills in art; and the Neolithic period which showed domesticated animals, food production, the arts of knitting, spinning and weaving cloth, starting fires through friction, building houses rather than living in caves, the development of institutions including the family, religion, and a form of government or the origin of the state.

Ancient civilizations were those cultures, which developed to a greater degree and were considered advanced. These included the following eleven with their major accomplishments.

Egypt made numerous significant contributions including construction of the great pyramids; development of hieroglyphic writing; preservation of bodies after death; making paper from papyrus; contributing to developments in arithmetic and geometry; the invention of the method of counting in groups of 1-10 (the decimal system); completion of a solar calendar; and laying the foundation for science and astronomy.

The ancient civilization of the **Sumerians** invented the wheel; developed irrigation through use of canals, dikes, and devices for raising water; devised the system of cuneiform writing; learned to divide time; and built large boats for trade. The Babylonians devised the famous Code of Hammurabi, a code of laws.

The ancient **Assyrians** were warlike and aggressive due to a highly organized military and used horse drawn chariots. The **Hebrews**, also known as the **ancient Israelites** instituted "monotheism," which is the worship of one God, Yahweh, and combined the 66 books of the Hebrew and Christian Greek scriptures into the Bible we have today.

The **Minoans** had a system of writing using symbols to represent syllables in words. They built palaces with multiple levels containing many rooms, water and sewage systems with flush toilets, bathtubs, hot and cold running water, and bright paintings on the walls.

The **Mycenaeans** changed the Minoan writing system to aid their own language and used symbols to represent syllables.

The **Phoenicians** were sea traders well known for their manufacturing skills in glass and metals and the development of their famous purple dye. They became so very proficient in the skill of navigation that they were able to sail by the stars at night. Further, they devised an alphabet using symbols to represent single sounds, which was an improved extension of the Egyptian principle and writing system.

In **India,** the caste system was developed, the principle of zero in mathematics was discovered, and the major religion of **Hinduism** was begun.

China began building the Great Wall; practiced crop rotation and terrace farming; increased the importance of the silk industry, and developed caravan routes across Central Asia for extensive trade. Also, they increased proficiency in rice cultivation and developed a written language based on drawings or pictographs (no alphabet symbolizing sounds as each word or character had a form different from all others).

The ancient **Persians** developed an alphabet; contributed the religions/philosophies of Zoroastrianism, Mithraism, and Gnosticism; and allowed conquered peoples to retain their own customs, laws, and religions.

Skill 3.1.b   Understand the important contributions of classical civilizations, including the non-Western world.

The classical civilization of **Greece** reached the highest levels in man's achievements based on the foundations already laid by such ancient groups as the Egyptians, Phoenicians, Minoans, and Mycenaeans. Among the more important contributions of Greece were the Greek alphabet derived from the Phoenician letters which formed the basis for the Roman and our present-day alphabets, extensive trading and colonization resulting in the spread of the Greek civilization; the love of sports with emphasis on a sound body, leading to the tradition of the Olympic games; the rise of independent, strong city-states; the complete contrast between independent, freedom-loving Athens with its practice of pure democracy (direct, personal, active participation in government by qualified citizens) and rigid, totalitarian, militaristic Sparta; important accomplishments in drama, epic and lyric poetry, fables, myths centered around the many gods and goddesses, science, astronomy, medicine, mathematics, philosophy, art, architecture, writing about and recording historical events; the conquests of Alexander the Great spreading Greek ideas to the areas he conquered and bringing to the Greek world many ideas from Asia; and above all, the value of ideas, wisdom, curiosity, and the desire to learn as much about the world as was possible.

The ancient civilization of **Rome** lasted approximately 1,000 years including the periods of republic and empire, although its lasting influence on Europe and its history was for a much longer period. There was a very sharp contrast between the curious, imaginative, inquisitive Greeks and the practical, simple, down-to-earth, no-nonsense Romans who spread and preserved the ideas of ancient Greece and other culture groups. The contributions and accomplishments of the Romans are numerous but their greatest included language, engineering and building, law, government, roads, trade, and the **"Pax Romana",** the long period of peace enabling free travel and trade, spreading people, cultures, goods, and ideas all over a vast area of the known world.

A most interesting and significant characteristic of the Greek, Hellenic, and Roman civilizations was **"secularism"** where emphasis shifted away from religion to the state. Men were not absorbed in or dominated by religion as had been the case in Egypt and the nations located in Mesopotamia. Religion and its leaders did not dominate the state and its authority was greatly diminished.

In **India, Hinduism** was a continuing influence along with the rise of Buddhism. Industry and commerce developed along with extensive trading with the Near East. Outstanding advances in the fields of science and medicine were made along with being one of the first to be active in navigation and maritime enterprises during this time.

China is considered by some historians as the oldest, uninterrupted civilization in the world and was in existence around the same time as the ancient civilizations found in Egypt, Mesopotamia, and the Indus Valley. The Chinese studied nature and weather; stressed the importance of education, family, and a strong central government; followed the religions of **Buddhism, Confucianism, and Taoism;** and invented such things as gunpowder, paper, printing, and the magnetic compass.

The civilization in **Japan** appeared during this time having borrowed much of their culture from China. It was the last of these classical civilizations to develop. Although they used, accepted, and copied Chinese art, law, architecture, dress, and writing, the Japanese refined these into their own unique way of life, including incorporating the religion of Buddhism into their culture.

The civilizations in **Africa** south of the Sahara were developing the refining and use of iron, especially for farm implements and later for weapons. Trading was overland using camels and at important seaports. The Arab influence was extremely important, as was their later contact with Indians, Christian Nubians, and Persians. In fact, their trading activities were probably the most important factor in the spread of and assimilation of different ideas and stimulation of cultural growth.

Skill 3.1.c   Demonstrate an understanding of the period known as the Middle Ages.

The official end of the **Roman Empire** came when Germanic tribes took over and controlled most of Europe. The five major tribes were the Visigoths, Ostrogoths, Vandals, Saxons, and the Franks. In later years, the Franks successfully stopped the invasion of southern **Europe** by Muslims by soundly defeating them under the leadership of Charles Martel at the Battle of Tours in 732 A. D. Thirty-six years later in 768 A. D., the grandson of Charles Martel became King of the Franks and is known in history as Charlemagne. Charlemagne was a man of war but was unique in his respect for and encouragement of learning. He made great efforts to rule fairly and ensure just treatment for his people.

The **Vikings** had a lot of influence at this time with spreading their ideas and knowledge of trade routes and sailing, accomplished first through their conquests and later through trade.

The purpose of the Crusades was to rid Jerusalem of Muslim control and these series of violent, bloody conflicts did affect trade and stimulated later explorations seeking the new, exotic products such as silks and spices. The **Crusaders** came into contact with other religions and cultures and learned and spread many new ideas.

During this time, the system of **feudalism** became the dominant feature. It was a system of loyalty and protection. The strong protected the weak that returned the service with farm labor, military service, and loyalty. Life was lived out on a vast estate, owned by a nobleman and his family, called a "manor." It was a complete village supporting a few hundred people, mostly peasants. Improved tools and farming methods made life more bearable although most never left the manor or traveled from their village during their lifetime.

Also coming into importance at this time was the era of **knighthood** and its code of chivalry as well as the tremendous influence of the Church (Roman Catholic). Until the period of the Renaissance, the Church was the only place where people could be educated. The **Bible** and other books were hand-copied by monks in the monasteries. Cathedrals were built and were decorated with art depicting religious subjects.

With the increase in trade and travel, cities sprang up and began to grow. Craft workers in the cities developed their skills to a high degree, eventually organizing **guilds** to protect the quality of the work and to regulate the buying and selling of their products. City government developed and flourished centered on strong town councils. Active in city government and the town councils were the wealthy businessmen who made up the rising middle class.

The end of the **feudal manorial system** was sealed by the outbreak and spread of the infamous Black Death, which killed over one-third of the total population of Europe. Those who survived and were skilled in any job or occupation were in demand and many serfs or peasants found freedom and, for that time, a decidedly improved standard of living. Strong nation-states became powerful and people developed a renewed interest in life and learning.

In other parts of the world were the **Byzantine and Saracenic** (or Islamic) civilizations, both dominated by religion. The major contributions of the Saracens were in the areas of science and philosophy. Included were accomplishments in astronomy, mathematics, physics, chemistry, medicine, literature, art, trade and manufacturing, agriculture, and a marked influence on the Renaissance period of history.

The Byzantines (Christians) made important contributions in art and the preservation of Greek and Roman achievements including architecture (especially in eastern Europe and Russia), the Code of Justinian and Roman law.

Skill 3.1.d   Demonstrate an understanding of the importance and accomplishments of the Renaissance and Reformation periods

The word "Renaissance" literally means "rebirth" and signaled the rekindling of interest in the glory of ancient classical Greece and Rome civilizations. It was the period in human history marking the start of many ideas and innovations leading to our modern age.

The **Renaissance** began in Italy with many of its ideas starting in Florence, controlled by the infamous Medici family. Education, especially for some of the merchants, required reading, writing, math, the study of law, and the writings of classical Greece and Rome. Contributions of the Italian Renaissance period were in:

- a) art - the more important artists were Giotto and his development of perspective in paintings; Leonardo da Vinci was not only an artist but also a scientist and inventor; Michelangelo was a sculptor, painter, and architect; and others including Raphael, Donatello, Titian, and Tintoretto

- b) political philosophy - the writings of Machiavelli

- c) literature - the writings of Petrarch and Boccaccio

- d) science – Galileo

      e)   medicine - the work of Brussels-born Andrea Vesalius earned him the title of "father of anatomy" and had a profound influence on the Spaniard Michael Servetus and the Englishman William Harvey

In Germany, Gutenberg's invention of the **printing press** with movable type facilitated the rapid spread of Renaissance ideas, writings and innovations, thus ensuring the enlightenment of most of Western Europe. Contributions were also made by Durer and Holbein in art and by Paracelsus in science and medicine.

The effects of the Renaissance in the Low Countries can be seen in the literature and philosophy of Erasmus and the art of van Eyck and Breughel the Elder. Rabelais and de Montaigne in France also contributed to literature and philosophy. In Spain, the art of El Greco and de Morales flourished, as did the writings of Cervantes and De Vega. In England, Sir Thomas More and Sir Francis Bacon wrote and taught philosophy and inspired by Vesalius. William Harvey made important contributions in medicine. The greatest talent was found in literature and drama and given to mankind by **Chaucer, Spenser, Marlowe, Jonson, and the incomparable Shakespeare.**

The **Reformation** period consisted of two phases: the Protestant Revolution and the Catholic Reformation. The Protestant Revolution came about because of religious, political, and economic reasons. The religious reasons stemmed from abuses in the Catholic Church including fraudulent clergy with their scandalous immoral lifestyles; the sale of religious offices, indulgences, and dispensations; different theologies within the Church; and frauds involving sacred relics.

The political reasons for the **Protestant Revolution** involved the increase in the power of rulers who were considered "absolute monarchs" wanting all power and control, especially over the Church; and the growth of "nationalism" or patriotic pride in one's own country.

Economic reasons included the greedy desire of ruling monarchs to possess and control all lands and wealth of the Church; deep animosity against the burdensome papal taxation; the rise of the affluent middle class and its clash with medieval Church ideals; and the increase of an active system of "intense" capitalism.

The Protestant Revolution began in Germany with the revolt of **Martin Luther** against Church abuses. It spread to Switzerland where it was led by Calvin. It began in England with the efforts of King Henry VIII to have his marriage to Catherine of Aragon annulled so he could wed another and have a male heir. The results were the increasing support given not only by the people but also by nobles and some rulers, and of course, the attempts of the Church to stop it.

The **Catholic Reformation** was undertaken by the Church to "clean up its act" and to slow or stop the Protestant Revolution. The major efforts to this end were supplied by the Council of Trent and the Jesuits. Six major results of the Reformation included:
- Religious freedom,
- Religious tolerance,
- More opportunities for education,
- Power and control of rulers limited,
- Increase in religious wars, and
- An increase in fanaticism and persecution.

Competency 3.2 Understand major social, intellectual, economic, and geopolitical developments of the First Global Age, the Age of Revolution, and the Industrial Revolution, from 1450 to 1850.

Skill 3.2.a   Understand the importance and results of the Age of Exploration.

A number of individuals and events led to the time of exploration and discoveries. The **Vivaldo brothers and Marco Polo** wrote of their travels and experiences, which signaled the early beginnings. From the Crusades, the survivors made their way home to different places in Europe bringing with them fascinating, new information about exotic lands, people, customs, and desired foods and goods such as spices and silks.

The Renaissance ushered in a time of curiosity, learning, and incredible energy sparking the desire for trade to procure these new, exotic products and to find better, faster, cheaper trade routes to get to them. The work of geographers, astronomers and mapmakers made important contributions and many studied and applied the work of such men as **Hipparchus of Greece, Ptolemy of Egypt, Tycho Brahe of Denmark, and Fra Mauro of Italy.**

Portugal made the start under the encouragement, support, and financing of Prince Henry the Navigator. The better known explorers who sailed under the flag of Portugal included **Cabral, Diaz, and Vasco da Gama,** who successfully sailed all the way from Portugal, around the southern tip of Africa, to Calcutta, India.

Christopher Columbus, sailing for Spain, is credited with the discovery of America although he never set foot on its soil. Magellan is credited with the first circumnavigation of the earth. Other Spanish explorers made their marks in parts of what are now the United States, Mexico, and South America.

For France, claims to various parts of North America were the result of the efforts of such men as **Verrazano, Champlain, Cartier, LaSalle, Father Marquette and Joliet.** Dutch claims were based on the work of one **Henry Hudson. John Cabot gave** England its stake in North America along with **John Hawkins, Sir Francis Drake, and the half-brothers Sir Walter Raleigh and Sir Humphrey Gilbert.**

Actually the first Europeans in the New World were Norsemen led by **Eric the Red** and later, his son **Leif the Lucky.** However, before any of these, the ancestors of today's **Native Americans and Latin American Indians** crossed the Bering Strait from Asia to Alaska, eventually settling in all parts of the Americas.

Skill 3.2.b   Understand the significance of revolutionary movements.

The time period of the 1700s and 1800s was characterized in Western countries by the opposing political ideas of **democracy and nationalism,** resulting in strong nationalistic feelings and people of common cultures asserting their belief in the right to have a part in their government.

The **American Revolution** resulted in the successful efforts of the English colonies in America, experienced in over one hundred years of mostly self-government and resentful of increased British meddling and ever-increasing control, in declaring their freedom, winning a war with aid from France, and forming a new independent nation.

The **French Revolution** was the revolt of the middle and lower classes against the gross political and economic excesses of the rulers and the supporting nobility. It ended with the establishment of the First in a series of French Republics. Conditions leading to revolt included extreme taxation, inflation, lack of food, and the total disregard for the impossible, degrading, and unacceptable condition of the people on the part of the rulers, nobility, and the Church.

The **Industrial Revolution,** which began in Great Britain and spread elsewhere, was the development of power-driven machinery (fueled by coal and steam) leading to the accelerated growth of industry with large factories replacing homes and small workshops as work centers. The lives of people changed drastically and a largely agricultural society changed to an industrial one. In Western Europe, the period of empire and colonialism began as the industrial nations seized and claimed parts of Africa and Asia in an effort to control and provide the raw materials needed to feed the industries and machines in the "mother country". Later developments included power based on electricity and internal combustion, replacing coal and steam.

The **Russian Revolution** occurred first in March (or February on the old calendar) 1917 with the abdication of Tsar Nicholas II and the establishment of a democratic government. The strength of the Bolsheviks, those who were the extreme Marxists and had a majority in Russia's socialist party, overcame opposition and in November (October on the old calendar) did away with the provisional democratic government and set up the world's first Marxist state.

The conditions in Russia in previous centuries led up to this. Russia's harsh climate, tremendous size, and physical isolation from the rest of Europe, along with the brutal despotic rule and control of the tsars over enslaved peasants, contributed to the final conditions leading to revolution. Despite the tremendous efforts of Peter the Great to bring his country up to the social, cultural, and economic standards of the rest of Europe, Russia always remained a hundred years or more behind. Autocratic rule, the existence of the system of serfdom or slavery of the peasants, lack of money, defeats in wars, lack of enough food and food production, little, if any, industrialization--all of these contributed to conditions ripe for revolt.

By 1914, Russia's industrial growth was even faster than Germany's and agricultural production was improving, along with better transportation. However, the conditions of poverty were horrendous. The Orthodox Church was steeped in political activities and the absolute rule of the tsar was the order of the day. By the time the nation entered World War I, conditions were just right for revolution. Marxist socialism seemed to be the solution or answer to all the problems. Russia had to stop participation in the war, although winning a big battle. Industry could not meet the military's needs.

Transportation by rail was severely disrupted and it was most difficult to procure supplies from the Allies. The people had had enough of war, injustice, starvation, poverty, slavery, and cruelty. The support for and strength of the Bolsheviks were mainly in the cities. After two or three years of civil war, fighting foreign invasions, and opposing other revolutionary groups, the Bolsheviks were finally successful in making possible a type of "pre-Utopia" for the workers and the people.

As succeeding **Marxist or Communist** leaders came to power, the effects of this violent revolution were felt all around the earth. From 1989 till 1991, Communism eventually gave way to various forms of democracies and free enterprise societies in Eastern Europe and the former Soviet Union. The foreign policies of all free Western nations were directly and immensely affected by the Marxist-Communist ideology. Its effect on Eastern Europe and the former Soviet Union was felt politically, economically, socially, culturally, and geographically. The people of ancient Russia simply exchanged one autocratic dictatorial system for another and its impact on all of the people on the earth is still being felt to this day.

Competency 3.3   Understand major political, geopolitical, social, cultural, and economic developments since 1850.

Skill 3.3.a   Understand the importance of the growth of nationalism.

The time from 1830 to 1914 is characterized by the extraordinary growth and spread of **patriotic pride** in a nation along with intense, widespread imperialism. Loyalty to one's nation included national pride; extension and maintenance of sovereign political boundaries; unification of smaller states with common language, history, and culture into a more powerful nation; or smaller national groups who, as part of a larger multi-cultural empire, wished to separate into smaller, political, cultural nations. Examples of major events of this time resulting from the insurgence of nationalism include:

In the United States, **territorial expansion** occurred in the expansion westward under the banner of **"Manifest Destiny."** In addition, the U.S. was involved in the War with Mexico, the Spanish-American War, and support of the Latin American colonies of Spain in their revolt for independence. In Latin America, the Spanish colonies were successful in their fight for independence and self-government.

In Europe, Italy and Germany were each totally united into one nation from many smaller states. There were revolutions in Austria and Hungary, the Franco-Prussian War, the dividing of Africa among the strong European nations, interference and intervention of Western nations in Asia, and the breakup of Turkish dominance in the Balkans.

In Africa, France, Great Britain, Italy, Portugal, Spain, Germany, and Belgium controlled the entire continent except Liberia and Ethiopia. In Asia and the Pacific Islands, only China, Japan, and present-day Thailand (Siam) kept their independence. The others were controlled by the strong European nations.

An additional reason for **European imperialism** was the harsh, urgent demand for the raw materials needed to fuel and feed the great Industrial Revolution. These resources were not available in the huge quantity so desperately needed which necessitated (and rationalized) the partitioning of the continent of Africa and parts of Asia. In turn, these colonial areas would purchase the finished manufactured goods.

Skill 3.3.b   Understand the causes and results of the wars of the 20th century.

World War I ☐ 1914 to 1918

Causes were: the surge of nationalism, the increasing strength of military capabilities, massive colonization for raw materials needed for industrialization and manufacturing, and military and diplomatic alliances.

The initial spark, which started the conflagration, was the assassination of Austrian Archduke Francis Ferdinand and his wife in Sarajevo.

There were 28 nations involved in the war, not including colonies and territories. It began July 28, 1914 and ended November 11, 1918 with the signing of the Treaty of Versailles. Economically, the war cost a total of $337 billion; increased inflation and huge war debts; and caused a loss of markets, goods, jobs, and factories. Politically, old empires collapsed; many monarchies disappeared; smaller countries gained temporary independence; Communists seized power in Russia; and, in some cases, nationalism increased. Socially, total populations decreased because of war casualties and low birth rates. There were millions of displaced persons and villages and farms were destroyed. Cities grew while women made significant gains in the work force and the ballot box. There was less social distinction and classes. Attitudes completely changed and old beliefs and values were questioned. The peace settlement established the League of Nations to ensure peace, but it failed to do so.

World War II ☐ 1939 to 1945

Causes were:

a) Ironically, **the Treaty of Paris,** the peace treaty ending World War I, ultimately led to the Second World War. Countries that fought in the first war were either dissatisfied over the "spoils" of war, or were punished so harshly that resentment continued building to an eruption twenty years later.

b) The **economic problems** of both winners and losers of the first war were never resolved and the worldwide Great Depression of the 1930s dealt the final blow to any immediate rapid recovery. Democratic governments in Europe were severely strained and weakened which in turn gave strength and encouragement to those political movements that were extreme and made promises to end the economic chaos in their countries.

c) **Nationalism,** which was a major cause of World War I, grew even stronger and seemed to feed the feelings of discontent, which became increasingly rampant.

d) Because of **unstable economic** conditions and political unrest, harsh dictatorships arose in several of the countries, especially where there was no history of experience in democratic government.

e) Countries such as Germany, Japan, and Italy began to **aggressively expand their borders** and acquire additional territory.

In all, 59 nations became embroiled in World War II, which began September 1, 1939 and ended September 2, 1945. These dates include both the European and Pacific Theaters of war. The horrible tragic results of this second global conflagration were more deaths and more destruction than in any other armed conflict. It completely uprooted and displaced millions of people. The end of the war brought renewed power struggles, especially in Europe and China, with many Eastern European nations as well as China coming under complete control and domination of the Communists, supported and backed by the Soviet Union. With the development of and two-time deployment of an atomic bomb against two Japanese cities, the world found itself in the nuclear age. The peace settlement established the United Nations Organization, still existing and operating today.

Korean War ☐ 1950 to 1953

Causes: Korea was under control of Japan from 1895 to the end of the Second World War in 1945. At war's end, the Soviet and U.S. military troops moved into Korea with the U.S. troops in the southern half and the Soviet troops in the northern half with the 38 degree North Latitude line as the boundary.

The General Assembly of the UN in 1947 ordered elections throughout all of Korea to select one government for the entire country. The Soviet Union would not allow the North Koreans to vote, so they set up a Communist government there. The South Koreans set up a democratic government but both claimed the entire country. At times, there were clashes between the troops from 1948 to 1950. After the U.S. removed its remaining troops in 1949 and announced in early 1950 that Korea was not part of its defense line in Asia, the Communists decided to act and invaded the south.

Participants were: North and South Korea, United States of America, Australia, New Zealand, China, Canada. France, Great Britain, Turkey, Belgium, Ethiopia, Colombia, Greece, South Africa, Luxembourg, Thailand, the Netherlands, and the Philippines. It was the first war in which a world organization played a major military role and it presented quite a challenge to the UN, which had only been in existence five years.

The war began June 25, 1950 and ended July 27, 1953. A truce was drawn up and an armistice agreement was signed ending the fighting. A permanent treaty of peace has never been signed and the country remains divided between the Communist North and the Democratic South. It was a very costly and bloody war destroying villages and homes, displacing and killing millions of people.

The Vietnam War
U.S. Involvement □ 1957 to 1973

Causes: U.S. involvement was the second phase of three in Vietnam's history. The first phase began in 1946 when the Vietnamese fought French troops for control of the country. Vietnam prior to 1946 had been part of the French colony of Indochina (since 1861 along with Laos and Kampuchea or Cambodia). In 1954, the defeated French left and the country became divided into Communist North and Democratic South. U.S. aid and influence continued as part of the U.S. "Cold War" foreign policy to help any nation threatened by Communism.

The second phase involved the U.S. commitment. The Communist Vietnamese considered the war one of national liberation, a struggle to avoid continual dominance and influence of a foreign power. A cease-fire was arranged in January 1973 and a few months later U.S. troops left for good. The third and final phase consisted of fighting between the Vietnamese but ended April 30, 1975, with the surrender of South Vietnam, the entire country being united under Communist ruler.

Participants were the United States of America, Australia, New Zealand, South and North Vietnam, South Korea, Thailand, and the Philippines. With active U.S. involvement from 1957 to 1973, it was the longest war participated in by the U.S.; was tremendously destructive and completely divided the American public in their opinions and feelings about the war. Many were frustrated and angered by the fact that it was the first war fought on foreign soil in which U.S. combat forces were totally unable to achieve their goals and objectives.

Returning veterans faced not only readjustment to normal civilian life but also faced bitterness, anger, rejection, and no heroes' welcomes. Many suffered severe physical and deep psychological problems. The war set a precedent with Congress and the American people actively challenging U.S. military and foreign policy. The conflict, though tempered markedly by time, still exists and still has a definite effect on people.

TEACHER CERTFICATION STUDY GUIDE

Skill 3.3.c Show an understanding of major contemporary world issues and trends.

The struggle between the **Communist world under Soviet Union** leadership and the non-Communist world under Anglo-American leadership resulted in what became known as the Cold War. Communism crept into the Western Hemisphere with Cuban leader Fidel Castro and his regime. Most colonies in Africa, Asia, and the Middle East gained independence from European and Western influence and control. In South Africa in the early 1990s, the system of racial segregation, called "apartheid," was abolished.

The Soviet Union was the first industrialized nation to successfully begin a program of **space flight and exploration,** launching Sputnik and putting the first man in space. The United States also experienced success in its space program successfully landing space crews on the moon. In the late 1980s and early 1990s, the Berlin Wall was torn down and Communism fell in the Soviet Union and Eastern Europe. The 15 republics of the former USSR became independent nations with varying degrees of freedom and democracy in government and together formed the Commonwealth of Independent States (CIS). The former Communist nations of Eastern Europe also emphasized their independence with democratic forms of government.

Tremendous progress in communication and transportation has tied all parts of the earth and drawn them closer. There are still vast areas of unproductive land, extreme poverty, food shortages, rampant diseases, violent friction between cultures, the ever-present nuclear threat, environmental pollution, rapid reduction of natural resources, urban over-crowding, acceleration in global terrorism and violent crimes, and a diminishing middle class.

Skill 3.3.d Know the differences between the world's major religions.

Eight common religions are practiced today. Interestingly, all of these religions have divisions or smaller sects within them. Not one of them is totally completely unified.

Judaism: the oldest of the eight and was the first to teach and practice the belief in one God, Yahweh.

Christianity: came from Judaism, grew and spread in the First Century throughout the Roman Empire, despite persecution. A later schism resulted in the Western (Roman Catholic) and Eastern (Orthodox) parts. Protestant sects developed as part of the Protestant Revolution. The name "Christian" means one who is a follower of Jesus Christ who started Christianity. Christians follow his teachings and examples, living by the laws and principles of the Bible.

HISTORY

Islam: founded in Arabia by Mohammed who preached about God, Allah. Islam spread through trade, travel, and conquest and followers of it fought in the Crusades. In addition, other wars against Christians and today against the Jewish nation of Israel. Followers of Islam, called Muslims, live by the teachings of the Koran, their holy book, and of their prophets.

Hinduism: begun by people called Aryans around 1500 BC and spread into India. The Aryans blended their culture with the culture of the Dravidians, natives they conquered. Today it has many sects, promotes worship of hundreds of gods and goddesses and belief in reincarnation. Though forbidden today by law, a prominent feature of Hinduism in the past was a rigid adherence to and practice of the infamous caste system.

Buddhism: developed in India from the teachings of Prince Gautama and spread to most of Asia. Its beliefs opposed the worship of numerous deities, the Hindu caste system and the supernatural. Worshippers must be free of attachment to all things worldly and devote themselves to finding release from life's suffering.

Confucianism: is a Chinese religion based on the teachings of the Chinese philosopher Confucius. There is no clergy, no organization, and no belief in a deity or in life after death. It emphasizes political and moral ideas with respect for authority and ancestors. Rulers were expected to govern according to high moral standards.

Taoism: a native Chinese religion with worship of more deities than almost any other religion. It teaches all followers to make the effort to achieve the two goals of happiness and immortality. Practices and ceremonies include meditation, prayer, magic, reciting scriptures, special diets, breath control, beliefs in witchcraft, fortune telling, astrology, and communicating with the spirits of the dead.

Shinto: the native religion of Japan developed from native folk beliefs worshipping spirits and demons in animals, trees, and mountains. According to its mythology, deities created Japan and its people, which resulted in worshipping the emperor as a god. Shinto was strongly influenced by Buddhism and Confucianism but never had strong doctrines on salvation or life after death.

TEACHER CERTFICATION STUDY GUIDE

SUBAREA IV: U.S. AND ILLINOIS HISTORY

Competency 4.1   Understand the development of colonial settlements in North America, the Revolutionary War, and the creation of the U.S. government.

Though not greatly differing from each other in degree of civilization, the native peoples north of Mexico varied widely in customs, housing, dress, and religion. Among the native peoples of North America there were at least 200 languages and 1500 dialects. Each of the hundreds of tribes was somewhat influenced by its neighbors. Communication between tribes that spoke different languages was conducted primarily through a very elaborate system of sign language. Several groups of tribes can be distinguished.

The Woods Peoples occupied the area from the Atlantic to the Western plains and prairies. They cultivated corn and tobacco, fished and hunted.

The Plains Peoples, who populated the area from the Mississippi River to the Rocky Mountains, were largely wandering and warlike, hunting buffalo and other game for food. After the arrival of Europeans and the re-introduction of the horse they became great horsemen.

The Southwestern Tribes of New Mexico and Arizona included Pueblos, who lived in villages constructed of *adobe* (sun-dried brick), cliff dwellers, and nomadic tribes. These tribes had the most advanced civilizations.

The California Tribes were separated from the influence of other tribes by the mountains. They lived primarily on acorns, seeds and fish, and were probably the least advanced civilizations.

The Northwest Coast Peoples of Washington, British Columbia and Southern Alaska were not acquainted with farming, but built large wooden houses and traveled in huge cedar canoes.

The Plateau Peoples who lived between the plains and the Pacific coast were simple people who lived in underground houses or brush huts and subsisted primarily on fish.

The native peoples of America, like other peoples of the same stage of development, believed that all objects, both animate and inanimate, were endowed with certain spiritual powers. They were intensely religious, and lived every aspect of their lives as their religion prescribed. They believed a soul inhabited every living thing. Certain birds and animals were considered more powerful and intelligent than humans and capable of influence for good or evil.

Most of the tribes were divided into clans of close blood relations, whose *totem* was a particular animal from which they were often believed to have descended. The sun and the four principal directions were often objects of worship. The *shaman*, a sort of priest, was often the *medicine-man* of a tribe. Sickness was often supposed to be the result of displeasing some spirit and was treated with incantations and prayer. Many of the traditional stories resemble those of other peoples in providing answers to primordial questions and guidance for life. The highest virtue was self-control. Hiding emotions and enduring pain or torture unflinchingly was required of each. Honesty was also a primary virtue, and promises were always honored no matter what the personal cost.

The communities did not have any strict form of government, for the most part. Each individual was responsible for governing himself or herself, particularly with regard to the rights of other members of the community. The chiefs generally carried out the will of the tribe. Each tribe was a discrete unit, with its own lands. Boundaries of tribal territories were determined by treaties with neighbors. There was an organized confederation among certain tribes, often called a nation. The Iroquois confederation was often referred to as The Five Nations (later The Six Nations).

Customs varied from tribe to tribe. One consistent cultural element was the smoking of the calumet, a stone pipe, at the beginning and end of a war. In Native American communities, no individual owned land. The plots of land that were cultivated were, however, respected. Wealth was sometimes an honor, but generosity was more highly valued. Agriculture was quite advanced and irrigation was practiced in some locations. Most tribes practiced unique styles of basket work, pottery and weaving, either in terms of shape or decoration.

The interactions among Native Americans, Europeans, and Africans in early North American colonial societies

Spain's influence was in Florida, the Gulf Coast from Texas all the way west to California and south to the tip of South America and some of the islands of the West Indies. French control centered from New Orleans north to what is now northern Canada including the entire Mississippi Valley, the St. Lawrence Valley, the Great Lakes, and the land that was part of the Louisiana Territory. A few West Indies islands were also part of France's empire. England settled the eastern seaboard of North America, including parts of Canada and from Maine to Georgia. Some West Indies islands also came under British control. The Dutch had New Amsterdam for a period but later ceded it into British hands. One interesting aspect of this was each of these three nations, especially England, the land claims extended partly or all the way across the continent, regardless of the fact that the others claimed the same land. The wars for dominance and control of power and influence in Europe would undoubtedly and eventually extend to the Americas, especially North America.

The part of North America claimed by **France** was called New France and consisted of the land west of the Appalachian Mountains. This area of claims and settlement included the St. Lawrence Valley, the Great Lakes, the Mississippi Valley, and the entire region of land westward to the Rocky Mountains. They established the permanent settlements of Montreal and New Orleans, thus giving them control of the two major gateways into the heart of North America, the vast, rich interior. The St. Lawrence River, the Great Lakes, and the Mississippi River along with its tributaries made it possible for the French explorers and traders to roam at will, virtually unhindered in exploring, trapping, trading, and furthering the interests of France.

Most of the French settlements were in Canada along the St. Lawrence River. Only scattered forts and trading posts were found in the upper Mississippi Valley and Great Lakes region. The rulers of France originally intended New France to have vast estates owned by nobles and worked by peasants who would live on the estates in compact farming villages--the New World version of the Old World's medieval system of feudalism. However, it didn't work out that way. Each of the nobles wanted his estate to be on the river for ease of transportation. The peasants working the estates wanted the prime waterfront location, also. The result of all this real estate squabbling was that New France's settled areas wound up mostly as a string of farmhouses stretching from Quebec to Montreal along the St. Lawrence and Richelieu Rivers.

In the non-settled areas in the interior were the French fur traders. They made friends with the friendly tribes of Indians, spending the winters with them getting the furs needed for trade. In the spring, they would return to Montreal in time to take advantage of trading their furs for the products brought by the cargo ships from France, which usually arrived at about the same time. Most of the wealth for New France and its "Mother Country" was from the fur trade, which provided a livelihood for many, many people. Manufacturers and workmen back in France, ship-owners and merchants, as well as the fur traders and their Indian allies all benefited. However, the freedom of roaming and trapping in the interior was a strong enticement for the younger, stronger men and resulted in the French not strengthening the areas settled along the St. Lawrence.

Into the 18th century, the rivalry with the British was getting stronger and stronger. New France was united under a single government and enjoyed the support of many Indian allies. The French traders were very diligent in not destroying the forests and driving away game upon which the Indians depended for life. It was difficult for the French to defend all of their settlements as they were scattered over half of the continent. However, by the early 1750s, in Western Europe, France was the most powerful nation. Its armies were superior to all others and its navy was giving the British stiff competition for control of the seas. The stage was set for confrontation in both Europe and America.

Spanish settlement had its beginnings in the Caribbean with the establishment of colonies on Hispaniola (at Santo Domingo which became the capital of the West Indies), Puerto Rico, and Cuba. There were a number of reasons for Spanish involvement in the Americas, to name just a few:

- the spirit of adventure,
- the desire for land,
- expansion of Spanish power, influence, and empire,
- the desire for great wealth,
- expansion of Roman Catholic influence and conversion of native peoples,

The first permanent settlement in what is now the United States was in 1565 at St. Augustine, Florida. A later permanent settlement in the southwestern United States was in 1609 at Santa Fe, New Mexico. At the peak of Spanish power, the area in the United States claimed, settled, and controlled by Spain included Florida and all land west of the Mississippi River--quite a piece of choice real estate. Of course, France and England also lay claim to the same areas. Nonetheless, ranches and missions were built and the Indians who came in contact with the Spaniards were introduced to animals, plants, and seeds from the Old World that they had never seen before. Animals brought in included: horses, cattle, donkeys, pigs, sheep, goats and poultry.

Spain's control over her New World colonies lasted more than 300 years, longer than England or France. To this day, Spanish influence remains in names of places, art, architecture, music, literature, law, and cuisine. The Spanish settlements in North America were not commercial enterprises but were for protection and defense of the trading and wealth from their colonies in Mexico and South America. The Russians hunting seals came down the Pacific coast, the English moved into Florida and west into and beyond the Appalachians, and the French traders and trappers were making their way from Louisiana and other parts of New France into Spanish territory. The Spanish never realized or understood that self-sustaining economic development and colonial trade was so important. Consequently, the Spanish settlements in the U.S. never really prospered.

Before 1763, when England was rapidly on the way to becoming the most powerful of the three major Western European powers, its thirteen colonies, located between the Atlantic and the Appalachians, physically occupied the least amount of land. Moreover, it is interesting that even before the Spanish Armada was defeated, two Englishmen, Sir Humphrey Gilbert and his half-brother Sir Walter Raleigh were unsuccessful in their attempts to build successful permanent colonies in the New World. Nonetheless, the thirteen English colonies were successful and, by the time they had gained their independence from Britain, were more than able to govern themselves.
They had a rich historical heritage of law, tradition, and documents leading the way to constitutional government conducted according to laws and customs.

The settlers in the British colonies highly valued individual freedom, democratic government, and getting ahead through hard work.

The English colonies, with only a few exceptions, were considered commercial ventures to make a profit for the crown or the company or whoever financed its beginnings. One was strictly a philanthropic enterprise and three others were primarily for religious reasons but the other nine were started for economic reasons. Settlers in these unique colonies came for different reasons:

   a) religious freedom,
   b) political freedom,
   c) economic prosperity, and
   d) land ownership.

The colonies were divided generally into the three regions of **New England**, **Middle Atlantic, and Southern**. The culture of each was distinct and affected attitudes, ideas towards politics, religion, and economic activities. The geography of each region also contributed to its unique characteristics.

The **New England colonies** consisted of Massachusetts, Rhode Island, Connecticut, and New Hampshire. Life in these colonies was centered on the towns. What farming was done was by each family on its own plot of land but a short summer growing season and limited amount of good soil gave rise to other economic activities such as manufacturing, fishing, shipbuilding, and trade. The vast majority of the settlers shared similar origins, coming from England and Scotland. Towns were carefully planned and laid out the same way. The form of government was the town meeting where all adult males met to make the laws. The legislative body, the General Court, consisted of an Upper and Lower House.

The **Middle or Middle Atlantic colonies** included New York, New Jersey, Pennsylvania, Delaware, and Maryland. New York and New Jersey were at one time the Dutch colony of New Netherlands and Delaware at one time was New Sweden. These five colonies, from their beginnings were considered "melting pots" with settlers from many different nations and backgrounds. The main economic activity was farming with the settlers scattered over the countryside cultivating rather large farms. The Indians were not as much of a threat as in New England so they did not have to settle in small farming villages. The soil was very fertile, the land was gently rolling, and a milder climate provided a longer growing season.

These farms produced a large surplus of food, not only for the colonists themselves but also for sale. This colonial region became known as the "breadbasket" of the New World and the New York and Philadelphia seaports were constantly filled with ships being loaded with meat, flour, and other foodstuffs for the West Indies and England. There were other economic activities such as shipbuilding, iron mines, and factories producing paper, glass, and textiles. The legislative body in Pennsylvania was unicameral or consisted of one house. In the other four colonies, the legislative body had two houses. Also units of local government were in counties and towns.

The **Southern colonies** were Virginia, North and South Carolina, and Georgia. Virginia was the first permanent successful English colony and Georgia was the last. The year 1619 was a very important year in the history of Virginia and the United States with three very significant events. First, sixty women were sent to Virginia to marry and establish families, Second, twenty Africans, the first of thousands, arrived, Third, most importantly, the Virginia colonists were granted the right to self-government and they began by electing their own representatives to the House of Burgesses, their own legislative body.

The major economic activity in this region was farming. Here the soil was very fertile and the climate was very mild with an even longer growing season. The large plantations eventually requiring large numbers of slaves were found in the coastal or tidewater areas. Although the wealthy slave-owning planters set the pattern of life in this region, most of the people lived inland away from coastal areas. They were small farmers and very few, it any, owned slaves.

The settlers in these four colonies came from diverse backgrounds and cultures. Virginia was colonized mostly by people from England while Georgia was started as a haven for debtors from English prisons. Pioneers from Virginia settled in North Carolina while South Carolina welcomed people from England and Scotland, French Protestants, Germans, and emigrants from islands in the West Indies. Products from farms and plantations included rice, tobacco, indigo, cotton, some corn and wheat. Other economic activities included lumber and naval stores (tar, pitch, rosin, and turpentine) from the pine forests and fur trade on the frontier. Cities such as Savannah and Charleston were important seaports and trading centers.

In the colonies, the daily life of the colonists differed greatly between the coastal settlements and the inland or interior. The Southern planters and the people living in the coastal cities and towns had a way of life similar to that in towns in England. The influence was seen and heard in how people dressed and talked. The architectural styles of houses and public buildings, and the social divisions or levels of society mimicked that of England. Both the planters and city dwellers enjoyed an active social life and had strong emotional ties to England.

On the other hand, life inland on the frontier had marked differences. All facets of daily living--clothing, food, housing, economic and social activities--were all connected to what was needed to sustain life and survive in the wilderness. Everything was produced practically themselves. They were self-sufficient and extremely individualistic and independent. There were little, if any, levels of society or class distinctions as they considered themselves to be the equal to all others, regardless of station in life. The roots of equality, independence, individual rights and freedoms were strong and well developed. People were not judged by their fancy dress, expensive house, eloquent language, or titles following their names.

The colonies had from 1607 to 1763 to develop, refine, practice, experiment, and experience life in a rugged, uncivilized land. The Mother Country had virtually left them on their own to take care of their selves all that time. When in 1763, Britain decided she needed to regulate and "mother" the "little ones," to her surprise she had a losing fight on her hands.

By the 1750s in Europe, Spain was "out of the picture," no longer the most powerful nation and not even a contender. The remaining rivalry was between Britain and France. For nearly 25 years, between 1689 and 1748, a series of "armed conflicts" involving these two powers had been taking place. These conflicts had spilled over into North America. The War of the League of Augsburg in Europe, 1689 to 1697, had been King William's War. The War of the Spanish Succession, 1702 to 1713, had been Queen Anne's War. The War of the Austrian Succession, 1740 to 1748, was called King George's War in the colonies. The two nations fought for possession of colonies, especially in Asia and North America, and for control of the seas, but none of these conflicts was decisive.

The final conflict, which decided once and for all who was the most powerful, began in North America in 1754, in the Ohio River Valley. It was known in America as the **French and Indian War** and in Europe as the Seven Years' War, since it began there in 1756. In America, both sides had advantages and disadvantages. The British colonies were well established and consolidated in a smaller area. British colonists outnumbered French colonists 23 to 1. Except for a small area in Canada, French settlements were scattered over a much larger area (roughly half of the continent) and were smaller. However, the French settlements were united under one government and were quick to act and cooperate when necessary. In addition, the French had many more Indian allies than the British. The British colonies had separate, individual governments and very seldom cooperated, even when needed. In Europe, at that time, France was the more powerful of the two nations.

The French depended on the St. Lawrence River for transporting supplies, soldiers, and messages-the link between New France and the Mother Country. Tied into this waterway system was the connecting links of the Great Lakes, Mississippi River and its tributaries along which were scattered French forts, trading posts, and small settlements.

In 1758, the British captured Louisburg on Cape Breton Island, New France was doomed. Louisburg gave the British navy a base of operations preventing French reinforcements and supplies getting to their troops. Other forts fell to the British: Frontenac, Duquesne, Crown Point, Ticonderoga, Niagara, those in the upper Ohio Valley, and, most importantly, Quebec and finally Montreal. Spain entered the war in 1762 to aid France but it was too late. British victories occurred all around the world: in India, in the Mediterranean, and in Europe.

In 1763 in Paris, Spain, France, and Britain met to draw up the Treaty of Paris. Great Britain got most of India and all of North America east of the Mississippi River, except for New Orleans. Britain received from Spain control of Florida and returned to Spain Cuba and the islands of the Philippines, taken during the war. France lost nearly all of its possessions in America. India and was allowed to keep four islands: Guadeloupe, Martinique, Haiti on Hispaniola, and Miquelon and St. Pierre. France gave Spain New Orleans and the vast territory of Louisiana, west of the Mississippi River. Britain was now the most powerful nation--period.

Where did all of this leave the British colonies? Their colonial militias had fought with the British and they too benefited. The militias and their officers gained much experience in fighting which was very valuable later. The thirteen colonies began to realize that cooperating with each other was the only way to defend themselves. They didn't really understand that until the war for independence and setting up a national government, but a start had been made. At the start of the war in 1754, Benjamin Franklin proposed to the thirteen colonies that they unite permanently to be able to defend themselves. This was after the French and their Indian allies had defeated Major George Washington and his militia at **Fort Necessity**. This left the entire northern frontier of the British colonies vulnerable and open to attack.

Delegates from seven of the thirteen colonies met at Albany, New York, along with the representatives from the **Iroquois Confederation** and British officials. Franklin's proposal, known as the Albany Plan of Union, was totally rejected by the colonists, along with a similar proposal from the British. They simply did not want each of the colonies to lose its right to act independently. However, the seed was planted.

American independence and the factors contributing to its success

The **War for Independence** occurred due to a number of changes, the two most important ones being economic and political. By the end of the French and Indian War in 1763, Britain's American colonies were 13 out of a total of 33 scattered around the earth. Like all other countries, Britain strove for having a strong economy and a favorable balance of trade. To have that delicate balance a nation needs wealth, self-sufficiency, and a powerful army and navy. The overseas colonies would provide raw materials for the industries in the Mother Country, be a market for the finished products by buying them and assist the Mother Country in becoming powerful and strong (as in the case of Great Britain). By having a strong merchant fleet, it would be a school for training the Royal Navy and provide bases of operation for the Royal Navy.

The foregoing explained the major reason for British encouragement and support of colonization, especially in North America. So between 1607 and 1763, at various times for various reasons, the British Parliament enacted different laws to assist the government in getting and keeping this trade balance. One series of laws required that most of the manufacturing be done only in England, such as: prohibition of exporting any wool or woolen cloth from the colonies, no manufacture of beaver hats or iron products. The colonists weren't concerned as they had no money and no highly skilled labor to set up any industries, anyway.

The **Navigation Acts** of 1651 put restrictions on shipping and trade within the British Empire by requiring that it was allowed only on British ships. This increased the strength of the British merchant fleet and greatly benefited the American colonists. Since they were British citizens, they could have their own vessels, building and operating them as well. By the end of the war in 1763, the shipyards in the colonies were building one third of the merchant ships under the British flag. There were quite a number of wealthy, American, colonial merchants.

The Navigation Act of 1660 restricted the shipment and sale of colonial products to England only. In 1663 another Navigation Act stipulated that the colonies had to buy manufactured products only from England and that any European goods going to the colonies had to go to England first. These acts were a protection from enemy ships and pirates and from competition from European rivals.

The New England and Middle Atlantic colonies at first felt threatened by these laws as they had started producing many of the products being produced in Britain. They soon found new markets for their goods and began what was known as a "triangular trade." Colonial vessels started the first part of the triangle by sailing for Africa loaded with kegs of rum from colonial distilleries.

On Africa's West Coast, the rum was traded for either gold or slaves. The second part of the triangle was from Africa to the West Indies where slaves were traded for molasses, sugar, or money. The third part of the triangle was home, bringing sugar or molasses (to make more rum), gold, and silver.

The major concern of the British government was that the trade violated the 1733 Molasses Act. Planters had wanted the colonists to buy all of their molasses in the British West Indies but these islands could give the traders only about one eighth of the amount of molasses needed for distilling the rum. The colonists were forced to buy the rest of what they needed from the French, Dutch, and Spanish islands, thus evading the law by not paying the high duty on the molasses bought from these islands. If Britain had enforced the Molasses Act, economic and financial chaos and ruin would have occurred. Nevertheless, for this act and all the other mercantile laws, the government followed the policy of "salutary neglect," deliberately failing to enforce the laws.

In 1763, after the war, money was needed to pay the British war debt, for the defense of the empire, and to pay for the governing of 33 colonies scattered around the earth. It was decided to adopt a new colonial policy and pass laws to raise revenue. It was reasoned that the colonists were subjects of the king and since the king and his ministers had spent a great deal of money defending and protecting them (this especially for the American colonists), it was only right and fair that the colonists should help pay the costs of their defense. The earlier laws passed had been for the purposes of regulating production and trade which generally put money into colonial pockets. These new laws would take some of that rather hard-earned money out of their pockets and it would be done, in colonial eyes, unjustly and illegally.

Before 1763, except for trade and supplying raw materials, the colonies had been left pretty much to themselves. England looked on them merely as part of an economic or commercial empire. Little consideration was given as to how they were to conduct their daily affairs, so the colonists became very independent, self-reliant, and extremely skillful at handling those daily affairs. This, in turn, gave rise to leadership, initiative, achievement, and vast experience. In fact, there was a far greater degree of independence and self-government in the British colonies in America than could be found in Britain or the major countries on the Continent or any other colonies anywhere. There were a number of reasons for this:

1. The religious and scriptural teachings of previous centuries put forth the worth of the individual and equality in God's sight. Keep in mind that freedom of worship and from religious persecution were major reasons to live in the New World.

2. European Protestants, especially Calvinists, believed and taught the idea that government originates from those governed, that rulers are required to protect individual rights and that the governed have the right and privilege to choose their rulers.

3. Trading companies put into practice the principle that their members had the right to make the decisions and shape the policies affecting their lives.

4. The colonists believed and supported the idea that a person's property should not be taken without his consent, based on that treasured English document, the Magna Carta, and English common law.

5. From about 1700 to 1750, population increases in America came about through immigration and generations of descendants of the original settlers. The immigrants were mainly Scots-Irish who hated the English, Germans who cared nothing about England, and black slaves who knew nothing about England. The descendants of the original settlers had never been out of America at any time.

6. In America, as new towns and counties were formed, there began the practice of representation in government. Representatives to the colonial legislative assemblies were elected from the district in which they lived, chosen by qualified property-owning male voters, and representing the interests of the political district from which they were elected. One thing to remember: each of the 13 colonies had a royal governor appointed by the king representing his interests in the colonies. Nevertheless, the colonial legislative assemblies controlled the purse strings having the power to vote on all issues involving money to be spent by the colonial governments.

Contrary to this was the governmental set-up in England. Members of Parliament were not elected to represent their own districts. They were considered representative of classes, not individuals. If some members of a professional or commercial class or some landed interests were able to elect representatives, then those classes or special interests were represented. It had nothing at all to do with numbers or territories. Some large population centers had no direct representation at all, yet the people there considered themselves represented by men elected from their particular class or interest somewhere else. Consequently, it was extremely difficult for the English to understand why the American merchants and landowners claimed they were not represented because they themselves did not vote for a Member of Parliament.

The colonists' protest of "no taxation without representation" was meaningless to the English. Parliament represented the entire nation, was completely unlimited in legislation, and had become supreme; and the colonists were incensed at the English attitude of "of course you have representation--everyone does." The colonists considered their colonial legislative assemblies equal to Parliament, totally unacceptable in England, of course. There were two different environments of the older traditional British system in the Mother Country and in America new ideas and different ways of doing things. In a new country, a new environment has little or no tradition, institutions or vested interests. New ideas and traditions grew extremely fast pushing aside what was left of the old ideas and old traditions. By 1763, Britain had changed its perception of its American colonies to their being a "territorial" empire. The stage was set and the conditions were right for a showdown.

In 1763, Parliament decided to have a standing army in North America to reinforce British control. In 1765, the **Quartering Act** was passed requiring the colonists to provide supplies and living quarters for the British troops. In addition, efforts by the British were made to keep the peace by establishing good relations with the Indians. Consequently, a proclamation was issued which prohibited any American colonists from making any settlements west of the Appalachians until provided for through treaties with the Indians.

The Sugar Act of 1764 required efficient collection of taxes on any molasses that were brought into the colonies. It also gave British officials free license to conduct searches of the premises of anyone suspected of violating the law. The colonists were taxed on newspapers, legal documents, and other printed matter under the Stamp Act of 1765. Although a stamp tax was already in use in England, the colonists would have none of it and after the ensuing uproar of rioting and mob violence, Parliament repealed the tax.

Of course, great exultation, jubilance, and wild joy resulted when news of the repeal reached America. However, what no one noticed was the small, quiet Declaratory Act attached to the repeal. This act plainly and unequivocally stated that Parliament still had the right to make all laws for the colonies. It denied their right to be taxed only by their own colonial legislatures--a very crucial, important piece of legislation but virtually overlooked and unnoticed at the time. Other acts leading up to armed conflict included the **Townshend Acts** passed in 1767 taxing lead, paint, paper, and tea brought into the colonies. This increased anger and tension resulting in the British sending troops to New York City and Boston.

In Boston, mob violence provoked retaliation by the troops thus bringing about the deaths of five people and the wounding of eight others. The so-called Boston Massacre shocked Americans and British alike. Subsequently, in 1770, Parliament voted to repeal all the provisions of the Townshend Acts with the exception of the tea tax. In 1773, the tax on tea sold by the British East India Company was substantially reduced, fueling colonial anger once more. This gave the company an unfair trade advantage and forcibly reminded the colonists of the British right to tax them. Merchants refused to sell the tea; colonists refused to buy and drink it; and a shipload of it was dumped into Boston Harbor--a most violent Tea Party.

In 1774, the passage of the Quebec Act extended the limits of that Canadian colony's boundary southward to include territory located north of the Ohio River. However, the punishment for Boston's Tea Party came in the same year with the Intolerable Acts. Boston's port was closed; the royal governor of the colony of Massachusetts was given increased power, and the colonists were compelled to house and feed the British soldiers. The propaganda activities of the patriot organizations **Sons of Liberty** and **Committees of Correspondence** kept the opposition and resistance before everyone. Delegates from twelve colonies met in Philadelphia September 5, 1774, in the First Continental Congress. They definitely opposed acts of lawlessness and wanted some form of peaceful settlement with Britain. They maintained American loyalty to the Mother Country and affirmed Parliament's power over colonial foreign affairs.

They insisted on repeal of the Intolerable Acts and demanded ending all trade with Britain until this took place. The reply from King George III, the last king of America, was an insistence of colonial submission to British rule or be crushed. With the start of the Revolutionary War April 19, 1775, the Second Continental Congress began meeting in Philadelphia May 10 that year to conduct the business of war and government for the next six years.

One historian explained that the British were interested only in raising money to pay war debts, regulate the trade and commerce of the colonies, and look after business and financial interests between the Mother Country and the rest of her empire. The establishment of overseas colonies was first, and foremost, a commercial enterprise, not a political one. The political aspect was secondary and assumed. The British took it for granted that Parliament was supreme, was recognized so by the colonists, and were very resentful of the colonial challenge to Parliament's authority. They were contemptuously indifferent to politics in America and had no wish to exert any control over it. As resistance and disobedience swelled and increased in America, the British increased their efforts to punish them and put them in their place.

The British had been extremely lax and totally inconsistent in enforcement of the mercantile or trade laws passed in the years before 1754. The government itself was not particularly stable so actions against the colonies occurred in anger and their attitude was one of a moral superiority, that they knew how to manage America better than the Americans did themselves. This of course points to a lack of sufficient knowledge of conditions and opinions in America. The colonists had been left on their own for nearly 150 years and by the time the Revolutionary War began, they were quite adept at self-government and adequately handling the affairs of their daily lives. The Americans equated ownership of land or property with the right to vote. Property was considered the foundation of life and liberty and, in the colonial mind and tradition, these went together.

Therefore when an indirect tax on tea was made, the British felt that since it wasn't a direct tax, there should be no objection to it. The colonists viewed any tax, direct or indirect, as an attack on their property. They felt that as a representative body, the British Parliament should protect British citizens, including the colonists, from arbitrary taxation. Since they felt they were not represented, Parliament, in their eyes, gave them no protection. So, war began. August 23, 1775, George III declared that the colonies were in rebellion and warned them to stop or else.

By 1776, the colonists and their representatives in the Second Continental Congress realized that things were past the point of no return. The Declaration of Independence was drafted and declared July 4, 1776. George Washington labored against tremendous odds to wage a victorious war. The turning point in the Americans' favor occurred in 1777 with the American victory at Saratoga. This victory decided for the French to align themselves with the Americans against the British. With the aid of Admiral deGrasse and French warships blocking the entrance to Chesapeake Bay, British General Cornwallis trapped at Yorktown, Virginia, surrendered in 1781 and the war was over. The Treaty of Paris officially ending the war was signed in 1783.

Articles of Confederation and the U.S. Constitution

Articles of Confederation - This was the first political system under which the newly independent colonies tried to organize themselves. It was drafted after the Declaration of Independence in 1776, was passed by the Continental Congress on November 15, 1777, ratified by the thirteen states, and took effect on March 1, 1781.

The newly independent states were unwilling to give too much power to a national government. They were already fighting Great Britain. They did not want to replace one harsh ruler with another. After many debates, the form of the Articles was accepted. Each state agreed to send delegates to the Congress. Each state had one vote in the Congress. The Articles gave Congress the power to declare war, appoint military officers, and coin money. The Congress was also responsible for foreign affairs. The Articles of Confederation limited the powers of Congress by giving the states final authority. Although Congress could pass laws, at least nine of the thirteen states had to approve a law before it went into effect. Congress could not pass any laws regarding taxes. To get money, Congress had to ask each state for it, no state could be forced to pay.

Thus, the Articles created a loose alliance among the thirteen states. The national government was weak, in part, because it didn't have a strong chief executive to carry out laws passed by the legislature. This weak national government might have worked if the states were able to get along with each other. However, many different disputes arose and there was no way of settling them. Thus, the delegates went to meet again to try to fix the Articles; instead they ended up scrapping them and created a new Constitution that learned from these earlier mistakes.

The central government of the new United States of America consisted of a Congress of two to seven delegates from each state with each state having just one vote. The government under the Articles solved some of the postwar problems but had serious weaknesses. Some of its powers included: borrowing and coining money, directing foreign affairs, declaring war and making peace, building and equipping a navy, regulating weights and measures, asking the states to supply men and money for an army. The delegates to Congress had no real authority as each state carefully and jealously guarded its own interests and limited powers under the Articles. Also, the delegates to Congress were paid by their states and had to vote as directed by their state legislatures. The serious weaknesses were the lack of power: to regulate finances, over interstate trade, over foreign trade, to enforce treaties, and military power. Something better and more efficient was needed.

In May of 1787, delegates from all states except Rhode Island began meeting in Philadelphia. At first, they met to revise the Articles of Confederation as instructed by Congress; but they soon realized that much more was needed. Abandoning the instructions, they set out to write a new Constitution, a new document, the foundation of all government in the United States and a model for representative government throughout the world.

The first order of business was the agreement among all the delegates that the convention would be kept secret. No discussion of the convention outside of the meeting room would be allowed. They wanted to be able to discuss, argue, and agree among themselves before presenting the completed document to the American people.

The delegates were afraid that if the people were aware of what was taking place before it was completed the entire country would be plunged into argument and dissension. It would be extremely difficult, if not impossible, to settle differences and come to an agreement. Between the official notes kept and the complete notes of future President James Madison, an accurate picture of the events of the Convention is part of the historical record.

The delegates went to Philadelphia representing different areas and different interests. They all agreed on a strong central government but not one with unlimited powers. They also agreed that no one part of government could control the rest. It would be a republican form of government (sometimes referred to as representative democracy) in which the supreme power was in the hands of the voters who would elect the men who would govern for them.

One of the first serious controversies involved the small states versus the large states over representation in Congress. Virginia's Governor Edmund Randolph proposed that state population determine the number of representatives sent to Congress, also known as the Virginia Plan. New Jersey delegate William Paterson countered with what is known as the New Jersey Plan, each state having equal representation.

After much argument and debate, the Great Compromise was devised, known also as the Connecticut Compromise, as proposed by Roger Sherman. It was agreed that Congress would have two houses. The Senate would have two Senators, giving equal powers in the Senate. The House of Representatives would have its members elected based on each state's population. Both houses could draft bills to debate and vote on with the exception of bills pertaining to money, which must originate in the House of Representatives.
Another controversy involved economic differences between North and South. One concerned the counting of the African slaves for determining representation in the House of Representatives. The southern delegates wanted this but didn't want it to determine taxes to be paid.

The northern delegates argued the opposite: count the slaves for taxes but not for representation. The resulting agreement was known as the "three-fifths" compromise. Three-fifths of the slaves would be counted for both taxes and determining representation in the House.

The last major compromise, also between North and South, was the Commerce Compromise. The economic interests of the northern part of the country were ones of industry and business whereas the south's economic interests were primarily in farming. The Northern merchants wanted the government to regulate and control commerce with foreign nations and with the states. Of course, Southern planters opposed this idea as they felt that any tariff laws passed would be unfavorable to them. The acceptable compromise to this dispute was that Congress was given the power to regulate commerce with other nations and the states, including levying tariffs on imports. However, Congress did not have the power to levy tariffs on any exports. This increased Southern concern about the effect it would have on the slave trade. The delegates finally agreed that the importation of slaves would continue for 20 more years with no interference from Congress. Any import tax could not exceed 10 dollars per person. After 1808, Congress would be able to decide whether to prohibit or regulate any further importation of slaves.

Of course, when work was completed and the document was presented, nine states needed to approve for it to go into effect. There was no little amount of discussion, arguing, debating, and haranguing. The opposition had three major objections:

1) The states seemed as if they were being asked to surrender too much power to the national government.
2) The voters did not have enough control and influence over the men who would be elected by them to run the government.
3) A lack of a "bill of rights" guaranteeing hard-won individual freedoms and liberties.

Eleven states finally ratified the document and the new national government went into effect. It was no small feat that the delegates were able to produce a workable document that satisfied all opinions, feelings, and viewpoints. The separation of powers of the three branches of government and the built-in system of checks and balances to keep power balanced were a stroke of genius. It provided for the individuals and the states as well as an organized central authority to keep a new inexperienced young nation on track. They created a system of government so flexible that it had continued in its basic form to this day. In 1789, the Electoral College unanimously elected George Washington as the first President and the new nation was on its way.

They created a government that as Benjamin Franklin said, *"though it may not be the best there is";* he said that he, *"wasn't sure that it could be possible to create one better".* A fact that might be true considering that the Constitution has lasted, through civil war, foreign wars, depression, and social revolution for over 200 years.

It is truly a living document because of its ability to remain strong while allowing itself to be changed with changing times.

Ratification of the U.S. Constitution was by no means a foregone conclusion. The representative government had powerful enemies, especially those who had seen firsthand the failure of the Articles of Confederation. The strong central government had powerful enemies, including some of the guiding lights of the American Revolution.

Those who wanted to see a strong central government were called Federalists, because they wanted to see a federal government reign supreme. Among the leaders of the Federalists were Alexander Hamilton and John Jay. These two, along with James Madison, wrote a series of letters to New York newspapers, urging that that state ratify the Constitution. These became known as the **Federalist Papers**.

In the Anti-Federalist camp were Thomas Jefferson and Patrick Henry. These men and many others like them were worried that a strong national government would descend into the kind of tyranny that they had just worked so hard to abolish. In the same way that they took their name from their foes, they wrote a series of arguments against the Constitution called the **Anti-Federalist Papers.**

In the end, both sides got most of what they wanted. The Federalists got their strong national government, which was held in place by the famous "checks and balances." The Anti-Federalists got the Bill of Rights, the first ten Amendments to the Constitution and a series of laws that protect some of the most basic of human rights. The states that were in doubt for ratification of the Constitution signed on when the Bill of Rights was promised.

Legislative – Article I of the Constitution established the legislative or law-making branch of the government called the Congress. It is made up of two houses, the House of Representatives and the Senate. Voters in all states elect the members who serve in each respective House of Congress. The Legislative branch is responsible for making laws, raising and printing money, regulating trade, establishing the postal service and federal courts, approving the President's appointments, declaring war and supporting the armed forces. The Congress also has the power to change the Constitution itself, and to *impeach* (bring charges against) the President. Charges for impeachment are brought by the House of Representatives, and are then tried in the Senate.

Executive – Article II of the Constitution created the Executive branch of the government, headed by the President, who leads the country, recommends new laws, and can veto bills passed by the legislative branch. As the chief of state, the President is responsible for carrying out the laws of the country and the treaties and declarations of war passed by the legislative branch. The President also appoints federal judges and is commander-in-chief of the military when it is called into service. Other members of the Executive branch include the Vice-President, also elected, and various cabinet members as he might appoint: ambassadors, presidential advisors, members of the armed forces, and other appointed and civil servants of government agencies, departments and bureaus. Though the President appoints them, they must be approved by the Legislative branch.

Judicial – Article III of the Constitution established the Judicial Branch of government headed by the Supreme Court. The Supreme Court has the power to rule that a law passed by the legislature, or an act of the Executive branch is illegal and unconstitutional. Citizens, businesses, and government officials can in an appeal capacity, ask the Supreme Court to review a decision made in a lower court if someone believes that the ruling by a judge is unconstitutional. The Judicial branch also includes lower federal courts known as federal district courts that have been established by the Congress. These courts try lawbreakers and review cases referred from other courts.

Powers delegated to the federal government	Powers reserved to the states:
1. To tax.	1. To regulate intrastate trade.
2. To borrow and coin money.	2. To establish local governments.
3. To establish postal service.	3. To protect general welfare.
4. To grant patents and copyrights.	4. To protect life and property.
5. To regulate interstate & foreign commerce.	5. To ratify amendments.
6. To establish courts.	6. To conduct elections.
7. To declare war.	7. To make state and local laws.
8. To raise and support the armed forces.	
9. To govern territories.	
10. To define and punish felonies and piracy on the high seas.	
11. To fix standards of weights and measures.	
12. To conduct foreign affairs.	

Concurrent powers of the federal government and states.

1. Both Congress and the states may tax.
2. Both may borrow money.
3. Both may charter banks and corporations.
4. Both may establish courts.
5. Both may make and enforce laws.
6. Both may take property for public purposes.
7. Both may spend money to provide for the public welfare.

Implied powers of the federal government.

1. To establish banks or other corporations implied from delegated powers to tax, borrow, and to regulate commerce.
2. To spend money for roads, schools, health, insurance, etc. implied from powers
3. to establish post roads, to tax to provide for general welfare and defense, and to regulate commerce.
4. To create military academies, implied from powers to raise and support an armed force.
5. To locate and generate sources of power and sell surplus implied from powers
6. To dispose of government property, commerce, and war powers.
7. To assist and regulate agriculture implied from power to tax and spend for general welfare and regulate commerce.

The first amendment guarantees the basic rights of freedom of religion, freedom of speech, freedom of the press, and freedom of assembly.

The next three amendments came out of the colonists' struggle with Great Britain. For example, the third amendment prevents Congress from forcing citizens to keep troops in their homes. Before the Revolution, Great Britain tried to coerce the colonists to house soldiers.

Amendments five through eight protect citizens who are accused of crimes and are brought to trial. Every citizen has the right to due process of law (due process as defined earlier, being that the government must follow the same fair rules for everyone brought to trial.) These rules include the right to a trial by an impartial jury, the right to be defended by a lawyer, and the right to a speedy trial.

The last two amendments limit the powers of the federal government to those that are expressly granted in the Constitution, any rights not expressly mentioned in the Constitution, thus, belong to the states or to the people. In regards to specific guarantees:

Freedom of Religion: Religious freedom has not been seriously threatened in the United States historically. The policy of the government has been guided by the premise that church and state should be separate. When religious practices have been at cross purposes with attitudes prevailing in the nation at particular times, there have been restrictions placed on these practices. Some of these have been restrictions against the practice of polygamy that is supported by certain religious groups. The idea of animal sacrifice that is promoted by some religious beliefs is generally prohibited. The use of mind altering illegal substances that some have used in religious rituals has been restricted. In the United States, all recognized religious institutions are tax-exempt in following the idea of separation of church and state, and therefore, there have been many quasi-religious groups that have in the past tried to take advantage of this fact. All of these issues continue, and most likely will continue to occupy both political and legal considerations for some time to come.

Freedom of Speech, Press, and Assembly: These rights historically have been given wide latitude in their practice though there has been instances when one or the other have been limited for various reasons. The classic limitation, for instance, in regards to freedom of speech, has been the famous precept that an individual is prohibited from yelling fire! in a crowded theatre. This prohibition is an example of the state saying that freedom of speech does not extend to speech that might endanger other people. There is also a prohibition against slander, or the knowingly stating of a deliberately falsehood against one party by another. Also there are many regulations regarding freedom of the press, the most common example are the various laws against libel, (or the printing of a known falsehood). In times of national emergency, various restrictions have been placed on the rights of press, speech and sometimes assembly.

All these ideas found their final expression in the United States Constitution's first ten amendments, known as the Bill of Rights. In 1789, the first Congress passed these first amendments and by December 1791, three-fourths of the states at that time had ratified them. The Bill of Rights protects certain liberties and basic rights. James Madison who wrote the amendments said that the Bill of Rights does not give Americans these rights. People, Madison said, already have these rights. They are natural rights that belong to all human beings. The Bill of Rights simply prevents the governments from taking away these rights.

Causes and Consequences of the War of 1812

United States' unintentional and accidental involvement in what was known as the **War of 1812** came about due to the political and economic struggles between France and Great Britain. Napoleon's goal was complete conquest and control of Europe, including and especially Great Britain. Although British troops were temporarily driven off the mainland of Europe, the navy still controlled the seas, the seas across which France had to bring the products needed. America traded with both nations, especially with France and its colonies. The British decided to destroy the American trade with France, mainly for two reasons: (a) Products and goods from the U.S. gave Napoleon what he needed to keep up his struggle with Britain. He and France was the enemy and it was felt that the Americans were aiding the Mother Country's enemy. (b) Britain felt threatened by the increasing strength and success of the U.S. merchant fleet. They were becoming major competitors with the ship owners and merchants in Britain.

The British issued the **Orders in Council** which was a series of measures prohibiting American ships from entering any French ports, not only in Europe but also in India and the West Indies. At the same time, Napoleon began efforts for a coastal blockade of the British Isles. He issued a series of Orders prohibiting all nations, including the United States, from trading with the British. He threatened seizure of every ship entering French ports after they stopped at any British port or colony, even threatening to seize every ship inspected by British cruisers or that paid any duties to their government. British were stopping American ships and impressing American seamen to service on British ships. Americans were outraged.

In 1807, Congress passed the Embargo Act forbidding American ships from sailing to foreign ports. It couldn't be completely enforced and it really hurt business and trade in America so, in 1809, it was repealed. Two additional acts passed by Congress after James Madison became president attempted to regulate trade with other nations and to get Britain and France to remove the restrictions they had put on American shipping. The catch was that whichever nation removed restrictions, the U.S. agreed not to trade with the other one. Clever Napoleon was the first to do this, prompting Madison to issue orders prohibiting trade with Britain, ignoring warnings from the British not to do so. Of course, this didn't work either and although Britain eventually rescinded the Orders in Council, war came in June of 1812 and ended Christmas Eve, 1814, with the signing of the Treaty of Ghent.

During the war, Americans were divided over not only whether or not it was necessary to even fight but also over what territories should be fought for and taken. The nation was still young and just not prepared for war. The primary American objective was to conquer Canada but it failed. Two naval victories and one military victory stand out for the United States. Oliver Perry gained control of Lake Erie and Thomas MacDonough fought on Lake Champlain. Both of these naval battles successfully prevented the British invasion of the United States from Canada. Nevertheless, the troops did land below Washington on the Potomac, marched into the city, and burned the public buildings, including the White House. Andrew Jackson's victory at New Orleans was a great morale booster to Americans, giving them the impression the U.S. had won the war. The battle actually took place after Britain and the United States had reached an agreement and it had no impact on the war's outcome. The peace treaty did little for the United States other than bringing peace, releasing prisoners of war, restoring all occupied territory, and setting up a commission to settle boundary disputes with Canada. Interestingly, the war proved to be a turning point in American history. European events had profoundly shaped U.S. policies, especially foreign policies.

During the colonial period, political parties, as the term is now understood, did not exist. The issues, which divided the people, were centered on the relations of the colonies to the mother country. There was initially little difference of opinion on these issues. About the middle of the 18th century, after England began to develop a harsher colonial policy, two factions arose in America. One favored the attitude of home government and the other declined to obey and demanded a constantly increasing level of self-government. The former came to be known as **Tories**, the latter as **Whigs**. During the course of the American Revolution a large number of Tories left the country either to return to England or move into Canada.

From the beginning of the Confederation, there were differences of opinion about the new government. One faction favored a loose confederacy in which the individual state would retain all powers of sovereignty except the absolute minimum required for the limited cooperation of all the states. (This approach was tried under the Articles of Confederation.) The other faction, which steadily gained influence, demanded that the central government be granted all the essential powers of sovereignty and the what should be left to the states was only the powers of local self-government. The inadequacy of the Confederation demonstrated that the latter were promoting a more effective point of view.

The first real party organization developed soon after the inauguration of Washington as President. His cabinet included people of both factions. Hamilton was the leader of the **Nationalists** – the **Federalist Party** – and Jefferson was the spokesman for the Anti-Federalists, later known as **Republicans**, **Democratic-Republicans**, and finally **Democrats**.

The Anti-Masonic Party came into being to oppose the Freemasons who they accused of being a secret society trying to take over the country. The Free Soil Party existed for the 1848 and 1852 elections only. They opposed slavery in the lands acquired from Mexico. The Liberty Party of this period was also abolitionist.

In the mid-1850s, the slavery issue was beginning to heat up and in 1854, those opposed to slavery, the Whigs, and some Northern Democrats opposed to slavery, united to form the Republican Party. Before the Civil War, the Democratic Party was more heavily represented in the South and was thus pro-slavery for the most part. The American Party was called the "Know Nothings." They lasted from 1854 to 1858 and were opposed to Irish-Catholic immigration.

The **Constitution Union Party** was formed in 1860. It was made up of entities from other extinguished political powers. They claim to support the Constitution above all and thought this would do away with the slavery issue. The **National Union Party** of 1864 was formed only for the purpose of the Lincoln election. That was the only reason for its existence.

Other political parties came and went in the post-Civil War era. The **Liberal Republican** Party formed in 1872 to oppose Ulysses S. Grant. They thought that Grant and his administration were corrupt and sought to displace them. The Anti-Monopoly Party of 1789 was more short-lived than the previous one. It billed itself as progressive and supported things like a graduated income tax system, the direct election of senators, etc. The **Greenback Party** was formed in 1878 and advocated the use of paper money. The Populist Party was a party consisting mostly of farmers who opposed the gold standard.

The process of political parties with short life spans continued in the twentieth century. Most of this is due to the fact that these parties come into existence in opposition to some policy or politician. Once the "problem" is gone, so is the party that opposed it. The Farmer-Labor Party was a Minnesota based political party. It supported farmers and labor and social security. It had moderate success in electing officials in Minnesota and merged with the Democratic Party in 1944.The Progressive Party was formed in 1912 due to a rift in the Republican Party that occurred when Theodore Roosevelt lost the nomination. This is not the same as the Progressive Party formed in 1924 to back LaFollette of Wisconsin. The Social Democratic Party was an outgrowth of a social movement and didn't have much political success.

There have also been other parties that have had a short termed life in the years following the Great Depression. The **American Labor Party** was a socialist party that existed in New York for a while. The American Workers Party was another socialist party based on Marxism. They also were short-lived. The **Progressive Party** came into being in 1948 to run candidates for President and Vice-President. The Dixicrats or States Rights Democratic Party also formed in 1948. They were a splinter group from the Democrats who supported Strom Thurmond. They also supported Wallace 1968. There have been various Workers' Parties that have come and gone. Most of these have had left-wing tendencies.

There are other political parties but they are not as strong as the Republicans and the Democrats. The Libertarian Party represents belief in the free rights of individuals to do as they wish without the interference of government. They favor a small government so propose a much lower level of government spending and services. The Libertarians are the third largest political party in America. The Socialist Party is also a political party. They run candidates in the elections. They favor the establishment of a radical democracy in which people control production and communities for all, not for the benefit of a few.

The **Communist Party** is also a political party advocating very radical changes in American society. They are concerned with the revolutionary struggle and moving through Marx's stages of history. There are many other parties. The American First Party is conservative as is the American Party. The American Nazi Party is also active in politics. Preaching fascism, they run candidates for elections and occasionally win. The Constitution Party is also representative of conservative views. The **Reform Party** was founded by Ross Perot, after his bid for President as an Independent. The list goes on and on. Many of these parties are regional and small and not on the national scene. Many of them form for a purpose, such as an election, and then dwindle.

Competency 4.2   Understand westward movement in U.S. history, major developments of the early national and Jacksonian periods, the Civil War, and Reconstruction.

One historian has stated that before 1865, the nation referred to itself as "the United States are ... ," but after 1865, "the United States is ..." It took the Civil War to finally, completely unify all states into one Union.

The drafting of the Constitution, its ratification and implementation, united 13 different, independent states into a Union under one central government. The two crucial compromises of the convention delegates concerning slaves pacified Southerners, especially the slave owners, but the issue of slavery was not settled and from then on **sectionalism** became stronger and more apparent each year putting the entire country on a collision course.

Slavery in the English colonies began in 1619 when 20 Africans arrived in the colony of Virginia at Jamestown. From then on, slavery had a foothold, especially in the agricultural South, where a large amount of slave labor was needed for the extensive plantations. Free men refused to work for wages on the plantations when land was available for settling on the frontier. Therefore, slave labor was the only recourse left. If it had been profitable to use slaves in New England and the Middle Colonies, then without doubt slavery would have been more widespread. However, it came down to whether or not slavery was profitable. It was in the South, but not in the other two colonial regions.

It is interesting that the West was involved in the controversy as well as the North and South. By 1860, the country was made up of these three major regions. The people in all three sections or regions had a number of beliefs and institutions in common. Of course, there were major differences with each region having its own unique characteristics. The basic problem was their development along very different lines.

The section of the North was industrial with towns and factories growing and increasing at a very fast rate. The South had become agricultural, eventually becoming increasingly dependent on the one crop of cotton. In the West, restless pioneers moved into new frontiers seeking land, wealth, and opportunity. Many were from the South and were slave owners, bringing their slaves with them. So between these three different parts of the country, the views on tariffs, public lands, internal improvements at federal expense, banking and currency, and the issue of slavery were decidedly, totally different. This period of U.S. history was a period of compromises, breakdowns of the compromises, desperate attempts to restore and retain harmony among the three sections, short-lived intervals of the uneasy balance of interests, and ever-increasing conflict.

At the Constitutional Convention, one of the slavery compromises concerned counting slaves for deciding the number of representatives for the House and the amount of taxes to be paid. Southerners pushed for counting the slaves for representation but not for taxes. The Northerners pushed for the opposite. The resulting compromise, sometimes referred to as the "three-fifths compromise," was that both groups agreed that three-fifths of the slaves would be counted for both taxes and representation.

The other compromise over slavery was part of the disputes over how much regulation the central government would control over commercial activities such as trade with other nations and the slave trade. It was agreed that Congress would regulate commerce with other nations including taxing imports. Southerners were worried about taxing slaves and the possibility of Congress prohibiting the slave trade altogether. The agreement reached allowed the states to continue importation of slaves for the next 20 years until 1808, at which time Congress would make the decision as to the future of the slave trade. During the 20-year period, no more than $10 per person could be levied on slaves coming into the country.

These two "slavery' compromises were a necessary concession to have Southern support and approval for the new document and new government. Many Americans felt that the system of slavery would eventually die out in the U.S., but by 1808, cotton was becoming increasingly important in the primarily agricultural South and the institution of slavery had become firmly entrenched in Southern culture. It is also evident that as early as the Constitutional Convention, active anti-slavery feelings and opinions were very strong, leading to extremely active groups and societies.

Democracy is loosely defined as "rule by the people," either directly or through representatives. Associated with the idea of democracy are freedom, equality, and opportunity. The basic concept of democracy existed in the 13 English colonies with the practice of independent self-government. The right of qualified persons to vote, hold office and actively participate in his or her government is sometimes referred to as "political" democracy. "Social" and "economic" democracy pertain to the idea that all have the opportunity to get an education, choose their own careers, and live as free men everyday all equal in the eyes of the law to everyone.

These three concepts of democracy were basic reasons why people came to the New World. The practices of these concepts continued through the colonial and revolutionary periods and were extremely influential in shaping the new central government under the Constitution. As the nation extended its borders into the lands west of the Mississippi, thousands of settlers streamed into the country. They brought with them ideas and concepts and adapted them to the development of the unique characteristics of the region. Equality for everyone, as stated in the Declaration of Independence, did not yet apply to minority groups, black Americans or American Indians. Voting rights and the right to hold public office were restricted in varying degrees in each state. All of these factors decidedly affected the political, economic, and social life of the country and these were focused in the attitudes towards slavery in three sections of the country.

The first serious clash between North and South occurred during 1819-1820 when James Monroe was in office as President and it was concerning admitting Missouri as a state. In 1819, the U.S. consisted of 21 states: 11 free states and 10 slave states. The Missouri Territory allowed slavery and if admitted would cause an imbalance in the number of U.S. Senators. Alabama had already been admitted as a slave state and that had balanced the Senate with the North and South each having 22 senators. The first Missouri Compromise resolved the conflict by approving the admission of Maine as a free state along with Missouri as a slave state. The balance of power in the Senate continued with the same number of free and slave states.

An additional provision of this compromise was that with the admission of Missouri, slavery would not be allowed in the rest of the Louisiana Purchase territory north of latitude 36 degrees 30'. This was acceptable to the Southern Congressmen since it was not profitable to grow cotton on land north of this latitude line anyway. It was thought that the crisis had been resolved but in the next year, it was discovered that in its state constitution, Missouri discriminated against the free blacks. Anti-slavery supporters in Congress went into an uproar, determined to exclude Missouri from the Union. Henry Clay, known as the Great Compromiser, then proposed a second Missouri Compromise, which was acceptable to everyone.

His proposal stated that the Constitution of the United States guaranteed protections and privileges to citizens of states and Missouri's proposed constitution could not deny these to any of its citizens. The acceptance in 1820 of this second compromise opened the way for Missouri's statehood--a temporary reprieve only.

The issue of tariffs also was a divisive factor during this period, especially between 1829 and 1833. The Embargo Act of 1807 and the War of 1812 had completely cut off the source of manufactured goods for Americans, so it was necessary to build factories to produce what was needed. After 1815, Great Britain proceeded to get rid of its industrial rivals by unloading its goods in America. To protect and encourage its own industries and their products, Congress passed the Tariff of 1816, which required high duties to be levied on manufactured goods coming into the United States. Southern leaders, such as John C. Calhoun of South Carolina, supported the tariff with the assumption that the South would develop its own industries.

For a brief period after 1815, the nation enjoyed the "Era of Good Feelings." People were moving into the West; industry and agriculture were growing; a feeling of national pride united Americans in their efforts and determination to strengthen the country. However, over-speculation in stocks and lands for quick profits backfired. Cotton prices were rising so many Southerners bought land for cultivation at inflated prices. Manufacturers in the industrial North purchased land to build more plants and factories as an attempt to have a part of this prosperity. Settlers in the West rushed to buy land to reap the benefits of the increasing prices of meat and grain. To have the money for all of these economic activities, all of these groups were borrowing heavily from the banks and the banks themselves encouraged this by giving loans on insubstantial security.

In late 1818, the Bank of the United States and its branches stopped renewal of personal mortgages and required state banks to immediately pay their bank notes in gold, silver, or in national bank notes. The state banks were unable to do this so they closed their doors and were unable to do any business at all. Since mortgages could not be renewed, people lost all their properties and foreclosures were rampant throughout the country. At the same time, as all of this was occurring, cotton prices collapsed in the English market. Its high price had caused the British manufacturers to seek cheaper cotton from India for their textile mills. With the fall of cotton prices, the demand for American manufactured goods declined, revealing how fragile the economic prosperity had been.

Congress passed a higher tariff in 1824 favoring the financial interests of the manufacturers in New England and the Middle Atlantic States. In addition, the 1824 tariff was closely tied to the presidential election of that year. Before becoming law, Calhoun had proposed the high tariffs in an effort to get Eastern business interests to vote with the agricultural interests in the South (who were against it). Supporters of candidate Andrew Jackson sided with whichever side served their best interests. Jackson himself would not be involved in any of this scheming.

The bill became law, to Calhoun's surprise, due mainly to the political maneuvering of Martin van Buren and Daniel Webster. By the time the higher 1828 tariff was passed, feelings were extremely bitter in the South, who believed that the New England manufacturers greatly benefited from it. Vice-President Calhoun, also speaking for his home state of South Carolina, promptly declared that if any state felt that a federal law was unconstitutional, that state could nullify it. In 1832, Congress took the action of lowering the tariffs to a degree but not enough to please South Carolina, which promptly declared the tariff null and void, threatening to secede from the Union.

In 1833, Congress lowered the tariffs again, this time at a level acceptable to South Carolina. Although President Jackson believed in states' rights, he also firmly believed in and determined to keep the preservation of the Union. A constitutional crisis had been averted but sectional divisions were getting deeper and more pronounced. The abolition movement was growing rapidly, becoming an important issue in the North.

The slavery issue was at the root of every problem, crisis, event, decision, and struggle from then on. The next crisis involved the issue concerning Texas. By 1836, Texas was an independent republic with its own constitution. During its fight for independence, Americans were sympathetic to and supportive of the Texans and some recruited volunteers who crossed into Texas to help the struggle. Problems arose when the state petitioned Congress for statehood. Texas wanted to allow slavery but Northerners in Congress opposed admission to the Union because it would disrupt the balance between free and slave states and give Southerners in Congress increased influence.
Others believed that granting statehood to Texas would lead to a war with Mexico. Mexico had refused to recognize Texas independence. For the time being, statehood was put on hold.

Friction increased between land-hungry Americans swarming into western lands and the Mexican government, which controlled these lands. The clash was not only political but also cultural and economic. The Spanish influence permeated all parts of southwestern life: law, language, architecture, and customs. By this time, the doctrine of Manifest Destiny was in the hearts and on the lips of those seeking new areas of settlement and a new life. Americans were demanding U.S. control of not only the Mexican Territory but also Oregon. Peaceful negotiations with Great Britain secured Oregon but it took two years of war to gain control of the southwestern U.S.

The Mexican government owed debts to U.S. citizens whose property was damaged or destroyed during its struggle for independence from Spain. By the time war broke out in 1845, Mexico had not paid its war debts. The government was weak, corrupt, irresponsible, torn by revolutions, and not in decent financial shape. Mexico was also bitter over American expansion into Texas and the 1836 revolution, which resulted in Texas independence. In the 1844 Presidential election, the Democrats pushed for annexation of Texas and Oregon and after winning, they started the procedure to admit Texas to the Union.

When statehood occurred, diplomatic relations between the U.S. and Mexico was ended. President Polk wanted U.S. control of the entire southwest, from Texas to the Pacific Ocean. He sent a diplomatic mission with an offer to purchase New Mexico and Upper California but the Mexican government refused to even receive the diplomat. Consequently, in 1846, each nation claimed aggression on the part of the other and war was declared. The treaty signed in 1848 and a subsequent one in 1853 completed the southwestern boundary of the United States, reaching to the Pacific Ocean, as President Polk wished.

The slavery issue flared again not to be done away with until the end of the Civil War. It was obvious that the newly acquired territory would be divided up into territories and later become states. Factions of Northerners advocated prohibition of slavery and Southerners favored slavery. A third faction arose supporting the doctrine of "popular sovereignty" which stated that people living in territories and states should be allowed to decide for themselves whether or not slavery should be permitted. In 1849, California applied for admittance to the Union and the furor began.

The result was the Compromise of 1850, a series of laws designed as a final solution to the issue. Concessions made to the North included the admission of California as a free state and the abolition of slave trading in Washington, D.C. The laws also provided for the creation of the New Mexico and Utah territories. As a concession to Southerners, the residents there would decide whether to permit slavery when these two territories became states. In addition, Congress authorized implementation of stricter measures to capture runaway slaves.

A few years later, Congress took up consideration of new territories between Missouri and present-day Idaho. Again, heated debate over permitting slavery in these areas flared up. Those opposed to slavery used the Missouri Compromise to prove their point showing that the land being considered for territories was part of the area the Compromise had designated as banned to slavery. On May 25, 1854, Congress passed the infamous Kansas-Nebraska Act which nullified the provision creating the territories of Kansas and Nebraska. This provided for the people of these two territories to decide for themselves whether or not to permit slavery to exist there. Feelings were so deep and divided that any further attempts to compromise would meet with little, if any, success. Political and social turmoil swirled everywhere. Kansas was called "Bleeding Kansas" because of the extreme violence and bloodshed throughout the territory because two governments existed there, one pro-slavery and the other anti-slavery.

The Supreme Court in 1857 handed down a decision guaranteed to cause explosions throughout the country. Dred Scott was a slave whose owner had taken him from slave state Missouri, then to free state Illinois, into Minnesota Territory, free under the provisions of the Missouri Compromise, then finally back to slave state Missouri. Abolitionists pursued the dilemma by presenting a court case, stating that since Scott had lived in a free state and free territory, he was in actuality a free man. Two lower courts had ruled before the Supreme Court became involved, one ruling in favor and one against. The Supreme Court decided that residing in a free state and free territory did not make Scott a free man because Scott (and all other slaves) was not an U.S. citizen or a state citizen of Missouri. Therefore, he did not have the right to sue in state or federal courts. The Court went a step further and ruled that the old Missouri Compromise was now unconstitutional because Congress did not have the power to prohibit slavery in the Territories.

Anti-slavery supporters were stunned. They had just recently formed the new Republican Party and one of its platforms was keeping slavery out of the Territories. Now, according to the decision in the Dred Scott case, this basic party principle was unconstitutional. The only way to ban slavery in new areas was by a Constitutional amendment, requiring ratification by three-fourths of all states. At this time, this was out of the question because the supporters would be unable to get a majority due to Southern opposition.

In 1858, Abraham Lincoln and Stephen A. Douglas were running for the office of U.S. Senator from Illinois and participated in a series of debates, which directly affected the outcome of the 1860 Presidential election. Douglas, a Democrat, was up for re-election and knew that if he won this race, he had a good chance of becoming President in 1860. Lincoln, a Republican, was not an abolitionist but he believed that slavery was wrong morally and he firmly believed in and supported the Republican Party principle that slavery must not be allowed to extend any further.

Douglas, on the other hand, originated the doctrine of "popular sovereignty" and was responsible for supporting and getting through Congress the inflammatory Kansas-Nebraska Act. In the course of the debates, Lincoln challenged Douglas to show that popular sovereignty reconciled with the Dred Scott decision. Either way he answered Lincoln, Douglas would lose crucial support from one group or the other. If he supported the Dred Scott decision, Southerners would support him but he would lose Northern support. If he stayed with popular sovereignty, Northern support would be his but Southern support would be lost. His reply to Lincoln, stating that Territorial legislatures could exclude slavery by refusing to pass laws supporting it, gave him enough support and approval to be re-elected to the Senate. But it cost him the Democratic nomination for President in 1860.

In 1859, abolitionist John Brown and his followers seized the federal arsenal at Harper's Ferry in what is now West Virginia. His purpose was to take the guns stored in the arsenal, give them to slaves nearby, and lead them in a widespread rebellion. He and his men were captured by Colonel Robert E. Lee of the United States Army and after a trial with a guilty verdict, he was hanged. Most Southerners felt that the majority of Northerners approved of Brown's actions but in actuality, most of them were stunned and shocked. Southern newspapers took great pains to quote a small but well-known minority of abolitionists who applauded and supported Brown's actions. This merely served to widen the gap between the two sections.

The final straw came with the election of Lincoln to the Presidency the next year. Due to a split in the Democratic Party, there were four candidates from four political parties. With Lincoln receiving a minority of the popular vote and a majority of electoral votes, the Southern states, one by one, voted to secede from the Union, as they had promised they would do if Lincoln and the Republicans were victorious. The die was cast.

It is ironic that South Carolina was the first state to secede from the Union and the first shots of the war were fired on Fort Sumter in Charleston Harbor. Both sides quickly prepared for war. The North had more in its favor: a larger population; superiority in finances and transportation facilities; manufacturing, agricultural, and natural resources. The North possessed most of the nation's gold, had about 92% of all industries, and almost all known supplies of copper, coal, iron, and various other minerals. Most of the nation's railroads were in the North and mid-West, men and supplies could be moved wherever needed; food could be transported from the farms of the mid-West to workers in the East and to soldiers on the battlefields. Trade with nations overseas could go on as usual due to control of the navy and the merchant fleet. The Northern states numbered 24 and included western (California and Oregon) and border (Maryland, Delaware, Kentucky, Missouri, and West Virginia) states.

The Southern states numbered 11 and included South Carolina, Georgia, Florida, Alabama, Mississippi, Louisiana, Texas, Virginia, North Carolina, Tennessee, and Arkansas, making up the Confederacy. Although outnumbered in population, the South was completely confident of victory. They knew that all they had to do was fight a defensive war and protect their own territory. The North had to invade and defeat an area almost the size of Western Europe. They figured the North would tire of the struggle and gave up. Another advantage of the South was that a number of its best officers had graduated from the U.S. Military Academy at West Point and had had long years of army experience. Many had exercised varying degrees of command in the Indian Wars and the war with Mexico. Men from the South were conditioned to living outdoors and were more familiar with horses and firearms than men from northeastern cities. Since cotton was such an important crop, Southerners felt that British and French textile mills were so dependent on raw cotton that they would be forced to help the Confederacy in the war.

The South had specific reasons and goals for fighting the war, more so than the North. The major aim of the Confederacy never wavered: to win independence, the right to govern themselves as they wished, and to preserve slavery. The Northerners were not as clear in their reasons for conducting war. At the beginning, most believed, along with Lincoln, that preservation of the Union was paramount. Only a few extremely fanatical abolitionists looked on the war as a way to end slavery. However, by war's end, more and more northerners had come to believe that freeing the slaves was just as important as restoring the Union.

The war strategies for both sides were relatively clear and simple. The South planned a defensive war, wearing down the North until it agreed to peace on Southern terms. The only exception was to gain control of Washington, D.C., go north through the Shenandoah Valley into Maryland and Pennsylvania in order to drive a wedge between the Northeast and mid-West, interrupt the lines of communication, and end the war quickly. The North had three basic strategies:

1. Blockade the Confederate coastline in order to cripple the South;
2. Seize control of the Mississippi River and interior railroad lines to split the Confederacy in two;
3. Seize the Confederate capital of Richmond, Virginia, driving southward joining up with Union forces coming east from the Mississippi Valley.

The South won decisively until the Battle of Gettysburg, July 1 - 3, 1863. Until Gettysburg, Lincoln's commanders, McDowell and McClellan, were less than desirable, Burnside and Hooker, not what was needed. Lee, on the other hand, had many able officers, Jackson and Stuart depended on heavily by him. Jackson died at Chancellorsville and was replaced by Longstreet. Lee decided to invade the North and depended on J.E.B. Stuart and his cavalry to keep him informed of the location of Union troops and their strengths. Four things worked against Lee at Gettysburg:

1) The Union troops gained the best positions and the best ground first, making it easier to make a stand there.

2) Lee's move into Northern territory put him and his army a long way from food and supply lines. They were more or less on their own.

3) Lee thought that his Army of Northern Virginia was invincible and could fight and win under any conditions or circumstances.

4) Stuart and his men did not arrive at Gettysburg until the end of the second day of fighting and by then, it was too little too late. He and the men had had to detour around Union soldiers and he was delayed getting the information Lee needed.

Consequently, he made the mistake of failing to listen to Longstreet and following the strategy of regrouping back into Southern territory to the supply lines. Lee felt that regrouping was retreating and almost an admission of defeat.

He was convinced the army would be victorious. Longstreet was concerned about the Union troops occupying the best positions and felt that regrouping to a better position would be an advantage. He was also very concerned about the distance from supply lines.

It was not the intention of either side to fight there, but the fighting began when a Confederate brigade who were looking for shoes, stumbled into a Union cavalry unit. The third and last day Lee launched the final attempt to break Union lines. General George Pickett sent his division of three brigades under Generals Garnet, Kemper, and Armistead against Union troops on Cemetery Ridge under command of General Winfield Scott Hancock. Union lines held and Lee and the defeated Army of Northern Virginia made their way back to Virginia. Although Lincoln's commander George Meade successfully turned back a Confederate charge, he and the Union troops failed to pursue Lee and the Confederates. This battle was the turning point for the North. After this, Lee never again had the troop strength to launch a major offensive.

The day after Gettysburg, on July 4, Vicksburg, Mississippi surrendered to Union General Ulysses Grant, thus severing the western Confederacy from the eastern part. In September 1863, the Confederacy won its last important victory at Chickamauga. In November, the Union victory at Chattanooga made it possible for Union troops to go into Alabama and Georgia, splitting the eastern Confederacy in two. Lincoln gave Grant command of all Northern armies in March of 1864. Grant led his armies into battles in Virginia while Phil Sheridan and his cavalry did as much damage as possible. In a skirmish at a place called Yellow Tavern, Virginia, Sheridan's and Stuart's forces met, with Stuart being fatally wounded.

The Union won the Battle of Mobile Bay and in May 1864, William Tecumseh Sherman began his march to successfully demolish Atlanta, then on to Savannah. He and his troops turned northward through the Carolinas to Grant in Virginia. On April 9, 1865, Lee formally surrendered to Grant at Appamattox Courthouse, Virginia.

The Civil War took more American lives than any other war in history, the South losing one-third of its' soldiers in battle compared to about one-sixth for the North. More than half of the total deaths were caused by disease and the horrendous conditions of field hospitals. Both sides paid a tremendous economic price but the South suffered more severely from direct damages. Destruction was pervasive with towns, farms, trade, industry, lives and homes of men, women, children all destroyed and an entire Southern way of life was lost. The South had no voice in the political, social, and cultural affairs of the nation, lessening to a great degree the influence of the more traditional Southern ideals. The Northern Yankee Protestant ideals of hard work, education, and economic freedom became the standard of the United States and helped influence the development of the nation into a modem, industrial power.

The effects of the Civil War were tremendous. It changed the methods of waging war and has been called the first modern war. It introduced weapons and tactics that, when improved later, were used extensively in wars of the late 1800s and 1900s. Civil War soldiers were the first to fight in trenches, first to fight under a unified command, first to wage a defense called "major cordon defense", a strategy of advance on all fronts. They were also the first to use repeating and breech loading weapons. Observation balloons were first used during the war along with submarines, ironclad ships, and mines. Telegraphy and railroads were put to use first in the Civil War. It was considered a modern war because of the vast destruction and was "total war", involving the use of all resources of the opposing sides. There was no *way* it could have ended other than total defeat and unconditional surrender of one side or the other.

By executive proclamation and constitutional amendment, slavery was officially ended, although there remained deep prejudice and racism, still raising its ugly head today. Also, the Union was preserved and the states were finally truly united. Sectionalism, especially in the area of politics, remained strong for another 100 years but not to the degree and with the violence as existed before 1861. It has been noted that the Civil War may have been American democracy's greatest failure for, from 1861 to 1865, calm reason, basic to democracy, fell to human passion. Yet, democracy did survive. The victory of the North established that no state has the right to end or leave the Union. Because of unity, the U.S. became a major global power. Lincoln never proposed to punish the South. He was most concerned with restoring the South to the Union in a program that was flexible and practical rather than rigid and unbending. In fact he never really felt that the states had succeeded in leaving the Union but that they had left the 'family circle" for a short time. His plans consisted of two major steps:

- All Southerners taking an oath of allegiance to the Union promising to accept all federal laws and proclamations dealing with slavery would receive a full pardon. The only ones excluded from this were men who had resigned from civil and military positions in the federal government to serve in the Confederacy, those who were part of the Confederate government, those in the Confederate army above the rank of lieutenant, and Confederates who were guilty of mistreating prisoners of war and blacks.

- A state would be able to write a new constitution, elect new officials, and return to the Union fully equal to all other states on certain conditions: a minimum number of persons (at least 10% of those who were qualified voters in their states before secession from the Union who had voted in the 1860 election) must take an oath of allegiance.

While the war dragged on to its bloody and destructive conclusion, Lincoln was very concerned and anxious to get the states restored to the Union. He showed flexibility in his thinking as he made changes to his Reconstruction program to make it as easy and painless as possible. Congress had final approval of many actions. It would be interesting to know how differently things might have turned out if Lincoln had lived to see some or all of his kind policies supported by fellow moderates, put into action. Unfortunately, it didn't turn out that way. After Andrew Johnson became President and the radical Republicans gained control of Congress, the harsh measures of radical Reconstruction were implemented.

The economic and social chaos in the South after the war was unbelievable with starvation and disease rampant, especially in the cities. The U.S. Army provided some relief of food and clothing for both white and blacks but the major responsibility fell to the Freedmen's Bureau. Though the bureau agents to a certain extent helped southern whites, their main responsibility was to the freed slaves. They were to assist the freedmen to become self-supporting and protect them from being taken advantage of by others. Northerners looked on it as a real, honest effort to help the South out of the chaos it was in. Most white Southerners charged the bureau with causing racial friction, deliberately encouraging the freedmen to consider former owners as enemies.

As a result, as southern leaders began to be able to restore life as it had once been, they adopted a set of laws known as "black codes", containing many of the provisions of the prewar "slave codes." There were certain improvements in the lives of freedmen, but the codes denied the freedmen their basic civil rights. In short, except for the condition of freedom and a few civil rights, white Southerners made every effort to keep the freedmen in a way of life subordinate to theirs.

Radicals in Congress pointed out these illegal actions by white Southerners as evidence that they were unwilling to recognize, accept, and support the complete freedom of black Americans and could not be trusted. Therefore, Congress drafted its own program of Reconstruction, including laws that would protect and further the rights of blacks. Three amendments were added to the Constitution: the 13th Amendment of 1865 outlawed slavery throughout the entire United States. The 14th Amendment of 1868 made blacks American citizens. The 15th Amendment of 1870 gave black Americans the right to vote and made it illegal to deny anyone the right to vote based on race.

Federal troops were stationed throughout the South and protected Republicans who took control of Southern governments. Bitterly resentful, white Southerners fought the new political system by joining a secret society called the Ku Klux Klan, using violence to keep black Americans from voting and getting equality. However, before being allowed to rejoin the Union, the Confederate states were required to agree to all federal laws. Between 1866 and 1870, all of them had returned to the Union, but Northern interest in Reconstruction was fading. Reconstruction officially ended when the last Federal troops left the South in 1877. It can be said that Reconstruction had a limited success as it set up public school systems and expanded legal rights of black Americans. Nevertheless, white supremacy came to be in control again and its bitter fruitage is still with us today.

Lincoln and Johnson had considered the conflict of Civil War as a "rebellion of individuals". Congressional Radicals, such as Charles Sumner in the Senate, considered the Southern states as complete political organizations and were now in the same position as any unorganized Territory and should be treated as such. Radical House leader Thaddeus Stevens considered the Confederate States, not as Territories, but as conquered provinces and felt they should be treated that way. President Johnson refused to work with Congressional moderates, insisting on having his own way. As a result the Radicals gained control of both houses of Congress and when Johnson opposed their harsh measures, they came within one vote of impeaching him. General Grant was elected President in 1868, serving two scandal-ridden terms. He was himself an honest, upright person but he greatly lacked political experience and his greatest weakness was a blind loyalty to his friends. He absolutely refused to believe that his friends were not honest and stubbornly would not admit to their using him to further their own interests. One of the sad results of the war was the rapid growth of business and industry with large corporations controlled by unscrupulous men. However, after 1877, some degree of normalcy returned and there was time for rebuilding, expansion, and growth.

There was a marked degree of industrialization before and during the Civil War, but at war's end, industry in America was small. After the war, dramatic changes took place. Machines replaced hand labor, extensive nationwide railroad service made possible the wider distribution of goods, invention of new products made available in large quantities, and large amounts of money from bankers and investors for expansion of business operations. American life was definitely affected by this phenomenal industrial growth. Cities became the centers of this new business activity resulting in mass population movements there and tremendous growth. This new boom in business resulted in huge fortunes for some Americans and extreme poverty for many others. The discontent this caused resulted in a number of new reform movements from which came measures controlling the power and size of big business and helping the poor.

Of course, industry before, during, and after the Civil War was centered mainly in the North, especially the tremendous industrial growth after. The late 1800s and early 1900s saw the increasing buildup of military strength and the U.S. becoming a world power.

The use of machines in industry enabled workers to produce a large quantity of goods much faster than by hand. With the increase in business, hundreds of workers were hired, assigned to perform a certain job in the production process. This was a method of organization called "division of labor" and by its increasing the rate of production, businesses lowered prices for their products making the products affordable for more people. As a result, sales and businesses were increasingly successful and profitable.

A great variety of new products or inventions became available such as: the typewriter, the telephone, barbed wire, the electric light, the phonograph, and the gasoline automobile. From this list, the one that had the greatest effect on America's economy was the automobile.

The increase in business and industry was greatly affected by the many rich natural resources that were found throughout the nation. The industrial machines were powered by the abundant water supply. The construction industry as well as products made from wood depended heavily on lumber from the forests. Coal and iron ore in abundance were needed for the steel industry, which profited and increased from the use of steel in such things as skyscrapers, automobiles, bridges, railroad tracks, and machines. Other minerals such as silver, copper, and petroleum played a large role in industrial growth, especially petroleum, from which gasoline was refined as fuel for the increasingly popular automobile.

U.S. imperialism and examine the experience of the United States as a colonial power

During the period of 1823 to the 1890s, the major interests and efforts of the American people were concentrated on expansion, settlement, and development of the continental United States. The Civil War, 1861-1865, preserved the Union and eliminated the system of slavery. From 1865 onward, the focus was on taming the West and developing industry. During this period, travel and trade between the United States and Europe were continuous. By the 1890s, American interests turned to areas outside the boundaries of the United States. The West was developing into a major industrial area and people in the United States became very interested in selling their factory and farm surplus to overseas markets. In fact, some Americans desired getting and controlling land outside the U.S. boundaries. Before the 1890s, the U.S. had little, if anything to do with foreign affairs, was not a strong nation militarily, and had inconsequential influence on international political affairs. In fact, the Europeans looked on the American diplomats as inept and bungling in their diplomatic efforts and activities. However, all of this changed and the **Spanish-American War of 1898** saw the entry of the United States as a world power.

It was the belief of many that the United States was destined to control all of the land between the two oceans or as one newspaper editor termed it, "Manifest Destiny." This mass migration westward put the U.S. government on a collision course with the Indians, Great Britain, Spain, and Mexico. The fur traders and missionaries ran up against the Indians in the northwest and the claims of Great Britain for the Oregon country.

In the American southwest, Spain had claimed this area since the 1540s, had spread northward from Mexico City, and, in the 1700s, had established missions, forts, villages, towns, and very large ranches. After the purchase of the Louisiana Territory in 1803, Americans began moving into Spanish territory. A few hundred American families in what is now Texas were allowed to live there but had to agree to become loyal subjects to Spain. In 1821, Mexico successfully revolted against Spanish rule, won independence, and chose to be more tolerant towards the American settlers and traders. The Mexican government encouraged and allowed extensive trade and settlement, especially in Texas. Many of the new settlers were southerners and brought with them their slaves. Slavery was outlawed in Mexico and technically illegal in Texas, although the Mexican government rather looked the other way.

With the influx of so many Americans and the liberal policies of the Mexican government, there came to be concern over the possible growth and development of an American state within Mexico. Settlement restrictions, cancellation of land grants, the forbidding of slavery and increased military activity brought everything to a head. The order of events included the fight for Texas independence, the brief Republic of Texas, eventual annexation of Texas, statehood, and finally war with Mexico.

The Texas controversy was not the sole reason for war. Since American settlers had begun, pouring into the Southwest the cultural differences played a prominent part. Language, religion, law, customs, and government were totally different and opposite between the two groups. A clash was bound to occur.

Friction increased between land-hungry Americans swarming into western lands and the Mexican government, which controlled these lands. The clash was not only political but also cultural and economic. The Spanish influence permeated all parts of southwestern life: law, language, architecture, and customs. By this time, the doctrine of Manifest Destiny was in the hearts and on the lips of those seeking new areas of settlement and a new life.

During the 1890s, Spain controlled such overseas possessions as Puerto Rico, the Philippines, and Cuba. Cubans rebelled against Spanish rule and the U.S. government found itself besieged by demands from Americans to assist the Cubans in their revolt. When the U.S. battleship Maine blew up off the coast of Havana, Cuba, Americans blamed the Spaniards for it and demanded American action against Spain. Two months later, Congress declared war on Spain and the U.S. quickly defeated them. The peace treaty gave the U.S. possession of Puerto Rico, the Philippines, Guam and Hawaii, which was annexed during the war.

Most students of American history are aware of the tremendous influx of immigrants to America during the 19th century. It is also a known fact that the majority settled in the ethnic neighborhoods and communities of the large cities, close to friends, relatives, and the work they were able to find. After the U.S. Congress passed the 1862 Homestead Act after the Civil War ended, the West began to open up for settlement. One interesting fact that some are not aware of is that more than half of the hardy pioneers who went to homestead and farm western lands were European immigrants: Swedes, Norwegians, Czechs, Germans, Danes, Finns, and Russians.

By far, the nation's immigrants were an important reason for America's phenomenal industrial growth from 1865 to 1900. They came seeking work and better opportunities for themselves and their families than what life in their native country could give them. What they found in America was suspicion and distrust because they were competitors with Americans for jobs, housing, and decent wages. Their languages, customs, and ways of living were different, especially between the different national and ethnic groups. Until the early 1880s, most immigrants were from the parts of northwestern Europe such as Germany, Scandinavia, the Netherlands, Ireland, and Great Britain.

After 1890, the new arrivals increasingly came from eastern and southern Europe. Chinese immigrants on the Pacific coast, so crucial to the construction of the western part of the first transcontinental railroad, were the first to experience this increasing distrust which eventually erupted into violence and bloodshed. From about 1879 to the present time, the U.S. Congress made, repealed, and amended numerous pieces of legislation concerning quotas, restrictions, and other requirements pertaining to immigrants. The immigrant laborers, both skilled and unskilled, were the foundation of the modern labor union movement as a means of gaining recognition, support, respect, rights, fair wages, and better working conditions.

Competency 4.3 *Understand industrialization in the United States and the effects of industrialization on U.S. economic, social, and political life.*

The tremendous change that resulted from the Industrial Revolution led to a demand for reform that would control the power wielded by big corporations. The gap between the industrial moguls and the working people was growing. This disparity between rich and poor resulted in a public outcry for reform at the same time that there was an outcry for governmental reform that would end the political corruption and elitism of the day.

This fire was fueled by the writings on investigative journalists – the "muckrakers" – who published scathing exposes of political and business wrongdoing and corruption. The result was the rise of a group of politicians and reformers who supported a wide array of populist causes. The period 1900 to 1917 came to be known as the Progressive Era. Although these leaders came from many different backgrounds and were driven by different ideologies, they shared a common fundamental belief that government should be eradicating social ills and promoting the common good and the equality guaranteed by the Constitution.

The reforms initiated by these leaders and the spirit of **Progressivism** were far-reaching. Politically, many states enacted the initiative and the referendum. The adoption of the recall occurred in many states. Several states enacted legislation that would undermine the power of political machines. On a national level the two most significant political changes were (1) the ratification of the 19th amendment, which required that all U.S. Senators be chosen by popular election, and (2) the ratification of the 19th Amendment, which granted women the right to vote.

Major economic reforms of the period included aggressive enforcement of the Sherman Antitrust Act; passage of the Elkins Act and the Hepburn Act, which gave the Interstate Commerce Commission greater power to regulate the railroads; the Pure Food and Drug Act prohibited the use of harmful chemicals in food; The Meat Inspection Act regulated the meat industry to protect the public against tainted meat; over 2/3 of the states passed laws prohibiting child labor; workmen's compensation was mandated; and the Department of Commerce and Labor was created.

Responding to concern over the environmental effects of the timber, ranching, and mining industries, Roosevelt set aside 238 million acres of federal lands to protect them from development. Wildlife preserves were established, the national park system was expanded, and the National Conservation Commission was created. The Newlands Reclamation Act also provided federal funding for the construction of irrigation projects and dams in semi-arid areas of the country. The Wilson Administration carried out additional reforms. The Federal Reserve Act created a national banking system, providing a stable money supply. The Sherman Act and the Clayton Antitrust Act defined unfair competition, made corporate officers liable for the illegal actions of employees, and exempted labor unions from antitrust lawsuits. The Federal Trade Commission was established to enforce these measures. Finally, the 16th amendment was ratified, establishing an income tax. This measure was designed to relieve the poor of a disproportionate burden in funding the federal government and make the wealthy pay a greater share of the nation's tax burden.

Literature and the arts during the twentieth century

Music. The 20th century experienced a revolution in music. In keeping with the exceptionally high value of individuality and unique personal expression, there was a quest for new and unique forms of musical expression.

The major forms inspired by classical music have continued, though with certain modifications. The symphony has continued in form, but with greater dissonance and great experimentation in rhythm. Major symphonic composers of the century include: Gustav Mahler, Jean Sibelius, Dmitry Shostakovich, Serge Prokofiev and Sergey Rachmaninov, as well as Leonard Bernstein. Opera began to change after WWII as composers began to incorporate other musical forms that were emerging during the century. Notable operatic composers include Benjamin Britten, Karlheinz Stockhausen, Virgil Thomson, Douglas Moore, Philip Glass and John Adams. Ballet tended to focus on music written specifically for its needs. This trend included such composers as Claude Debussy, Maurice Ravel and R. Strauss. Igor Stravinsky's *The Rite of Spring*, however was internationally recognized for its violent rhythms and dissonance. The second half of the century was marked by the tendency to re-stage ballets with existing music. The exceptions were Aaron Copland Has Werner Henze and Benjamin Britten.

Musical Theater was an evolution from the operettas of the Romantic Period and the traditions of the European music hall and American vaudeville. Most notable in this form are Leonard Bernstein and Steven Sondheim. Film Music also developed during this century. The soundtracks for films were either adaptations of classical music or new compositions from composers like Elmer Bernstein, Bernard Herrman, Max Steiner and Dmitri Tiomkin.

American Popular music evolved from folk music. This was the music of the first half of the century, characterized by a consistent structure of two verses, a chorus, and a repetition of the chorus. The songs were written to be sung by average persons, and the tunes were usually harmonized. Much of this music originated in New York's Tin Pan Alley. Particularly notable during this period were Irving Berlin, George and Ira Gershwin, and a host of others. After WWII, teen music began to dominate. New forms emerged from various ethnic and regional groups including Blues, Rhythm and Blues and Rap from the African American community; Country music from the south and the southwest, folk music, jazz, rock and roll, and rock.

In art, the primary expression of the first half of the decade was Modernism. The avant garde perspective encouraged all types of innovation and experimentation. Key elements of this movement have been abstraction, cubism, surrealism, realism, and abstract expressionism. Notable among the artists of this period for the birth or perfection of particular styles are Henri Matisse, Pablo Picasso, George Rouault, Gustav Klimt, George Braque, Salvador Dali, Hans Arp, Rene Magrite, and Marcel Duchamp. In the U.S. realism tended to find regional expressions including the Ashcan School and Robert Henri, Midwestern Regionalism and Grant Wood. Other particularly notable painters are Edward Hopper and Georgia O'Keeffe. The New York School came to be known for a style known as Abstract Expressionism and included such artists as Jackson Pollock, Willem de Kooning, Larry Rivers. Other painters of the period were Mark Rothko, Clement Greenberg, Ellsworth Kelly and the Op Art Movement.

In sculpture, many of the same patterns and trends were applied. Innovations included the exploration of empty space (Henry Moore), the effort to incorporate cubism in three dimensions (Marcel Duchamp), and the use of welded metal to create kinetic sculpture (Alexander Calder).

Postmodernism has been the description of the expansion of forms and the valuing of innovation since 1950. This has included Minimalism, Figurative Styles, Pop Art, Conceptual Art and Installation Art. Photography has developed as an art form, as well, during the 20th century.

The literature of this period has been an attempt to come to terms with the nature and the cost of war, of the meaning of the human struggle for freedom and the ability to enjoy basic human and civil rights. Literature has cried out against change and it has embraced change. By the beginning of the 20th century literature was reflecting the struggle of the modern individual to find a place and a meaning in a new world that seemed like a jungle. Literature has reflected the observation that not only does the modern human not know how to find meaning, he/she does not actually know what he/she is seeking. It is this crisis of identity that has been the subject of most modern literature. This can be seen is the writings of Joseph Conrad, Sigmund Freud, James Joyce, Eugene O'Neill, Luigi Pirandello, Samuel Beckett, George Bernard Shaw, T.S. Eliot, Kafka, Camus, Pasternak, Graham Greene, Tennessee Williams, and a host of others.

The historical record of African-Americans is known to all. Sold into slavery by rival tribes, they were brought against their will to the West Indies and southern America to slave on the plantations in a life-long condition of servitude and bondage. The 13th Constitutional Amendment abolished slavery; the 14th gave them U.S. citizenship; and the 15th gave them the right to vote. Efforts of well-known African-Americans resulted in some improvements although the struggle was continuous without let-up. Many were outspoken and urged and led protests against the continued onslaught of discrimination and inequality.

The leading black spokesman from 1890 to 1915 was educator **Booker T. Washington**. He recognized the need of vocational education for African-Americans, educating them for skills and training for such areas as domestic service, farming, the skilled trades, and small business enterprises. He founded and built in Alabama the famous Tuskegee Institute.

W.E.B. DuBois, another outstanding African-American leader and spokesman, believed that only continuous and vigorous protests against injustices and inequalities coupled with appeals to black pride would effect changes. The results of his efforts was the formation of the Urban League and the NAACP (the National Association for the Advancement of Colored People) which today continue to eliminate discriminations and secure equality and equal rights.

Others who made significant contributions were **Dr. George Washington Carver's** work improving agricultural techniques for both black and white farmers; the writers **William Wells Brown, Paul L. Dunbar, Langston Hughes**, and **Charles W. Chesnutt**; the music of **Duke Ellington, W.C. Handy, Marion Anderson, Louis Armstrong, Leontyne Price, Jessye Norman, Ella Fitzgerald**, and many, many others.

Students of American history are greatly familiar with the accomplishments and contributions of American women. Previous mention has been made of the accomplishments of such 19th century women as: writer **Louisa Mae Alcott**; abolitionist **Harriet Beecher Stowe**; women's rights activists **Elizabeth Cady Stanton** and **Lucretia Mott**; physician **Dr. Elizabeth Blackwell**; wonen's education activists **Mary Lyon, Catharine Esther Beecher**, and **Emma Hart Willard**; prison and asylum reform activist **Dorothea Dix**; social reformer, humanitarian, pursuer of peace **Jane Addams**; aviatrix **Amelia Earhart**; women's suffrage activists **Susan B. Anthony, Carrie Chapman Catt**, and **Anna Howard Shaw**; Supreme Court Associate Justices **Sandra Day O'Connor** and **Ruth Bader Ginsberg**; and many, many more who have made tremendous contributions in science, politics and government, music and the arts (such as **Jane Alexander** who is National Chairperson of the National Endowment for the Arts), education, athletics, law, etc.

Competency 4.4 Understand political and diplomatic developments, economic trends, and social movements in the United States from World War I to the present.

The American isolationist mood was given a shocking and lasting blow in 1941 with the Japanese attack on Pearl Harbor. The nation arose and forcefully entered the international arena as never before. Declaring itself "the arsenal of democracy", it entered the Second World War and emerged not only victorious, but also as the *strongest power* on the Earth. It would now, like it or not, have a permanent and leading place in world affairs.

In the aftermath of the Second World War, with the Soviet Union having emerged as the *second* strongest power on Earth, the United States embarked on a policy known as "Containment" of the Communist menace. This involved what came to be known as the "Marshall Plan" and the "Truman Doctrine". The Marshall Plan involved the economic aid that was sent to Europe in the aftermath of the Second World War aimed at preventing the spread of communism. To that end, the US has devoted a larger and larger share of its foreign policy, diplomacy, and both economic and military might to combating it.

The Truman Doctrine offered military aid to those countries that were in danger of communist upheaval. This led to the era known as the Cold War in which the United States took the lead along with the Western European nations against the Soviet Union and the Eastern Bloc countries. It was also at this time that the United States finally gave up on George Washington's' advice against "European entanglements" and joined the North Atlantic Treaty Organization or NATO. This was formed in 1949 and was comprised of the United States and several Western European nations for the purposes of opposing communist aggression.

The United Nations was also formed at this time (1945) to replace the defunct League of Nations for the purposes of ensuring world peace. Even with American involvement, would prove largely ineffective in maintaining world peace.
In the 1950s, the United States embarked on what was called the "Eisenhower Doctrine", after the then President Eisenhower. This aimed at trying to maintain peace in a troubled area of the world, the Middle East. However, unlike the Truman Doctrine in Europe, it would have little success.

The United States also became involved in a number of world conflicts in the ensuing years. Each had at the core the struggle against communist expansion. Among these were the Korean War (1950-1953), the Vietnam War (1965-1975), and various continuing entanglements in Central and South America and the Middle East. By the early 1970's under the leadership of then Secretary of State, Henry Kissinger, the United States and its allies embarked on the policy that came to be known as "Détente". This was aimed at the easing of tensions between the United States and its allies and the Soviet Union and its allies.

By the 1980s, the United States embarked on what some saw as a renewal of the Cold War. This owed to the fact that the United States was becoming more involved in trying to prevent communist insurgency in Central America. A massive expansion of its armed forces and the development of space-based weapons systems were undertaken at this time. As this occurred, the Soviet Union, with a failing economic system and a foolhardy adventure in Afghanistan, found itself unable to compete. By 1989, events had come to a head. This ended with the breakdown of the Communist Bloc, the virtual end of the monolithic Soviet Union, and the collapse of the communist system by the early 1990's.

Now the United States remains active in world affairs in trying to promote peace and reconciliation, with a new specter rising to challenge it and the world, the specter of nationalism.

The Cold War was, more than anything else was, an ideological struggle between proponents of democracy and those of communism. The two major players were the United States and the Soviet Union, but other countries were involved as well. It was a "cold" war because no large-scale fighting took place directly between the two big protagonists.

It wasn't just form of government that was driving this war, either. Economics were a main concern as well. A concern in both countries was that the precious resources (such as oil and food) from other like-minded countries wouldn't be allowed to flow to "the other side." These resources didn't much flow between the U.S. and Soviet Union, either.

The Soviet Union kept much more of a tight leash on its supporting countries, including all of Eastern Europe, which made up a military organization called the **Warsaw Pact**. The Western nations responded with a military organization of their own, NATO. Another prime battleground was Asia, where the Soviet Union had allies in China, North Korea, and North Vietnam and the U.S. had allies in Japan, South Korea, Taiwan, and South Vietnam. The Korean War and Vietnam War were major conflicts in which both big protagonists played big roles but didn't directly fight each other. The main symbol of the Cold War was the arms race, a continual buildup of missiles, tanks, and other weapons that became ever more technologically advanced and increasingly more deadly. The ultimate weapon, which both sides had in abundance, was the nuclear bomb. Spending on weapons and defensive systems eventually occupied great percentages of the budgets of the U.S. and the USSR, and some historians argue that this high level of spending played a large part in the end of the latter.

The war was a cultural struggle as well. Adults brought up their children to hate "the Americans" or "the Communists." Cold War tensions spilled over into many parts of life in countries around the world. The ways of life in countries on either side of the divide were so different that they served entirely foreign to outside observers.

The Cold War continued in varying degrees from 1947 to 1991, when the Soviet Union collapsed. Other Eastern European countries had seen their communist governments overthrown by this time as well, marking the shredding of the "Iron Curtain."

The major thrust of U.S. foreign policy from the end of World War II to 1990 was the post-war struggle between non-Communist nations, led by the United States, and the Soviet Union and the Communist nations who were its allies. It was referred to as a "Cold War" because its conflicts did not lead to a major war of fighting, or a "hot war." Both the Soviet Union and the United States embarked on an arsenal buildup of atomic and hydrogen bombs as well as other nuclear weapons. Both nations had the capability of destroying each other but because of the continuous threat of nuclear war and accidents, extreme caution was practiced on both sides. The efforts of both sides to serve and protect their political philosophies and to support and assist their allies resulted in a number of events during this 45-year period.

Pre-war empires lost tremendous amounts of territories as well as the wealth of natural resources in them. New, independent nations were formed and some predominately ethnic areas came under control of nations of different cultural backgrounds. Some national boundary changes overlapped and created tensions and hard feelings as well as political and economic confusion. The wishes and desires of every national or cultural group could not possibly be realized and satisfied, resulting in disappointments for both; those who were victorious and those who were defeated. Germany received harsher terms than expected from the treaty which weakened its post-war government and, along with the world-wide depression of the 1930s, set the stage for the rise of Adolf Hitler and his Nationalist Socialist Party and World War II.

The world after World War II was a complicated place. The Axis powers were defeated, but the Cold War had sprung up in its place. Many countries struggled to get out of the debt and devastation that their Nazi occupiers had wrought. The American Marshall Plan helped the nations of Western Europe get back on their feet. The Soviet Union helped the Eastern European nations return to greatness, with Communist governments at the helm. The nations of Asia were rebuilt as well, with Communism taking over China and Americanization taking over Japan and Taiwan. East and West struggled for control in this arena, especially in Korea and Southeast Asia. When Communism fell in the USSR and Eastern Europe, it remained in China, North Korea, and Vietnam; Vietnam's neighbors, however set their own path to government.

The United Nations, a more successful successor to the League of Nations (which couldn't prevent World War II) began in the waning days of the war. It brought the nations of the world together to discuss their problems, rather than fight about them. Another successful method of keeping the peace since the war has been the atomic bomb. On a more pacific note, UNICEF, a world wide children's fund has been able to achieve great things in just a few decades of existence. Other peace-based organizations like the Red Cross and Doctors Without Borders have seen their membership and their efficacy rise during this time as well.

In America, President Wilson lost in his efforts to get the U.S. Senate to approve the peace treaty. The Senate at the time was a reflection of American public opinion and its rejection of the treaty was a rejection of Wilson. The approval of the treaty would have made the U.S. a member of the League of Nations but Americans had just come off a bloody war to ensure that democracy would exist throughout the world. Americans just did not want to accept any responsibility that resulted from its new position of power and were afraid that membership in the League of Nations would embroil the U.S. in future disputes in Europe.

The kind of nationalism that Europe saw in the 19th Century spilled over into the mid-20th Century, with former colonies of European powers declaring themselves independent all the time, especially in Africa. India, a longtime British protectorate, also achieved independence at this time. With independence, these countries continued to grow. Some of these nations now experience severe overcrowding and dearth of precious resources. Some who can escape do; others have no way to escape.

The Middle East has been an especially violent part of the world since the war and the inception of the State of Israel. The struggle for supremacy in the Persian Gulf area has brought about a handful of wars as well. Oil, needed to power the world's devastatingly large transportation and manufacturing engines, is king of all resources.

Competency 4.5 Understand major developments in Illinois history.

Illinois was inhabited by Native Americans, among them the powerful **Illini**. This word was actually a French mangling of "Hileni" or "Illiniwek" as Illinois. This "name" notwithstanding, the Illini built one of the most powerful confederations the continent ever saw.

The five most populous tribes were the **Peoria, Kaskaskia, Tamaroa, Cahokia, and Michigamea**. They grew pumpkins, squash, and maize. They got fish from the Illinois River and participated in annual buffalo hunts.

Jacques Marquette and **Louis Joliet** explored much of the area in 1673. Also entering the picture in the late seventeenth century was René-Robert Cavelier, Sieur de La Salle. These explorers built forts and missions throughout what is now Illinois and claimed most of it for France.

In 1712, the Illinois River became the boundary of France's Louisiana Territory. For many years, the Illini Confederation fought the French. These struggles weakened both sides, making the British victory in the French and Indian War even easier.
After the British victory, the Illinois territory changed hands, from France to Great Britain. In 1771, the people of Illinois met at **Kaskaskia** and demanded a form of self-government; Great Britain refused, continuing to insist that all officials must be appointed by the British king.

The territory was soon part of battle again, during the Revolutionary War. George Rogers Clark captured Kaskaskia, Cahokia, and Vincennes, all strategic locations. After the American victory in 1783, Virginia claimed Illinois; one year later, the state turned it over to the federal government.

The Northwest Territory, formed in 1787, included Illinois. So did the Indiana Territory, formed in 1800. Three years later, **Fort Dearborn** was built near what is now Chicago. In 1809, the Illinois Territory was officially created, with Kaskaskia as its capital. Fur trappers and other settlers began to put down roots in the new territory, which included all of Wisconsin except the northern part of the Green Bay peninsula, a large part of Michigan, and all of Minnesota east of the Mississippi.

Illinois was also a battleground during the War of 1812. Native Americans killed many Americans at Fort Dearborn. With the American victory, in 1814, Illinois was secure.

The territory had, with the permission of the U.S. Congress in 1812, chosen a representative assembly and elected a territorial delegate to Congress. Eager to keep Kaskaskia, Vincennes, and other important cities in American hands, the United States put Illinois statehood on the fast track.

On December 3, 1818, Illinois became the 21st state. Its capital was Kaskaskia. The period after statehood was full of growing pains and war. The Black War in 1832 caused a great deal of strife. Mormons fled the state in 1844 after their leader, Joseph Smith, was killed.

Illinois was the scene of a famous series of political discussions known as the Lincoln-Douglas Debates. Senator **Stephen A. Douglas** and his challenger, **Abraham Lincoln**, traveled the state, debating the issues of the day. Douglas won re-election in 1858, but Lincoln became president two years later.

Lincoln's election prompted a large handful of Southern states to secede. This, and the attack on Fort Sumter, began the Civil War. Illinois was still part of the Union during the war, even though many citizens had Southern loyalties. Illinois contributed large numbers of men, weapons, iron, and food to the war effort.

Despite the Civil War death toll, the Great Chicago Fire of 1871, and other nineteenth century disasters, Illinois was by 1880, the fourth most populous state in the Union. Chicago and the rest of the state continued to grow. The state became a focal point for labor as well. The Haymarket Square riot and the Pullman strike emphasized the need for full disclosure on working conditions and salaries.

The dawn of the twentieth century brought continued industrialization and progress in Illinois. Meatpacking industries, in particular, were a big business. Workplace reforms and outside competition eventually led to a decline in this industry. Chicago was known for its bootlegging and gangsters during the Roaring Twenties. The state itself was known as a major manufacturing center during both world wars. The World's Fair in 1933 and the opening of the St. Lawrence Seaway in 1959 made Chicago a household name around the world. The erection of the Sears Tower, in 1973, helped in this regard as well.

The civil rights movement of the 1950s and 1960s was a particularly difficult time in Illinois history. Large populations of African-Americans living in Chicago and other urban centers met with resistance to their drive toward equality (although this resistance was not as determined or fierce as that in the South).

Chicago and Illinois today are very much symbols of their surroundings. Moreso Chicago and the state's inner cities but also the rest of the state is a Melting Pot of ethnicities and industries, chugging ahead on into the twenty first century.

Bibliography

Adams, James Truslow. (2006). "The March of Democracy," Vol 1. "The Rise of the Union". New York: Charles Scribner's Sons, Publisher.

Barbini, John & Warshaw, Steven. (2006). "The World Past and Present." New York: Harcourt, Brace, Jovanovich, Publishers.

Berthon, Simon & Robinson, Andrew. (2006. "The Shape of the World." Chicago: Rand McNally, Publisher.

Bice, David A. (2006). "A Panorama of Florida II". (Second Edition). Marceline, Missouri: Walsworth Publishing Co., Inc.

Bram, Leon (Vice-President and Editorial Director). (2006). "Funk and Wagnalls New Encyclopedia." United States of America.

Burns, Edward McNall & Ralph, Philip Lee. (2006. "World Civilizations Their History and Culture" (5th ed.). New York: W.W. Norton & Company, Inc., Publishers.

Dauben, Joseph W. (2006). "The World Book Encyclopedia." Chicago: World Book Inc. A Scott Fetzer Company, Publisher.

De Blij, H.J. & Muller, Peter O. (2006). "Geography Regions and Concepts" (Sixth Edition). New York: John Wiley & Sons, Inc., Publisher.

Encyclopedia Americana. (2006). Danbury, Connecticut: Grolier Inc, Publisher.

Heigh, Christopher (Editor). (2006). "The Cambridge Historical Encyclopedia of Great Britain and Ireland." Cambridge: Cambridge University Press, Publisher.

Hunkins, Francis P. & Armstrong, David G. (2006). "World Geography People and Places." Columbus, Ohio: Charles E. Merrill Publishing Co. A Bell & Howell Company, Publishers.

Jarolimek, John; Anderson, J. Hubert & Durand, Loyal, Jr. (2006). "World Neighbors." New York: Macmillan Publishing Company. London: Collier Macmillan Publishers.

McConnell, Campbell R. (2006). "Economics-Principles, Problems, and Policies" (Tenth Edition). New York: McGraw-Hill Book Company, Publisher.

Millard, Dr. Anne & Vanags, Patricia. (2006). "The Usborne Book of World History." London: Usborne Publishing Ltd., Publisher.

Novosad, Charles (Executive Editor). (2006). "The Nystrom Desk Atlas." Chicago: Nystrom Division of Herff Jones, Inc., Publisher.

Patton, Clyde P.; Rengert, Arlene C.; Saveland, Robert N.; Cooper, Kenneth S. & Cam, Patricia T. (2006). "A World View." Morristown, N.J.: Silver Burdette Companion, Publisher.

Schwartz, Melvin & O'Connor, John R. (2006). "Exploring A Changing World." New York: Globe Book Company, Publisher.

"The Annals of America: Selected Readings on Great Issues in American History 1620-1968." (2006). United States of America: William Benton, Publisher.

Tindall, George Brown & Shi, David E. (2006). "America-A Narrative History" (Fourth Edition). New York: W.W. Norton & Company, Publisher.

Todd, Lewis Paul & Curti, Merle. (2006). "Rise of the American Nation" (Third Edition). New York: Harcourt, Brace, Jovanovich, Inc., Publishers.

Tyler, Jenny; Watts, Lisa; Bowyer, Carol; Trundle, Roma & Warrender, Annabelle (2006) 'The Usbome Book of World Geography." London: Usbome Publishing Ltd., Publisher.

Willson, David H. (2006). "A History of England." Hinsdale, Illinois: The Dryder Press, inc., Publisher

Sample Test

1. Which one of the following is not a reason why Europeans came to the New World?

   A. To find resources in order to increase wealth

   B. To establish trade

   C. To increase a ruler's power and importance

   D. To spread Christianity

2. The study of human origins has been a major contribution of:

   A. Evans

   B. Schliemann

   C. Margaret Mead

   D. The Leakeys

3. Downstream for the flow of the Yangtze River is primarily:

   A. North

   B. South

   C. East

   D. West

4. The results of the Renaissance, Enlightenment, Commercial and Industrial Revolutions were more unfortunate for the people of:

   A. Asia

   B. Latin America

   C. Africa

   D. Middle East

5. Government regulation of economic activities for favorable balance of trade was the first major economic theory. It was called:

   A. Laissez-faire

   B. Globalism

   C. Mercantilism

   D. Syndicalism

6. The first ancient civilization to introduce and practice monotheism was the:

   A. Sumerians

   B. Minoans

   C. Phoenicians

   D. Hebrews

7. **Which one of the following does not affect climate?**

   A. Elevation or altitude

   B. Ocean currents

   C. Latitude

   D. Longitude

8. **The foundation of modern constitutionalism is embodied in the idea that government is limited by law. This was stated by:**

   A. John Locke

   B. Rousseau

   C. St. Thomas Aquinas

   D. Montesquieu

9. **The only colony not founded and settled for religious, political or business reasons was:**

   A. Delaware

   B. Virginia

   C. Georgia

   D. New York

10. **The "father of political science" is considered to be:**

    A. Aristotle

    B. John Locke

    C. Plato

    D. Thomas Hobbes

11. **Bathtubs, hot and cold running water, and sewage systems with flush toilets were developed by the:**

    A. Minoans

    B. Mycenaeans

    C. Phoenicians

    D. Greeks

12. In Western Europe, the achievements of the Renaissance were unsurpassed and made these countries outstanding cultural centers on the continent. All of the following were accomplishments except:

    A. Investment of the printing press

    B. A rekindling of interest in the learning of classical Greece and Rome

    C. Growth in literature, philosophy and art

    D. Better military tactics

13. Of the thirteen English colonies, the greatest degree of religious toleration was found in:

    A. Archaeology

    B. Geography

    C. Sociology

    D. Anthropology

14. The chemical process of radiocarbon dating would be most useful and beneficial in the field of:

    A. Archaeology

    B. Geography

    C. Sociology

    D. Anthropology

15. Which one of the following is not an important legacy of the Byzantine Empire?

    A. It protected Western Europe from various attacks from the East by such groups as the Persians, Ottoman Turks, and Barbarians

    B. It played a part in preserving the literature, philosophy, and language of ancient Greece

    C. Its military organization was the foundation for modern armies

    D. It kept the legal traditions of Roman government, collecting and organizing many ancient Roman laws

16. In the United States, federal investigations into business activities are handled by the:

    A. Department of Treasury

    B. Security & Exchange Commission

    C. Government Accounting Office

    D. Federal Trade Commission

17. The makeup of today's modern newspapers including comics, puzzles, sports, and columnists was a technique first used by:

    A. William Randolph Hearst

    B. Edward W. Scripps

    C. Joseph Pulitzer

    D. Charles A. Dana

18. Which French Renaissance writer wrote about the dangers of absolute powers and later examined himself in an effort to make inquiries into humankind and nature?

    A. Francois Rabelais

    B. Desiderius Erasmus

    C. Michel de Montaigne

    D. Sir Francis Bacon

19. Which of the following contributed to the severity of the Great Depression in California?

    A. An influx of Chinese immigrants.

    B. The dust bowl drove People out of the cities.

    C. An influx of Mexican immigrants.

    D. An influx of Oakies.

20. Downstream for the flow of the Nile River is:

    A. North

    B. South

    C. East

    D. West

21. The year 1619 was a memorable for the colony of Virginia. Three important events occurred resulting in lasting effects on US history. Which one of the following is not one of the events?

    A. Twenty African slaves arrived.

    B. The London Company granted the colony a charter making itn independent.

    C. The colonists were given the right by the London Company to govern themselves through representative government in the Virginia House of Burgesses

    D. The London Company sent to the colony 60 women who werequickly married, establishing families and stability in the colony.

22. Of all the major causes of both World Wars I and II, the most significant one is considered to be:

    A. Extreme nationalism

    B. Military buildup and aggression

    C. Political unrest

    D. Agreements and alliances

23. The end to hunting, gathering, and fishing of prehistoric people was due to:

    A. Domestication of animals

    B. Building crude huts and houses

    C. Development of agriculture

    D. Organized government in villages

24. In the United States government, power or control over public education, marriage, and divorce is:

    A. Implied or suggested

    B. Concurrent or shared

    C. Delegated or expressed

    D. Reserved

25. The principle of "popular sovereignty" allowing people in any territory to make their own decision concerning slavery was stated by;

    A. Henry Clay

    B. Daniel Webster

    C. John C. Calhoun

    D. Stephen A. Douglas

26. Under the brand new Constitution, the most urgent of the many problems facing the new federal government was that of:

    A. Maintaining a strong army and navy

    B. Establishing a strong foreign policy

    C. Raising money to pay salaries and war debts

    D. Setting up courts, passing federal laws, and providing for law enforcement officers

27. Which one of the following was not a reason why the United States went to war with Great Britain in 1812?

    A. Resentment by Spain over the sale exploration, and settlement of the Louisiana Territory

    B. The westward movement of farmers because of the need for more land

    C. Canadian fur traders were agitating the northwestern Indians to fight American expansion

    D. Britain continued to seize American ships on the high seas and force American seamen to serve aboard British ships

28. "Participant observation" is a method of study most closely associated with and used in:

    A. Anthropology

    B. Archaeology

    C. Sociology

    D. Political Science

29. The early ancient civilizations developed systems of government:

    A. To provide for defense against attack

    B. To regulate trade

    C. To regulate and direct the economic activities of the people as they worked together in groups

    D. To decide on the boundaries of the different fields during planting seasons

30. The "divine right" of kings was the key political characteristic of:

    A. The Age of Absolutism

    B. The Age of Reason

    C. The Age of Feudalism

    D. The Age of Despotism

31. The principle of zero in mathematics is the discovery of the ancient civilization found in:

    A. Egypt

    B. Persia

    C. India

    D. Babylon

32. The Ganges River empties into the:

    A. Bay of Bengal

    B. Arabian Sea

    C. Red Sea

    D. Arafura Sea

33. One South American country quickly and easily gained independence in the 19th century from European control; was noted for the uniqueness of its political stability and gradual orderly changes. This most unusual Latin American country is:

    A. Chile

    B. Argentina

    C. Venezuela

    D. Brazil

34. In which of the following disciplines would the study of physical mapping, modern or ancient, and the plotting of points and boundaries be least useful?

    A. Sociology

    B. Geography

    C. Archaeology

    D. History

35. US foreign minister Robert R. Livingstone said, "From this day the United States takes their place among the greatest powers." He was referring to the action taken by President Thomas Jefferson:

    A. Who had authorized the purchase of the Louisiana Purchase

    B. Who sent the US Marines and naval ships to fight the Barbary pirates

    C. Who had commissioned the Lewis and Clark expedition

    D. Who repealed the Embargo Act

36. The only Central American country with no standing army, a freely elected government, and considered the oldest democracy in the region is:

   A. Costa Rica

   B. Belize

   C. Honduras

   D. Guatemala

37. During the 1920s, the United States almost completely stopped all immigration. One of the reasons was:

   A. Plentiful cheap unskilled labor was no longer needed by industrialists

   B. War debts from World War I made it difficult to render financial assistance

   C. European nations were reluctant to allow people to leave since there was a need to rebuild populations and economic stability

   D. The United States did not become a member of the League of Nations

38. Seventeen sixty-three was the year of Great Britain's total victory over her European rivals and the establishment of a global empire. Of the American colonies, a European statesman accurately prophesied that these colonies no longer needed English protection and would soon gain independence. He was:

   A. Edmund Burke

   B. Comte de Rochambeau

   C. Count Vergennes

   D. William Pitt

39. Colonial expansion by Western European powers in the 18th and 19th centuries was due primarily to:

   A. Building and opening the Suez Canal

   B. The Industrial Revolution

   C. Marked improvements in transportation

   D. Complete independence of all the Americas and loss of European domination and influence

40. America's weak foreign policy and lack of adequate diplomacy during the 1870s and 1880s led to the comment that "a special Providence takes care of fools, drunkards, and the United States" is attributed to:

   A. Otto von Bismarck

   B. Benjamin Disraeli

   C. William Gladstone

   D. Paul von Hindenburg

41. It can be reasonably stated that the change in the United States from primarily an agricultural country into an industrial power was due to all of the following except:

   A. Tariffs on foreign imports

   B. Millions of hardworking immigrants

   C. An increase in technological developments

   D. The change from steam to electricity for powering industrial machinery

42. Many American authors were noted for "local Color" writings about the way of life in certain regions. Which one of the following was not associated with the other three in writing about life in the mining camps of the West?

   A. Hamlin Garland

   B. Joaquin Miller

   C. Bret Harte

   D. Mark Twain

43. There is no doubt of the vast improvement of the US Constitution over the weak Articles of Confederation. Which one of the four accurate statements below is a unique yet eloquent description of the document?

   A. The establishment of a strong central government in no way lessened or weakened the individual states.

   B. Individual rights were protected and secured.

   C. The Constitution is the best representation of the results of the American genius for compromise.

   D. Its flexibility and adaptation to change gives it a sense of timelessness.

44. The study of a people's language and writing would be part of all of the following except:

    A. Sociology

    B. Archaeology

    C. History

    D. Geography

45. The changing focus during the Renaissance when artists and scholars were less concerned with religion but centered their efforts on a better understanding of people and the world was called:

    A. Realism

    B. Humanism

    C. Individualism

    D. Intellectualism

46. The "father of anatomy" is considered to be:

    A. Vesalius

    B. Servetus

    C. Galen

    D. Harvey

47. In the US government, the power of coining money is:

    A. Implied or suggested

    B. Concurrent or shared

    C. Delegated or expressed

    D. Reserved

48. The source of authority for national, state, and local governments in the US is:

    A. The will of the people

    B. The US Constitution

    C. Written laws

    D. The Bill of Rights

49. India's greatest ruler is considered to be:

    A. Akbar

    B. Asoka

    C. Babur

    D. Jahan

50. "Poverty is the parent of revolution and crime" was from the writings of:

    A. Plato

    B. Aristotle

    C. Cicero

    D. Gaius

51. Geography was first studied in an organized manner by:

    A. The Egyptians

    B. The Greeks

    C. The Romans

    D. The Arabs

52. From about 1870 to 1900 the settlement of America's "last frontier", the West, was completed. One attraction for settlers was free land but it would have been to no avail without:

    A. Better farming methods and technology

    B. Surveying to set boundaries

    C. Immigrants and others to seek new land

    D. The railroad to get them there

53. Meridians, or lines of longitude, not only help in pinpointing locations but are also used for:

    A. Measuring distance from the Poles

    B. Determining direction of ocean currents

    C. Determining the time around the world

    D. Measuring distance on the equator

54. Historians state that the West helped to speed up the Industrial Revolution. Which one of the following statements was not a reason for this?

   A. Food supplies for the ever increasing urban populations came from farms in the West

   B. A tremendous supply of gold and silver from western mines provided the capital needed to built industries

   C. Descendants of western settlers, educated as engineers, geologists, and metallurgists in the East, returned to the West to mine the mineral resources needed for industry

   D. Iron, copper, and other minerals from western mines were important resources in manufacturing products

55. In the United States government, the power of taxation and borrowing is:

   A. Implied or suggested

   B. Concurrent or shared

   C. Delegated or expressed

   D. Reserved

56. The post-Civil War years were a time of low public morality, a time of greed, graft, and dishonesty. Which one of the reasons listed would not be accurate?

   A. The war itself because of the money and materials needed to carry on the War

   B. The very rapid growth of industry and big business after the War

   C. The personal example set by President Grant

   D. Unscrupulous heads of large impersonal corporations

57. Studies in astronomy, skills in mapping, and other contributions to geographic knowledge came from:

   A. Galileo

   B. Columbus

   C. Eratosthenes

   D. Ptolemy

58. Which one of the following would not be considered a result of World War II?

A. Economic depressions and slow resumption of trade and financial aid

B. Western Europe was no longer the center of world power

C. The beginnings of new power struggles not only in Europe but in Asia as well

D. Territorial and boundary changes for many nations, especially in Europe

59. The study of the ways in which different societies around the world deal with the problems of limited resources and unlimited needs and wants is in the area of:

A. Economics

B. Sociology

C. Anthropology

D. Political Science

60. Nineteenth century imperialism by Western European nations had important and far-reaching effects on the colonial peoples they ruled. All four of the following are the result of this. Which one was most important and had lasting effects on key 20th century events?

A. Local wars were ended

B. Living standards were raised

C. Demands for self government and feelings of nationalism surfaced

D. Economic developments occurred

61. After the War of 1812, Henry Clay and others proposed economic measures, including raising tariffs to protect American farmers and manufacturers from foreign competition. These measures were proposed in the period known as:

A. Era of Nationalism

B. American Expansion

C. Era of Good Feeling

D. American System

62. "These are the times that try men's souls" were words penned by:

    A. Thomas Jefferson

    B. Samuel Adams

    C. Benjamin Franklin

    D. Thomas Paine

63. The Age of Exploration begun in the 1400s was led by:

    A. The Portuguese

    B. The Spanish

    C. The English

    D. The Dutch

64. Which one of the following is not a function or responsibility of the US political parties?

    A. Conducting elections or the voting process

    B. Obtaining funds needed for election campaigns

    C. Choosing candidates to run for public office

    D. Making voters aware of issues and other public affairs information

65. The economist who disagreed with the idea that free markets lead to full employment and prosperity and suggested that increasing government spending would end depressions was:

    A. Keynes

    B. Malthus

    C. Smith

    D. Friedman

66. The study of social behavior of minority groups would be in the area of:

    A. Anthropology

    B. Psychology

    C. Sociology

    D. Cultural Geography

67. An extensive knowledge of surgery and medicine as well as principles of irrigation, fertilization and terrace farming was unique to:

    A. The Mayans

    B. The Atacamas

    C. The Incas

    D. The Tarapacas

68. The idea of universal peace through world organization was a philosophy of:

    A. Rousseau

    B. Immanuel Kant

    C. Montesquieu

    D. John Locke

69. Which ancient civilization is credited with being the first to develop irrigation techniques through the use of canals, dikes, and devices for raising water?

    A. The Sumerians

    B. The Egyptians

    C. The Babylonians

    D. The Akkadians

70. The study of past human cultures based on physical artifacts is:

    A. History

    B. Anthropology

    C. Cultural Geography

    D. Archaeology

71. The "father" of modern economics is considered by most economists to be:

    A. Thomas Robert Malthus

    B. John Stuart Mill

    C. Adam Smith

    D. John Maynard Keynes

72. The ideas and innovations of the period of the Renaissance were spread throughout Europe mainly because of:

    A. Extensive exploration

    B. Craft workers and their guilds

    C. The invention of the printing press

    D. Increased travel and trade

73. The American labor union movement started gaining new momentum:

    A. During the building of the railroads

    B. After 1865 with the growth of cities

    C. With the rise of industrial giants such as Carnegie and Vanderbilt

    D. During the war years of 1861-1865

74. **Soil erosion is most likely to occur in large amounts in:**

    A. Mountain ranges

    B. Deserts

    C. Tropical rainforests

    D. River valleys

75. **Who is considered to be the most important figure in the spread of Protestantism across Switzerland?**

    A. Calvin

    B. Zwingli

    C. Munzer

    D. Leyden

76. **The principle that "men entrusted with power tend to abuse it" is attributed to:**

    A. Locke

    B. Rousseau

    C. Aristotle

    D. Montesquieu

77. **After 1783, the largest "land owner" in the Americas was:**

    A. Britain

    B. Spain

    C. France

    D. United States

78. **The purchase of goods or services on one market for immediate resale on another market is:**

    A. Output

    B. Enterprise

    C. Arbitrage

    D. Mercantile

79. **After the Civil War, the US adapted an attitude of isolation from foreign affairs. But the turning point marking the beginning of the US becoming a world power was:**

    A. World War I

    B. Expansion of business and trade overseas

    C. The Spanish-American War

    D. The building and financial of the Panama Canal

80. The programs such as unemployment insurance and health insurance for the elderly are the responsibility of:

    A. Federal government

    B. Local government

    C. State government

    D. Communal government

81. The English explorer who gave England its claim to North American was:

    A. Raleigh

    B. Hawkins

    C. Drake

    D. Cabot

82. The three day Battle of Gettysburg was the turning point of the Civil War for the North leading to ultimate victory. The battle in the West reinforcing the North's victory and sealing the South's defeat was the day after Gettysburg at:

    A. Perryville

    B. Vicksburg

    C. Stones River

    D. Shiloh

83. The study of the exercise of power and political behavior in human society today would be conducted by experts in:

    A. History

    B. Sociology

    C. Political Science

    D. Anthropology

84. During the period of Spanish colonialism, which of the following was not a key to the goal of exploiting, transforming and including the native people?

    A. Missions

    B. Ranchos

    C. Presidios

    D. Pueblos

85. Potential customers for any product or service are not only called consumers but can also be called a:

    A. Resource

    B. Base

    C. Commodity

    D. Market

86. An early cultural group was so skillful in navigating on the seas that they were able to sail at night guided by stars. They were the:

   A. Greeks

   B. Persians

   C. Minoans

   D. Phoenicians

87. One method of trade restriction used by some nations is:

   A. Limited treaties

   B. Floating exchange rate

   C. Bill of exchange

   D. Import quotas

88. A political system in which the laws and traditions put limits on the powers of government is:

   A. Federalism

   B. Constitutionalism

   C. Parliamentary system

   D. Presidential system

89. Which one of the following did not contribute to the early medieval European civilization?

   A. The heritage from the classical cultures

   B. The Christian religion

   C. The influence of the German Barbarians

   D. The spread of ideas through trade and commerce

90. The Roman Empire gave so much to the world, especially the Western world. Of the legacies below, the most influential, effective and lasting is:

   A. The language of Latin

   B. Roman law, justice, and political system

   C. Engineering and building

   D. The writings of its poets an historians

91. Charlemagne's most important influence on Western civilization is seen today in:

    A. Relationship of church and state

    B. Strong military for defense

    C. The criminal justice system

    D. Education of women

92. Public administration, such as public officials in the areas of budget, accounting, distribution of public funds, and personnel management, would be part of the field of:

    A. Anthropology

    B. Sociology

    C. Law and Taxation

    D. Political Science and Economics

93. "Marbury vs Madison (1803)" was an important Supreme Court case which set the precedent for:

    A. The elastic clause

    B. Judicial review

    C. The supreme law of the land

    D. Popular sovereignty in the territories

94. Which one of the following is not a use for a region's wetlands?

    A. Produces fresh clean water

    B. Provides habitat for wildlife

    C. Provides water for hydroelectric power

    D. Controls floods

95. The philosopher who coined the term "sociology" also stated that social behavior and events could be measured scientifically. He is identified as:

    A. Auguste Comte

    B. Herbert Spencer

    C. Rousseau

    D. Kant

96. The belief that the United States should control all of North America was called:

    A. Westward Expansion

    B. Pan Americanism

    C. Manifest Destiny

    D. Nationalism

97. A well-known World War II figure who said that democracy was like a rotting corpse that had to be replaced by a superior way of life and more efficient government was:

    A. Hitler

    B. Stalin

    C. Tojo

    D. Mussolini

98. The Radical Republicans who pushed the harsh Reconstruction measures through Congress after Lincoln's death lost public and moderate Republican support when they went too far:

    A. In their efforts to impeach the President

    B. By dividing ten southern states into military-controlled districts

    C. By making the ten southern states give freed African Americans the right to vote

    D. Sending carpetbaggers into the South to build up support for Congressional legislation

99. The economic system promoting individual ownership of land, capital, and businesses with minimal governmental regulations is called:

    A. Macro-economy

    B. Micro-economy

    C. Laissez-faire

    D. Free enterprise

100. A political philosophy favoring or supporting rapid social changes in order to correct social and economic inequalities is called:

    A. Nationalism

    B. Liberalism

    C. Conservatism

    D. Federalism

101. China's last imperial ruling dynasty was one of its most stable and successful and, under its rule, Chinese culture made an outstanding impression on Western nations. This dynasty was:

    A. Min

    B. Manchu

    C. Han

    D. Chou

102. Development of a solar calendar, invention of the decimal system, and contributions to the development of geometry and astronomy are all the legacy of:

   A. The Babylonians

   B. The Persians

   C. The Sumerians

   D. The Egyptians

103. The study of "spatial relationships and interaction" would be done by people in the field of:

   A. Political Science

   B. Anthropology

   C. Geography

   D. Sociology

104. The circumference of the earth, which greatly contributed to geographic knowledge was calculated by:

   A. Ptolemy

   B. Eratosthenes

   C. Galileo

   D. Strabo

105. The first European to see Florida and sail along its coast was:

   A. Cabot

   B. Columbus

   C. Ponce de Leon

   D. Narvaez

106. Which one of the following events did not occur during the period known as the "Era of Good Feeling?"

   A. President Monroe issued the Monroe Doctrine

   B. Spain ceded Florida to the United States

   C. The building of the National Road

   D. The charter of the second Bank of the United States

107. Native communities in early California are commonly divided into several cultural areas. How many cultural areas?

   A. 4

   B. 5

   C. 6

   D. 7

108. The world religion which includes a caste system is:

    A. Buddhism

    B. Hinduism

    C. Sikhism

    D. Jainism

109. The idea that continued population growth would, in future years, seriously affect a nation's productive capabilities was stated by:

    A. Keynes

    B. Mill

    C. Malthus

    D. Friedman

110. After World War II, the United States:

    A. Limited its involvement in European affairs

    B. Shifted foreign policy emphasis from Europe to Asia

    C. Passed significant legislation pertaining to aid to farmers and tariffs on imports

    D. Entered the greatest period of economic growth in its history

111. France decided in 1777 to help the American colonies in their war against Britain. This decision was based on:

    A. The naval victory of John Paul Jones over the British ship Serapis"

    B. The survival of the terrible winter at Valley Forge

    C. The success of colonial guerilla fighters in the South

    D. The defeat of the British at Saratoga

112. What event sparked a great migration of people from all over the world to California?

    A. The birth of Labor Unions

    B. California statehood

    C. The invention of the automobile

    D. The gold rush

113. Which of the following does not differentiate provisions of the California constitution from the U.S. constitution?

   A. The governor of California has the pocket veto

   B. In California representation in both houses of the legislature is based on population

   C. The Governor and Lt. Governor are elected separately

   D. The equivalent of cabinet positions are elected rather than appointed.

114. A number of women worked hard in the first half of the 19th century for women's rights but decisive gains did not come until after 1850. The earliest accomplishments were in:

   A. Medicine

   B. Education

   C. Writing

   D. Temperance

115. Nineteenth century German unification was the result of the hard work of:

   A. Otto von Bismarck

   B. Kaiser William II

   C. Von Moltke

   D. Hindenburg

116. The geographical drought stricken region of Africa south of the Sahara and extending east and west from Senegal to Somalia is:

   A. The Kalahari

   B. The Namib

   C. The Great Rift Valley

   D. The Sahel

117. The idea or proposal for more equal division of profits among employers and workers was put forth by:

   A. Karl Marx

   B. Thomas Malthus

   C. Adam Smith

   D. John Stuart Mill

118. The term that best describes how the Supreme Court can block laws that may be unconstitutional from being enacted is:

   A. Jurisprudence

   B. Judicial Review

   C. Exclusionary Rule

   D. Right of Petition

119. On the spectrum of American politics, the label that most accurately describes voters to the "right of center" is:

   A. Moderates

   B. Liberals

   C. Conservatives

   D. Socialists

120. Marxism believes which two groups are in continual conflict?

   A. Farmers and landowners

   B. Kings and the nobility

   C. Workers and owners

   D. Structure and superstructure

121. The United States legislature is bi-cameral, this means:

   A. It consists of several houses

   B. It consists of two houses

   C. The Vice-President is in charge of the legislature when in session

   D. It has an upper and lower house

122. What Supreme Court ruling established the principal of judicial review?

   A. Jefferson vs Madison

   B. Lincoln vs Douglas

   C. Marbury vs Madison

   D. Marbury vs Jefferson

123. To be eligible to be elected President one must:

   A. Be a citizen for at least five years

   B. Be a citizen for seven years

   C. Have been born a citizen

   D. Be a naturalized citizen

124. The international organization established to work for world peace at the end of the Second World War is the:

    A. League of Nations

    B. United Federation of Nations

    C. United Nations

    D. United World League

125. Which of the following is an example of a direct democracy?

    A. Elected representatives

    B. Greek city-states

    C. The United States Senate

    D. The United States House of Representative

Answer Key

1. B	41. A	81. D	121. B
2. D	42. A	82. B	122. C
3. C	43. C	83. C	123. C
4. C	44. A	84. B	124. C
5. C	45. B	85. D	125. B
6. D	46. A	86. D	
7. D	47. C	87. D	
8. C	48. A	88. B	
9. C	49. A	89. D	
10. A	50. B	90. B	
11. A	51. B	91. A	
12. D	52. D	92. D	
13. B	53. C	93. B	
14. A	54. C	94. C	
15. C	55. B	95. A	
16. D	56. C	96. C	
17. C	57. D	97. D	
18. C	58. A	98. A	
19. D	59. A	99. D	
20. A	60. C	100. B	
21. B	61. D	101. B	
22. A	62. D	102. D	
23. C	63. A	103. C	
24. D	64. A	104. B	
25. D	65. A	105. A	
26. C	66. C	106. A	
27. A	67. C	107. C	
28. A	68. B	108. B	
29. C	69. A	109. C	
30. A	70. D	110. D	
31. C	71. C	111. D	
32. A	72. C	112. D	
33. D	73. B	113. A	
34. A	74. C	114. B	
35. A	75. A	115. A	
36. A	76. D	116. D	
37. A	77. B	117. D	
38. C	78. C	118. B	
39. B	79. C	119. C	
40. A	80. C	120. C	

TEACHER CERTFICATION STUDY GUIDE

Rationales for Sample Questions

1. Which one of the following is not a reason why Europeans came to the New World?

    A. To find resources in order to increase wealth

    B. To establish trade

    C. To increase a ruler's power and importance

    D. To spread Christianity

Answer:

B. To establish trade

The Europeans came to the New World for a number of reasons; often they came to find new natural resources to extract for manufacturing. The Portuguese, Spanish and English were sent over to increase the monarch's power and spread influences such as religion (Christianity) and culture. Therefore, the only reason given that Europeans didn't come to the New World was to establish trade.

TEACHER CERTFICATION STUDY GUIDE

2. The study of human origins has been a major contribution of:

    A. Evans

    B. Schliemann

    C. Margaret Mead

    D. The Leakeys

Answer:

D. The Leakeys

Although each of the above-mentioned people made significant contributions to the study of people's history, (A) English archeologist Sir Arthur Evans (1851-1941) has been primarily associated with the excavation of the Knossos on the island of Crete. (B) Heinrich Schliemann (1922-1890) was the German archeologist most well known for the excavation of the ruins of Troy. (C) Margaret Mead (1901-1978) was a cultural anthropologist most acclaimed for her 1928 book *Coming of Age in Samoa*, besides authoring numerous books, she was also the curator of ethnology at the American Museum of Natural History in New York City. (D) The Leakeys, Louis (1903-1972), Mary (1913-1976) and son Richard (1944-), discovered fossils in East Africa that changed the world consensus about the age of humans and also discovered ancient fossils in Olduvai Gorge, Tanzania. The Leakeys, however, were most concerned with the study of early human origins.

3. Downstream for the flow of the Yangtze River is primarily:

	A. North

	B. South

	C. East

	D. West

Answer:

C. East

The Yangtze River runs from Tibet through China and flows eastward to the Pacific Ocean. The Yangtze River is an important travel and trade route through China and meets the Pacific at Shanghai.

TEACHER CERTFICATION STUDY GUIDE

4. The results of the Renaissance, Enlightenment, Commercial and the Industrial Revolutions were more unfortunate for the people of:

    A. Asia

    B. Latin America

    C. Africa

    D. Middle East

Answer:

C. Africa

The results of the Renaissance, Enlightenment, Commercial and Industrial Revolutions were quite beneficial for many people in much of the world. New ideas of humanism, religious tolerance, and secularism were spreading. Increased trade and manufacturing were surging economies in much of the world. The people of Africa, however, suffered during these times as they became largely left out of the developments. Also, the people of Africa were stolen, traded, and sold into slavery to provide a cheap labor force for the growing industries of Europe and the New World.

5. **Government regulation of economic activities for favorable balance of trade was the first major economic theory. It was called:**

    A. Laissez-faire

    B. Globalism

    C. Mercantilism

    D. Syndicalism

Answer:

C. Mercantilism

(A) Laissez-faire is the doctrine that calls for no government interference in economic and political policy. (B) Globalism is not an economic or political theory, nor is it an actual word in the English language. Globalization is the idea that we are all increasingly connected in a worldwide system. (D) Syndicalism is similar to anarchism claiming that workers should control and govern economic policies and regulations as opposed to state control. Therefore, (C) mercantilism is the best regulation of economic activities for a favorable balance of trade.

TEACHER CERTFICATION STUDY GUIDE

6. The first ancient civilization to introduce and practice monotheism was the:

    A. Sumerians

    B. Minoans

    C. Phoenicians

    D. Hebrews

Answer:

D. Hebrews

The (A) Sumerians and (C) Phoenicians both practiced religions in which many gods and goddesses were worshipped. Often these Gods/Goddesses were based on a feature of nature such as a sun, moon, weather, rocks, water, etc. The (B) Minoan culture shared many religious practices with the Ancient Egyptians. It seems that the king was somewhat of a god figure and the queen, a goddess. Much of the Minoan art point to worship of multiple gods. Therefore, only the (D) Hebrews introduced and fully practiced monotheism, or the belief in one god.

7. Which one of the following does not affect climate?

    A. Elevation and altitude

    B. Ocean currents

    C. Latitude

    D. Longitude

Answer:

D. Longitude

Latitude is the primary influence of earth climate as it determines the climatic region in which an area lies. Elevation or altitude and ocean currents are considered to be secondary influences on climate. Longitude is considered to have no important influence over climate.

HISTORY 215

TEACHER CERTFICATION STUDY GUIDE

8. The foundation of modern constitutionalism is embodied in the idea that government is limited by law. This law was stated by:

    A. John Locke

    B. Rousseau

    C. St. Thomas Aquinas

    D. Montesquieu

Answer:

C. St. Thomas Aquinas

(A) John Locke (1632-1704), whose book *Two Treatises of Government* has long been considered a founding document on the rights of people to rebel against an unjust government, was an important figure in the founding of the US Constitution and on general politics of the American Colonies. (D) Montesquieu (1689-1755) and (B) Rousseau (1712-1778) were political philosophers who explored the idea of what has come to be known as liberalism. They pushed the idea that through understanding the interconnectedness of economics, geography, climate and psychology that changes could be made to improve life. Therefore, it was St. Thomas Aquinas (1225-1274) who merged Aristotelian ideas with Christianity, who helped lay the ideas of modern constitutionalism and the limiting of government by law.

TEACHER CERTFICATION STUDY GUIDE

9. The only colony not founded and settled for religious, political, or business reasons was:

   A. Delaware

   B. Virginia

   C. Georgia

   D. New York

Answer:

C. Georgia

The Swedish and the Dutch established Delaware and New York as Middle Colonies. They were established with the intention of growth by economic prosperity from farming across the countryside. The English, with the intention of generating a strong farming economy settled Virginia, a Southern Colony. Georgia was the only one of these colonies not settled for religious, political or business reasons as it was started as a place for debtors from English prisons.

TEACHER CERTFICATION STUDY GUIDE

10. The "father of political science" is considered to be:

   A. Aristotle

   B. John Locke

   C. Plato

   D. Thomas Hobbes

Answer:

A. Aristotle

(D) Thomas Hobbes (1588-1679) wrote the important work *Leviathan* in which he pointed out that people are by all means selfish, individualistic animals that will always look out for themselves and therefore, the state must combat this nature desire. (B) John Locke (1632-1704) whose book *Two Treatises of Government* has long been considered a founding document on the rights of people to rebel against an unjust government was an important figure in the founding of the US Constitution and on general politics of the American Colonies. (C) Plato (427-347 B.C.) and Aristotle (384-322 B.C.) both contributed to the field of political science.

Both believed that political order would result in the greatest stability. In fact, Aristotle studied under Plato. Both Plato and Aristotle studied the ideas of causality and the Prime Mover, but their conclusions were different. Aristotle, however, is considered to be "the father of political science" because of his development of systems of political order the true development, a scientific system to study justice and political order.

TEACHER CERTFICATION STUDY GUIDE

11. Bathtubs, hot and cold running water, and sewage systems with flush toilets were developed by the:

    A. Minoans

    B. Mycenaeans

    C. Phoenicians

    D. Greeks

Answer:

A. Minoans

The (A) Minoans were one of the earliest Greek cultures and existed on the island of Crete and flourished from about 1600 B.C. to about 1400 B.C. During this time, the (B) Mycenaean were flourishing on the mainland of what is now Greece. However, it was the Minoans on Crete that are best known for their advanced ancient civilization in which such advances as bathtubs, hot and cold running water, sewage systems and flush toilets were developed. The (C) Phoenicians also flourished around 1250 B.C., however, their primary development was in language and arts. The Phoenicians created an alphabet that has still considerable influence in the world today. The great developments off the (D) Greeks were primarily in the fields of philosophy, political science, and early ideas of democracy.

TEACHER CERTFICATION STUDY GUIDE

12. **In Western Europe, the achievements of the Renaissance were unsurpassed and made these countries outstanding cultural centers on the continent. All of the following were accomplishments except:**

    A. Invention of the printing press

    B. A rekindling of interest in the learning of classical Greece & Rome

    C. Growth in literature, philosophy, and art

    D. Better military tactics

Answer:

D. Better military tactics

The Renaissance in Western Europe produced many important achievements that helped push immense progress among European civilization. Some of the most important developments during the Renaissance were Gutenberg's invention of the printing press in Germany and a reexamination of the ideas and philosophies of classical Greece and Rome that eventually helped Renaissance thinkers to approach more modern ideas. Also important during the Renaissance was the growth in literature (Petrarch, Boccaccio, Erasmus), philosophy (Machiavelli, More, Bacon) and art (Van Eyck, Giotto, da Vinci). Therefore, improved military tactics is the only possible answer as it was clearly not a characteristic of the Renaissance in Western Europe.

13. **Of the thirteen English colonies, the greatest degree of religious toleration was found in:**

   A. Maryland

   B. Rhode Island

   C. Pennsylvania

   D. Delaware

Answer:

B. Rhode Island

The greatest degree of religious tolerance in all of the colonies was found in Rhode Island. Roger Williams, founder of Providence and Rhode Island, had objected to the Massachusetts colonial seizure of Indian lands and settlements and the relationship between these seizures and the Church of England. Williams was banished from Massachusetts and purposely set up Rhode Island as the first colony with a true separation of church and state.

14. **The chemical process of radiocarbon dating would be most useful and beneficial in the field of:**

   A. Archaeology

   B. Geography

   C. Sociology

   D. Anthropology

Answer:

A. Archaeology

Radiocarbon dating is a chemical process that helps generate a more absolute method for dating artifacts and remains by measuring the radioactive materials present in them today and calculating how long it takes for certain materials to decay. Since geographers mainly study locations and special properties of earth's living things and physical features, sociologists mostly study human society and social conditions and anthropologists generally study human culture and humanity, the answer is archaeology because archeologists study past human cultures by studying their remains.

15. Which one of the following is not an important legacy of the Byzantine Empire?

    A. It protected Western Europe from various attacks from the East by such groups as the Persians, Ottoman Turks, and Barbarians

    B. It played a part in preserving the literature, philosophy, and language of ancient Greece

    C. Its military organization was the foundation for modern armies

    D. It kept the legal traditions of Roman government, collecting and organizing many ancient Roman laws.

Answer:

C. Its military organization was the foundation for modern armies

The Byzantine Empire (1353-1453) was the successor to the Roman Empire in the East and protected Western Europe from invaders such as the Persians and Ottomans. The Byzantine Empire was a Christian incorporation of Greek philosophy, language, and literature along with Roman government and law. Therefore, although regarded as having a strong infantry, cavalry, and Engineering corps along with excellent morale amongst its soldiers, the Byzantine Empire is not particularly considered a foundation for modern armies.

TEACHER CERTFICATION STUDY GUIDE

16. **In the United States, federal investigations into business activities are handled by the:**

    A. Department of Treasury

    B. Security and Exchange Commission

    C. Government Accounting Office

    D. Federal Trade Commission

Answer:
D. Federal Trade Commission

The Department of Treasury (A), established in 1789, is an executive government agency that is responsible for advising the president on fiscal policy. There is no such thing as a Government Accounting Office. In the United States, Federal Trade Commission or FTC handles federal investigations into business activities. The establishment of the FTC in 1915 as an independent government agency was done so as to assure fair and free competition among businesses.

17. **The makeup of today's modern newspapers – including comics, puzzles, sports, and columnists – was a technique first used by:**

    A. William Randolph Hearst

    B. Edward W. Scripps

    C. Joseph Pulitzer

    D. Charles A. Dana

Answer:
C. Joseph Pulitzer

(A) William Randolph Hearst (1863-1951) was better known for his vast "empire" of publications, mostly newspapers and magazines. (B) Edward W. Scripps (1854-1926) set up the first chain of newspapers in the United States called the Scripps-McRae League and later set up the Scripps-Howard chain. (D) Charles A. Dana (1819-1897) was a newspaper editor most well known for his strong stance on the Civil War and his relentless pursuit of exposing corruption in the post-Civil War administration of Grant. The answer is, therefore, Joseph Pulitzer (1847-1911). His papers, *New York World* and *Evening World*, were the first to include such modern techniques as comics, puzzles, columnists, illustrations, and sports.

18. Which French Renaissance writer wrote about the dangers of absolute powers and later examined himself in an effort to make inquiries into humankind and nature?

    A. Francois Rabelais

    B. Desiderius Erasmus

    C. Michel de Montaigne

    D. Sir Francis Bacon

Answer:

C. Michel de Montaigne

(A) Francois Rabelais (1490-1553) was a French writer and physician who was both a practicing monk (first Franciscan then later Benedictine) and a respected humanist thinker of the Renaissance. (B) Desiderius Erasmus (1466-1536) was a Dutch humanist who was very critical of the Catholic Church but was equally conflicted with Luther's Protestant Reformation. Although Luther had once considered him an ally, Erasmus opposed Luther's break from the church and favored a more internal reform to corruption, he never left the Catholic Church. (D) Sir Francis Bacon (1561-1626) was an English philosopher and writer who pushed the idea that knowledge must come from thorough scientific knowledge and experiment, and insufficient data must not be used in reaching conclusions. (C) Michel de Montaigne (1533-1592), a French essayist from a mixed background, half Catholic and half Jewish, did write some about the dangers of absolute powers, primarily monarchs but also of the Church. His attitude changed as his examination of his own life developed into a study of mankind and nature.

TEACHER CERTFICATION STUDY GUIDE

19. Which of the following contributed to the severity of the Great Depression in California?

    A. An influx of Chinese immigrants.

    B. The dust bowl drove People out of the cities.

    C. An influx of Mexican immigrants.

    D. An influx of Oakies.

Answer:

D. An influx of Oakies

The answer is "An influx of Oakies" (D). The Dust Bowl of the Great Plains destroyed agriculture in the area. People living in the plains areas lost their livelihood and many lost their homes and possessions in the great dust storms that resulted from a period of extended drought. People from all of the states affected by the Dust Bowl made their way to California in search of a better life. Because the majority of the people were from Oklahoma, they were all referred to as "Oakies." These migrants brought with them their distinctive plains culture. The great influx of people seeking jobs exacerbated the effects of the Great Depression in California.

20. Downstream for the flow of the Nile River is:

    A. North

    B. South

    C. East

    D. West

Answer:

A. North

The Nile River flows from Central Africa, north to the Mediterranean Sea. The Nile River Delta is in Egypt.

21. **The year 1619 was a memorable year for the colony of Virginia. Three important events occurred resulting in lasting effects on US history. Which one of the following was not one of the events?**

    A. Twenty African slaves arrived.

    B. The London Company granted the colony a charter making it independent.

    C. The colonists were given the right by the London Company to govern themselves through representative government in the Virginia House of Burgesses.

    D. The London Company sent to the colony 60 women who were quickly married, establishing families and stability in the colony.

Answer:

B. The London Company granted the colony a charter making it independent.

In the year 1619, the Southern colony of Virginia had an eventful year including the first arrival of twenty African slaves, the right to self-governance through representative government in the Virginia House of Burgesses (their own legislative body), and the arrival of sixty women sent to marry and establish families in the colony. The London Company did not, however, grant the colony a charter in 1619.

22. **Of all the major causes of both World Wars I and II, the most significant one is considered to be:**

   A. Extreme nationalism

   B. Military buildup and aggression

   C. Political unrest

   D. Agreements and alliances

Answer:

A. Extreme nationalism

Although military buildup and aggression, political unrest, and agreements and alliances were all characteristic of the world climate before and during World War I and World War II, the most significant cause of both wars was extreme nationalism. Nationalism is the idea that the interests and needs of a particular nation are of the utmost and primary importance above all else. Some nationalist movements could be liberation movements while others were oppressive regimes, much depends on their degree of nationalism. The nationalism that sparked WWI included a rejection of German, Austro-Hungarian, and Ottoman imperialism by Serbs, Slavs and others culminating in the assassination of Archduke Ferdinand by a Serb nationalist in 1914. Following WWI and the Treaty of Versailles, many Germans and others in the Central Alliance Nations, malcontent at the concessions and reparations of the treaty started a new form of nationalism. Adolf Hitler and the Nazi regime led this extreme nationalism. Hitler's ideas were an example of extreme, oppressive nationalism combined with political, social and economic scapegoating and was the primary cause of WWII.

23. **The end to hunting, gathering, and fishing of prehistoric people was due to:**

   A. Domestication of animals

   B. Building crude huts and houses

   C. Development of agriculture

   D. Organized government in villages

Answer:

C. Development of agriculture

Although the domestication of animals, the building of huts and houses and the first organized governments were all very important steps made by early civilizations, it was the development of agriculture that ended the once dominant practices of hunting, gathering, and fishing among prehistoric people. The development of agriculture provided a more efficient use of time and for the first time a surplus of food. This greatly improved the quality of life and contributed to early population growth.

24. **In the United States government, power or control over public education, marriage, and divorce is:**

   A. Implied or suggested

   B. Concurrent or shared

   C. Delegated or expressed

   D. Reserved

Answer:

D. Reserved

In the United States government, power or control over public education, marriage, and divorce is reserved. This is to say that these powers are reserved for the people of the states to decide for themselves.

TEACHER CERTFICATION STUDY GUIDE

25. The principle of "popular sovereignty", allowing people in any Territory to make their own decision concerning slavery was stated by:

    A. Henry Clay

    B. Daniel Webster

    C. John C. Calhoun

    D. Stephen A. Douglas

Answer:

D. Stephen A. Douglas

(A) Henry Clay (1777-1852) and (B) Daniel Webster (1782-1852) were prominent Whigs whose main concern was keeping the United States one nation. They opposed Andrew Jackson and his Democratic party around the 1830s in favor of promoting what Clay called "the American System". (C) John C. Calhoun (1782-1850) served as Vice-President under John Quincy Adams and Andrew Jackson, and then as a state senator from South Carolina. He was very pro-slavery and a champion of states' rights. The principle of "popular sovereignty", in which people in each territory could make their own decisions concerning slavery, was the doctrine of (D) Stephen A. Douglas (1813-1861). Douglas was looking for a middle ground between the abolitionists of the North and the pro-slavery Democrats of the South. However, as the polarization of pro- and anti-slavery sentiments grew, he lost the presidential election to Republican Abraham Lincoln, who later abolished slavery.

26. **Under the brand new Constitution, the most urgent of the many problems facing the new federal government was that of:**

    A. Maintaining a strong army and navy

    B. Establishing a strong foreign policy

    C. Raising money to pay salaries and war debts

    D. Setting up courts, passing federal laws, and providing for law enforcement officers

Answer:

C. Raising money to pay salaries and war debts

Maintaining strong military forces, establishment of a strong foreign policy, and setting up a justice system were important problems facing the United States under the newly ratified Constitution. However, the most important and pressing issue was how to raise money to pay salaries and war debts from the Revolutionary War. Alexander Hamilton (1755-1804) then Secretary of the Treasury proposed increased tariffs and taxes on products such as liquor. This money would be used to pay off war debts and to pay for internal programs. Hamilton also proposed the idea of a National Bank.

27. **Which one of the following was not a reason why the United States went to war with Great Britain in 1812?**

   A. Resentment by Spain over the sale, exploration, and settlement of the Louisiana Territory

   B. The westward movement of farmers because of the need for more land

   C. Canadian fur traders were agitating the northwestern Indians to fight American expansion

   D. Britain continued to seize American ships on the high seas and force American seamen to serve aboard British ships

Answer:

A. Resentment by Spain over the sale, exploration, and settlement of the Louisiana Territory

The United States went to war with Great Britain in 1812 for a number of reasons including the expansion of settlers westward and the need for more land, the agitation of Indians by Canadian fur traders in eastern Canada, and the continued seizures of American ships by the British on the high seas. Therefore, the only statement given that was not a reason for the War of 1812 was the resentment by Spain over the sale, exploration and settlement of the Louisiana Territory. In fact, the Spanish continually held more hostility towards the British than towards the United States. The War of 1812 is often considered to be the second American war for independence.

28. "Participant observation" is a method of study most closely associated with and used in:

   A. Anthropology

   B. Archaeology

   C. Sociology

   D. Political science

Answer:

A. Anthropology

"Participant observation" is a method of study most closely associated with and used in (A) anthropology or the study of current human cultures. (B) Archaeologists typically the study of the remains of people, animals or other physical things. (C) Sociology is the study of human society and usually consists of surveys, controlled experiments, and field studies. (D) Political science is the study of political life including justice, freedom, power and equality in a variety of methods.

TEACHER CERTFICATION STUDY GUIDE

29. The early ancient civilizations developed systems of government:

    A. To provide for defense against attack

    B. To regulate trade

    C. To regulate and direct the economic activities of the people as they worked together in groups

    D. To decide on the boundaries of the different fields during planting seasons

Answer:

C. To regulate and direct the economic activities of the people as they worked together in groups

Although ancient civilizations were concerned with defense, trade regulation and the maintenance of boundaries in their fields, they could not have done any of them without first regulating and directing the economic activities of the people as they worked in groups. This provided for a stable economic base from which they could trade and actually had something worth providing defense for.

30. The "divine right" of kings was the key political characteristic of:

    A. The Age of Absolutism

    B. The Age of Reason

    C. The Age of Feudalism

    D. The Age of Despotism

Answer:

A. The Age of Absolutism

The "divine right" of kings was the key political characteristic of The Age of Absolutism and was most visible in the reign of King Louis XIV of France, as well as during the times of King James I and his son, Charles I. The divine right doctrine claims that kings and absolute leaders derive their right to rule by virtue of their birth alone. They see this both as a law of God and of nature.

HISTORY

TEACHER CERTFICATION STUDY GUIDE

31. **The principle of zero in mathematics is the discovery of the ancient civilization found in:**

    A. Egypt

    B. Persia

    C. India

    D. Babylon

Answer:

C. India

Although the Egyptians practiced algebra and geometry, the Persians developed an alphabet, and the Babylonians developed Hammurabi's Code, which would come to be considered among the most important contributions of the Mesopotamian civilization, it was the Indians that created the idea of zero in mathematics changing drastically our ideas about numbers.

32. **The Ganges River empties into the:**

    A. Bay of Bengal

    B. Arabian Sea

    C. Red Sea

    D. Arafura Sea

Answer:

A. Bay of Bengal

The Ganges River runs 1,560 miles, northeast through India across the plains to the Bay of Bengal in Bangladesh. The Ganges is considered to be the most sacred river in India according to the Hindus.

33. One South American country quickly and easily gained independence in the 19th century from European control; was noted for the uniqueness of its political stability and gradual orderly changes. This most unusual Latin American country is:

    A. Chile

    B. Argentina

    C. Venezuela

    D. Brazil

Answer:

D. Brazil

While Chile, Argentina, and Venezuela all have had histories marred by civil wars, dictatorships, and numerous violent coups during their quests for independence, Brazil experienced a more rapid independence. Independence was gained quickly and more easily than the other countries due to a bloodless revolution in 1889 that officially made Brazil a republic and the economic stability they had in place from a strong coffee and rubber based economy.

34. **In which of the following disciplines would the study of physical mapping, modern or ancient, and the plotting of points and boundaries be least useful?**

    A. Sociology

    B. Geography

    C. Archaeology

    D. History

Answer:

A. Sociology

In geography, archaeology, and history, the study of maps and plotting of points and boundaries is very important as all three of these disciplines hold value in understanding the spatial relations and regional characteristics of people and places. Sociology, however, mostly focuses on the social interactions of people and while location is important, the physical location is not as important as the social location such as the differences between studying people in groups or as individuals.

35. U.S. foreign minister Robert R. Livingstone said, "From this day the United States take their place among the greatest powers." He was referring to the action taken by President Thomas Jefferson:

- A. Who had authorized the purchase of the Louisiana Territory
- B. Who sent the US Marines and naval ships to fight the Barbary pirates
- C. Who had commissioned the Lewis and Clark expedition
- D. Who repealed the Embargo Act

Answer:

A. Who had authorized the purchase of the Louisiana Territory

Livingstone's claim that "from this day, the United States takes their place among the greatest powers" was a reference to Jefferson's authorization and acquisition of the Louisiana Territory. What he meant was that now the United States was beginning to fulfill what would later become known as "Manifest Destiny", and it would be this growth of physical size and political power that put the United States on course to be a world super power.

36. **The only Central American country with no standing army, a freely elected government, and considered the oldest democracy in the region is:**

    A. Costa Rica

    B. Belize

    C. Honduras

    D. Guatemala

Answer:

A. Costa Rica

Belize, Guatemala, and Honduras have all struggled over the past few hundred years. Efforts for independence from colonial powers such as Spain and Great Britain proved difficult and brought up many difficult issues such as the violent border disputes between Guatemala and Belize as late as the 1980s and 1990s that created strong tensions and almost all out war. Honduras experienced many bloody civil wars since its quest for independence began in the early 19th century. Even today, Honduras struggles as one of the poorest nations in the world and has continued to experience serious exploitation and abuses of workers by first world multinational corporations. Since the late 18th century, Costa Rica on the other hand, has experienced longstanding democracy and stability. They have no army and despite a couple of breakdowns in the political system, most notably in 1917 and 1948, it is considered the longest standing democracy in Central America.

37. During the 1920s, the United States almost completely stopped all immigration. One of the reasons was:

    A. Plentiful cheap, unskilled labor was no longer needed by industrialists

    B. War debts from World War I made it difficult to render financial assistance

    C. European nations were reluctant to allow people to leave since there was a need to rebuild populations and economic stability

    D. The United States did not become a member of the League of Nations

Answer:

A. Plentiful cheap, unskilled labor was no longer needed by industrialists

The primary reason that the United States almost completely stopped all immigration during the 1920s was because their once, much needed, cheap, unskilled labor jobs, made available by the once booming industrial economy, were no longer needed. This has much to do with the increased use of machines to do the work once done by cheap, unskilled laborers.

38. **1763 was the year of Great Britain's total victory over her European rivals and the establishment of a global empire. Of the American colonies, a European statesman accurately prophesied that these colonies no longer needed English protection and would soon gain independence. He was:**

    A. Edmund Burke

    B. Comte de Rochambeau

    C. Count Vergennes

    D. William Pitt

Answer:

C. Count Vergennes

Edmund Burke (1729-1797) was a British statesman that did believe in some political reforms in Great Britain's dealing with the American colonies but still believed in the needed guidance and power of the crown in maintaining order. He supported the Declaratory Acts that reasserted Great Britain's control over the colonies in 1766. Burke was important in both the American and French Revolutions. Comte de Rochambeau (1725-1807) was a French marshal who helped George Washington during the American Revolution. William Pitt (1759-1806) was a British statesman who was also a liberal in terms of his ideas for change in economic policy but he never speculated about the future independence of the American colonies. Count Vergennes or Charles Gravier Vergennes (1717-1787) was the French statesman who made the accurate prophecy that the American Colonies would soon be independent from Great Britain. Vergennes not only supported the American Revolution but also helped negotiate the Treaty of Paris in 1783 that secured independence for the colonies.

39. **Colonial expansion by Western European powers in the 18th and 19th centuries was due primarily to:**

    A. Building and opening the Suez Canal

    B. The Industrial Revolution

    C. Marked improvements in transportation

    D. Complete independence of all the Americas and loss of European domination and influence

Answer:

B. The Industrial Revolution

Colonial expansion by Western European powers in the late 18th and 19th centuries was due primarily to the Industrial Revolution in Great Britain that spread across Europe and needed new natural resources and therefore, new locations from which to extract the raw materials needed to feed the new industries.

TEACHER CERTFICATION STUDY GUIDE

40. America's weak foreign policy and lack of adequate diplomacy during the 1870s and 1880s led to the comment that "a special Providence takes care of fools, drunkards, and the United States" is attributed to:

   A. Otto von Bismarck

   B. Benjamin Disraeli

   C. William Gladstone

   D. Paul von Hindenburg

Answer:

A. Otto Von Bismarck

Benjamin Disraeli (1804-1881), a conservative, and William Gladstone (1809-1898), a liberal, were political rivals in Great Britain. Gladstone was greatly disliked by both his rival Disraeli and his Queen for being such a staunch political and economic reformer. Paul von Hindenberg (1847-1934) was a German field marshal and president (1925-1934) who fought against the Americans in World War I.

However, it was Otto von Bismarck (1815-1898), the German statesman who came to be known as the Iron Chancellor, who once said "a special Providence takes care of fools, drunkards, and the United States". Bismarck was saying that despite the United States' shortcomings in foreign policy, leadership and military strength, they continued to grow and gained power in the face of much better run governments, armies and foreign policy makers.

TEACHER CERTFICATION STUDY GUIDE

41. It can be reasonably stated that the change in the United States from primarily an agricultural country into an industrial power was due to all of the following except:

   A. Tariffs on foreign imports

   B. Millions of hardworking immigrants

   C. An increase in technological developments

   D. The change from steam to electricity for powering industrial machinery

Answer:

A. Tariffs on foreign imports

It can be reasonably stated that the change in the United States from primarily an agricultural country into an industrial power was due to a great degree of three of the reasons listed above. It was a combination of millions of hard-working immigrants, an increase in technological developments, and the change from steam to electricity for powering industrial machinery. The only reason given that really had little effect was the tariffs on foreign imports.

42. Many American authors were noted for "local color" writings about the way of life in certain regions. Which one of the following was not associated with the other three in writing about life in the mining camps of the West?

    A. Hamlin Garland

    B. Joaquin Miller

    C. Bret Harte

    D. Mark Twain

Answer:

A. Hamlin Garland

Hamlin Garland (1860-1940), unlike the other three authors mentioned, grew up in the mid-western farmlands and wrote stories that were bitter pictures of the difficulties of farm life. He also wrote political critiques. Joaquin Miller (1839-1913), an American poet, moved in 1852 to the Oregon frontier where he wrote about life in gold-mining camps, experiences with Native Americans, and painted an overall energetic and pleasant picture of frontier life. Bret Harte (1836-1902) moved to California at age 19 and wrote local-color short stories of life in mining camps and on the western frontiers of California. Mark Twain (1835-1910), however, was perhaps the most well known and celebrated novelist of early American. Twain, also known as Samuel Langhorne Clemens, was born in Missouri and lived in a variety of places before making it out West, first to Carson City, Nevada, and then later to Sacramento. Twain would return to Hartford, Connecticut, where he spent his later years and wrote *Roughing It* in 1887, about the difficult lives he saw lived on the Western frontier. Twain is best known for his books *The Adventures of Huckleberry Finn* and *The Adventures of Tom Sawyer*, the former of which is considered by many to be the first truly great American novel.

TEACHER CERTFICATION STUDY GUIDE

43. There is no doubt of the vast improvement of the U.S. Constitution over the weak Articles of Confederation. Which one of the four statements below is not a description of the document?

   A. The establishment of a strong central government in no way lessened or weakened the individual states

   B. Individual rights were protected and secured

   C. The Constitution demands unquestioned respect and subservience to the federal government by all states and citizens

   D. Its flexibility and adaptation to change gives it a sense of timelessness

Answer:

C. The Constitution demands unquestioned respect and subservience to the federal government by all states and citizens.

The U.S. Constitution was indeed a vast improvement over the Articles of Confederation and the authors of the document took great care to assure longevity. It clearly stated that the establishment of a strong central government in no way lessened or weakened the individual states. In the Bill of Rights, citizens were assured that individual rights were protected and secured. Possibly the most important feature of the new Constitution was its flexibility and adaptation to change which assured longevity.

Therefore, the only statement made that doesn't describe some facet of the Constitution is "The Constitution demands unquestioned respect and subservience to the federal government by all states and citizens". On the contrary, the Constitution made sure that citizens could critique and make changes to their government and encourages such critiques and changes as necessary for the preservation of democracy.

44. The study of a people's language and writing would be part of all of the following except:

    A. Sociology

    B. Archaeology

    C. History

    D. Geography

Answer:

A. Sociology

The study of a people's language and writing would be a part of studies in the disciplines of sociology (study of social interaction and organization), archaeology, (study of ancient artifacts including written works), and history (the study of the past). Language and writing would be less important to geography that tends to focus more on locations and spatial relations than on the people in those regions and their languages or writings.

45. The changing focus during the Renaissance when artists and scholars were less concerned with religion but centered their efforts on a better understanding of people and the world was called:

A. Realism

B. Humanism

C. Individualism

D. Intellectualism

Answer:

B. Humanism

Realism is a medieval philosophy that contemplated independence of existence of the body, the mind, and God. The idea of individualism is usually either a reference to an economic or political theory. Intellectualism is the placing of great importance and devotion to the exploring of the intellect. Therefore, the changing focus during the Renaissance when artists and scholars were less concerned with religion but centered their efforts on a better understanding of people and the world was called humanism.

46. The "father of anatomy" is considered to be:

A. Vesalius

B. Servetus

C. Galen

D. Harvey

Answer:

A. Vesalius

Andreas Vesalius (1514-1564) is considered to be the "father of anatomy" as a result of his revolutionary work on the human anatomy based on dissections of human cadavers. Prior to Vesalius, men such as Galen, (130-200) had done work in the field of anatomy, but they had based the majority of their work on animal studies.

47. In the United States government, the power of coining money is:

   A. Implied or suggested

   B. Concurrent or shared

   C. Delegated or expressed

   D. Reserved

Answer:

C. Delegated or expressed

In the United States government, the power of coining money is delegated or expressed. Therefore, only the United States government may coin money, the states may not coin money for themselves.

48. The source of authority for national, state, and local governments in the United States is:

   A. The will of the people

   B. The United States Constitution

   C. Written laws

   D. The Bill of Rights

Answer:

A. The will of the people

The source of authority for national, state, and local governments in the United States is the will of the people. Although the United States Constitution, the Bill of Rights, and the other written laws of the land are important guidelines for authority, they may ultimately be altered or changed by the will of the people.

49. India's greatest ruler is considered to be:

A. Akbar

B. Asoka

C. Babur

D. Jahan

Answer:

A. Akbar

Akbar (1556-1605) is considered to be India's greatest ruler. He combined a drive for conquest with a magnetic personality and went so far as to invent his own religion, Dinillahi, a combination of Islam, Christianity, Zoroastrianism, and Hinduism. Asoka (273 B.C.-232 B.C.) was also an important ruler as he was the first to bring together a fully united India. Babur (1483-1540) was both considered to be a failure as he struggled to maintain any power early in his reign, but later to be somewhat successful in his quest to reunite Northern India. Jahan's (1592-1666) rule of India is considered to be the golden age of art and literature in the region.

50. "Poverty is the parent of revolution and crime" was from the writings of:

A. Plato

B. Aristotle

C. Cicero

D. Gaius

Answer:

B. Aristotle

Aristotle once wrote "Poverty is the parent of revolution and crime", a comment that is probably as relevant today as it was in Aristotle's day. It showed his true insight as one of the great political and social commentators and philosophers of all time.

TEACHER CERTFICATION STUDY GUIDE

51. Geography was first studied in an organized manner by the:

- A. Egyptians
- B. Greeks
- C. Romans
- D. Arabs

Answer:

B. Greeks

The Greeks were the first to study geography, possibly because of the difficulties they faced as a result of geographic conditions. Greece had difficulty uniting early on as their steep, treacherous, mountainous terrain made it difficult for the city-states to be united. As the Greeks studied their geography, it became possible to defeat more powerful armies on their home turf, such as the great victory over the Persians at Marathon.

52. From about 1870 to 1900, the last settlement of America's "last frontier", the West, was completed. One attraction for settlers was free land but it would have been to no avail without:

- A. Better farming methods and technology
- B. Surveying to set boundaries
- C. Immigrants and others to see new lands
- D. The railroad to get them there

Answer:

D. The railroad to get them there

From about 1870 to 1900, the settlement for America's "last frontier" in the West was made possible by the building of the railroad. Without the railroad, the settlers never could have traveled such distances in an efficient manner.

TEACHER CERTFICATION STUDY GUIDE

53. Meridians, or lines of longitude, not only help in pinpointing locations, but are also used for:

    A. Measuring distance from the Poles

    B. Determining direction of ocean currents

    C. Determining the time around the world

    D. Measuring distance on the Equator

Answer:

C. Determining the time around the world

Meridians, or lines of longitude, are the determining factor in separating time zones and determining time around the world.

54. Historians state that the West helped to speed up the Industrial Revolution. Which one of the following statements was not a reason for this?

   A. Food supplies for the ever-increasing urban populations came from farms in the West.

   B. A tremendous supply of gold and silver from western mines provided the capital needed to build industries.

   C. Descendants of western settlers, educated as engineers, geologists, and metallurgists in the East, returned to the West to mine the mineral resources needed for industry.

   D. Iron, copper, and other minerals from western mines were important resources in manufacturing products.

Answer:

C. Descendants of western settlers, educated as engineers, geologists, and metallurgists in the East, returned to the West to mine the mineral resources needed for industry.

The West helped to speed up the Industrial Revolution in a number of important and significant ways. First, the land yielded crops for the growing urban populations. Second, the gold and silver supplies coming out of the Western mines provided the capital needed to build industries. Also, resources such as iron and copper were extracted from the mines in the West and provided natural resources for manufacturing. The descendants of western settlers typically didn't become educated and then returned to the West as miners. The miners were typically working class with little or no education.

55. In the United States government, the power of taxation and borrowing is:

    A. Implied or suggested

    B. Concurrent or shared

    C. Delegated or expressed

    D. Reserved

Answer:

B. Concurrent or shared

In the United States government, the power of taxation is concurrent or shared with the states. An example of this is the separation of state and federal income tax and the separate filings of tax returns for each.

56. **The post-Civil War years were a time of low public morality, a time of greed, graft, and dishonesty. Which one of the reasons listed would not be accurate?**

   A. The war itself because of the money and materials needed to carry on war

   B. The very rapid growth of industry and big business after the war

   C. The personal example set by President Grant

   D. Unscrupulous heads of large impersonal corporations

Answer:

C. The personal example set by President Grant

The post-Civil War years were a particularly difficult time for the nation and public morale was especially low. The war had plunged the country into debt and ultimately into a recession by the 1890s. Racism was rampant throughout the South and the North where freed Blacks were taking jobs for low wages. The rapid growth of industry and big business caused a polarization of rich and poor, workers and owners. Many people moved into the urban centers to find work in the new industrial sector, jobs were typically low-wage, long hours, and poor working conditions. The heads of large impersonal corporations were arrogant in treating their workers inhumanely and letting morale drop to a record low. The heads of corporations showed their greed and malice towards the workingman by trying to prevent and disband labor unions.

TEACHER CERTFICATION STUDY GUIDE

57. Studies in astronomy, skills in mapping, and other contributions to geographic knowledge came from:

A. Galileo

B. Columbus

C. Eratosthenes

D. Ptolemy

Answer:

D. Ptolemy

Ptolemy (2nd century AD) was important in the fields of astronomy and geography. His theory stated that the earth was the center of the universe and all the other planets rotated around it, a theory that was later proven false. Ptolemy, however was important for his contributions to the fields of mapping, mathematics, and geography. Galileo (1564-1642) was also important in the field of astronomy but did not make the mapping and geographic contributions of Ptolemy. He invented and used the world's first telescope and advanced Copernicus' theory that the earth revolved around the sun, much to the dismay of the Church.

TEACHER CERTFICATION STUDY GUIDE

58. Which one of the following would not be considered a result of World War II?

    A. Economic depressions and slow resumption of trade and financial aid

    B. Western Europe was no longer the center of world power

    C. The beginnings of new power struggles not only in Europe but in Asia as well

    D. Territorial and boundary changes for many nations, especially in Europe

Answer:

A. Economic depressions and slow resumption of trade and financial aid

Following World War II, the economy was vibrant and flourished from the stimulant of war and an increased dependence of the world on United States industries. Therefore, World War II didn't result in economic depressions and slow resumption of trade and financial aid. Western Europe was no longer the center of world power. New power struggles arose in Europe and Asia and many European nations underwent changing territories and boundaries.

59. The study of ways in which different societies around the world deal with the problems of limited resources and unlimited needs and wants is in the area of:

   A. Economics

   B. Sociology

   C. Anthropology

   D. Political Science

Answer:

A. Economics

The study of the ways in which different societies around the world deal with the problems of limited resources and unlimited needs and wants is a study of Economics. Economists consider the law of supply and demand as fundamental to the study of the economy. However, Sociology and Political Science also consider the study of economics and its importance in understanding social and political systems.

TEACHER CERTFICATION STUDY GUIDE

60. **Nineteenth century imperialism by Western Europe nations had important and far-reaching effects on the colonial peoples they ruled. All four of the following are the results of this. Which one was the most important and had lasting effects on key 20th century events?**

    A. Local wars were ended

    B. Living standards were raised

    C. Demands for self-government and feelings of nationalism surfaced

    D. Economic developments occurred

Answer:

C. Demands for self-government and feelings of nationalism surfaced

The 19th century imperialism by Western European nations had some very serious and far-reaching effects. The most important and lasting effect on events of the 20th century is the demands for self-government and the rise of nationalism. Both World War I and World War II were caused to a large degree by the rise of nationalist sentiment across Europe and Asia. Nationalism has also fueled numerous liberation movements and revolutionary movements across the globe from Central and South America to the South Pacific to Africa and Asia.

61. After the War of 1812, Henry Clay and others proposed economic measures, including raising tariffs to protect American farmers and manufacturers from foreign competition. These measures were proposed in the period known as:

   A. Era of Nationalism

   B. American Expansion

   C. Era of Good Feeling

   D. American System

Answer:

D. American System

Although there is no official (A) "Era of Nationalism", it could be used to describe the time leading up to and including the First and Second World Wars, as nationalism was on the rise. (B) American Expansion describes the movement of American settlers across the frontier towards the West. The so-called (C) "Era of Good Feeling" is the period after the War of 1812 but doesn't describe the policies proposed by Clay. The economic measures, including raising tariffs to protect American farmers and manufacturers from foreign competition, was known as the (D) American System.

62. "These are the times that try men's souls" were words penned by:

A. Thomas Jefferson

B. Samuel Adams

C. Benjamin Franklin

D. Thomas Paine

Answer:

D. Thomas Paine

Thomas Paine (1737-1809), the great American political theorist, wrote "these are the times that try men's souls" in his 16 part pamphlet *The Crisis*. Paine's authoring of *Common Sense* was an important step in spreading information to the American colonists about their need for independence from Great Britain.

63. The Age of Exploration begun in the 1400s was led by:

A. The Portuguese

B. The Spanish

C. The English

D. The Dutch

Answer:

A. The Portuguese

Although the Age of Exploration had many important players among them, the Dutch, Spanish and English, it was the Portuguese who sent the first explorers to the New World.

64. Which one of the following is not a function or responsibility of the US political parties?

- A. Conducting elections or the voting process
- B. Obtaining funds needed for election campaigns
- C. Choosing candidates to run for public office
- D. Making voters aware of issues and other public affairs information

Answer:

A. Conducting elections or the voting process

The US political parties have numerous functions and responsibilities. Among them are obtaining funds needed for election campaigns, choosing the candidates to run for office, and making voters aware of the issues. The political parties, however, do not conduct elections or the voting process, as that would be an obvious conflict of interest.

65. The economist who disagreed with the idea that free markets lead to full employment and prosperity and suggested that increasing government spending would end depressions was:

A. Keynes

B. Malthus

C. Smith

D. Friedman

Answer:

A. Keynes

John Maynard Keynes (1883-1946) advocated an economic system in which government regulations and spending on public works would stimulate the economy and lead to full employment. This broke from the classical idea that free markets would lead to full employment and prosperity. He was still a firm believer in capitalism, but in a less classical sense than Adam Smith (1723-1790), whose *Wealth of Nations* advocated for little or no government interference in the economy.

Smith claimed that an individual's self-interest would bring about the public's welfare. It is important to note that Smith was firmly against the free market systems of monopoly power and warned that the private sector, particularly large manufacturers, if left unregulated could potentially stand in opposition to the public welfare.

TEACHER CERTFICATION STUDY GUIDE

66. **The study of the social behavior of minority groups would be in the area of:**

    A. Anthropology

    B. Psychology

    C. Sociology

    D. Cultural Geography

Answer:

C. Sociology

The study of social behavior in minority groups would be primarily in the area of Sociology, as it is the discipline most concerned with social interaction and being. However, it could be argued that Anthropology, Psychology, and Cultural Geography could have some interest in the study as well.

67. **An extensive knowledge of surgery and medicine as well as principles of irrigation, fertilization and terrace farming was unique to:**

    A. The Mayans

    B. The Atacamas

    C. The Incas

    D. The Tarapacas

Answer:

C. The Incas

The Incas of Peru had an extensive knowledge of surgery and medicine as well as principles of irrigation, fertilization, and terrace farming. These were unique achievements for an ancient civilization.

HISTORY

TEACHER CERTFICATION STUDY GUIDE

68. **The idea of universal peace through world of organization was a philosophy of:**

    A. Rousseau

    B. Immanuel Kant

    C. Montesquieu

    D. John Locke

Answer:

B. Immanuel Kant

Immanuel Kant (1724-1804) was the German metaphysician and philosopher, who was a founding proponent of the idea that world organization was the means for achieving universal peace. Kant's ideas helped to found such world peace organizations as the League of Nations in the wake of World War I.

69. **Which ancient civilization is credited with being the first to develop irrigation techniques through the use of canals, dikes, and devices for raising water?**

    A. The Sumerians

    B. The Egyptians

    C. The Babylonians

    D. The Akkadians

Answer:

A. The Sumerians

The ancient (A) Sumerians of the Fertile Crescent of Mesopotamia are credited with being the first to develop irrigation techniques through the use of canals, dikes, and devices for raising water. The (B) Egyptians also practiced controlled irrigation but that was primarily through the use of the Nile's predictable flooding schedule. The (C) Babylonians were more noted for their revolutionary systems of law than their irrigation systems.

TEACHER CERTFICATION STUDY GUIDE

70. The study of past human cultures based on physical artifacts is:

    A. History

    B. Anthropology

    C. Cultural Geography

    D. Archaeology

Answer:

D. Archaeology

Archaeology is the study of past human cultures based on physical artifacts such as fossils, carvings, paintings, and engraved writings.

TEACHER CERTFICATION STUDY GUIDE

71. **The "father" of modern economics is considered by most economists today to be:**

   A. Thomas Robert Malthus

   B. John Stuart Mill

   C. Adam Smith

   D. John Maynard Keynes

Answer:

C. Adam Smith

Adam Smith (1723-1790) is considered by many to be the "father" of modern economics. In the *Wealth of Nations,* Smith advocated for little or no government interference in the economy. Smith claimed that individuals' self-interest would bring about the public's welfare. It is important to note that Smith was firmly against the free market systems of monopoly power and warned that the private sector, particularly large manufacturers, if left unregulated could potentially stand in opposition to the public welfare. John Maynard Keynes 1883-1946) was also an important economist. He advocated an economic system in which government regulations and spending on public works would stimulate the economy and lead to full employment. John Stuart Mill (1806-1873) was a progressive British philosopher and economist, whose ideas came closer to socialism than to the classical capitalist ideas of Adam Smith. Mill constantly advocated for political and social reforms, including emancipation for women, labor organizations, and farming cooperatives. Thomas Malthus (1766-1834) was a British economist who introduced the study of population and early on considered famine, war, and disease to be the primary checks on world population. He later modified his views and recognized his early theoretical shortcomings and shifted his focus to the causes of unemployment.

72. **The ideas and innovations of the period of the Renaissance were spread throughout Europe mainly because of:**

    A. Extensive exploration

    B. Craft workers and their guilds

    C. The invention of the printing press

    D. Increased travel and trade

Answer:

C. The invention of the printing press

The ideas and innovations of the Renaissance were spread throughout Europe for a number of reasons. While exploration, increased travel, and spread of craft may have aided the spread of the Renaissance to small degrees, nothing was as important to the spread of ideas as Gutenberg's invention of the printing press in Germany.

73. **The American labor union movement started gaining new momentum:**

    A. During the building of the railroads

    B. After 1865 with the growth of cities

    C. With the rise of industrial giants such as Carnegie and Vanderbilt

    D. During the war years of 1861-1865

Answer:

B. After 1865 with the growth of cities

The American Labor Union movement had been around since the late 18th and early 19th centuries. The Labor movement began to first experience persecution by employers in the early 1800s. The American Labor Movement remained relatively ineffective until after the Civil War. In 1866, the National Labor Union was formed, pushing such issues as the eight-hour workday and new policies of immigration. This gave rise to the Knights of Labor and eventually the American Federation of Labor (AFL) in the 1890s and the Industrial Workers of the World (1905). Therefore, it was the period following the Civil War that empowered the labor movement in terms of numbers, militancy, and effectiveness.

74. Soil erosion is most likely to occur in large amounts in:

A. Mountain ranges

B. Deserts

C. Tropical rainforests

D. River valleys

Answer:

C. Tropical rainforests

Soil erosion is most likely to occur in tropical rainforests as the large amount of constant rainfall moves the soil at a greater rate across a greater area. Mountain ranges and river valleys experience some soil erosion but don't have the levels of precipitation found in a tropical rainforest. Deserts have virtually no soil erosion due to their climate.

TEACHER CERTFICATION STUDY GUIDE

75. Who is considered to be the most important figure in the spread of Protestantism across Switzerland?

   A. Calvin

   B. Zwingli

   C. Munzer

   D. Leyden

Answer:

A. Calvin

While Huldreich Zwingli (1484-1531) was the first to spread the Protestant Reformation in Switzerland around 1519, it was John Calvin (1509-1564), whose less radical approach to Protestantism who really made the most impact in Switzerland. Calvin's ideas separated from the Lutherans over the "Lord's Supper" debate over the sacrament, and his branch of Protestants became known as Calvinism. Calvin certainly built on Zwingli's early influence but really made the religion widespread throughout Switzerland. Thomas Munzer (1489-1525) was a German Protestant reformer whose radical and revolutionary ideas about God's will to overthrow the ruling classes and his siding with the peasantry got him beheaded. Munzer has since been studied and admired by Marxists for his views on class. Leyden (or Leiden) was a founder of the University of Leyden, a Protestant place for study in the Netherlands.

TEACHER CERTFICATION STUDY GUIDE

76. **The principle that "men entrusted with power tend to abuse it" is attributed to:**

    A. Locke

    B. Rousseau

    C. Aristotle

    D. Montesquieu

Answer:

D. Montesquieu

The principle that "men entrusted with power tend to abuse it" is attributed to Montesquieu (1689-1755), the great French philosopher whose ideas based much on Locke's ideas, along with Rousseau, had a strong influence on the French Revolution of 1789. Although it would be reasonable to assume that Locke, Rousseau, and Aristotle would probably agree with the statement, all four of these men had profound impacts on the ideas of the Enlightenment, from humanism to constitutionals.

77. **After 1783, the largest "land owner" in the Americas was:**

    A. Britain

    B. Spain

    C. France

    D. United States

Answer:

A. Spain

Despite the emergence of the United States as an independent nation in control of the colonies over the British, and the French control of Canada, Spain remained the largest "land owner" in the Americas controlling much of the southwest as well as much of Central and South America.

HISTORY

78. The purchase of goods or services on one market for immediate resale on another market is:

 A. Output

 B. Enterprise

 C. Arbitrage

 D. Mercantile

Answer:

C. Arbitrage

Output is an amount produced or manufactured by an industry. Enterprise is simply any business organization. Mercantile is one of the first systems of economics in which goods were exchanged. Therefore, arbitrage is an item or service that an industry produces. The dictionary definition of arbitrage is the purchase of securities on one market for immediate resale on another market in order to profit from a price discrepancy.

TEACHER CERTFICATION STUDY GUIDE

79. **After the Civil War, the United States adapted an attitude of isolation from foreign affairs. But the turning point marking the beginning of the US becoming a world power was:**

    A. World War I

    B. Expansion of business and trade overseas

    C. The Spanish-American War

    D. The building and financing of the Panama Canal

Answer:

C. The Spanish-American War

The turning point marking the beginning of the United States becoming a super power was the Spanish-American War. This was seen as an extension of the Monroe doctrine, calling for United States dominance in the Western Hemisphere and removal of European powers in the region. The United States' relatively easy defeat of Spain in the Spanish-American War marked the beginning of a continuing era of dominance for the United States. In addition, in the post-Civil War era, Spain was the largest land owner in the Americas. Their easy defeat at the hands of the United States in Cuba, the Philippines, and elsewhere showed the strength of the United States across the globe.

80. **The programs such as unemployment insurance and health insurance for the elderly are the responsibility of:**

    A. Federal Government

    B. Local Government

    C. State Government

    D. Communal Government

Answer:

C. State Government

Assistance programs, such as unemployment insurance and free health insurance for the elderly is the responsibility of state governments.

TEACHER CERTFICATION STUDY GUIDE

81. The English explorer who gave England its claim to North America was:

    A. Raleigh

    B. Hawkins

    C. Drake

    D. Cabot

Answer:

D. Cabot

Sir Walter Raleigh (1554-1618) was an English explorer and navigator, who was sent to the New World in search of riches. He founded the lost colony at Roanoke, Virginia, and was later imprisoned for a supposed plot to kill the King for which he was later released. Sir John Hawkins (1532-1595) and Sir Francis Drake (1540-1596) were both navigators who worked in the slave trade, made some voyages to the New World, and commanded ships against and defeated the Spanish Armada in 1588. John Cabot (1450-1498) was the English explorer who gave England claim to North America.

TEACHER CERTFICATION STUDY GUIDE

82. The three-day Battle of Gettysburg was the turning point of the Civil War for the North leading to ultimate victory. The battle in the West reinforcing the North's victory and sealing the South's defeat was the day after Gettysburg at:

   A. Perryville

   B. Vicksburg

   C. Stones River

   D. Shiloh

Answer:

B. Vicksburg

The Battle of Vicksburg was crucial in reinforcing the North's victory and sealing the south's defeat for a couple of reasons. First, the Battle of Vicksburg potentially gave the Union full control of the Mississippi River. More importantly, the battle split the Confederate Army and allowed General Grant to reach his goal of restoring commerce to the important northwest area.

83. **The study of the exercise of power and political behavior in human society today would be conducted by experts in:**

    A. History

    B. Sociology

    C. Political Science

    D. Anthropology

Answer:

C. Political Science

Experts in the field of political science today would likely conduct the study of exercise of power and political behavior in human society. However, it is also reasonable to suggest that such studies would be important to historians (study of the past, often in an effort to understand the present), sociologists (often concerned with power structure in the social and political worlds), and even some anthropologists (study of culture and their behaviors).

84. During the period of Spanish colonialism, which of the following was not a key to the goal of exploiting, transforming and including the native people?

   A. Missions

   B. Ranchos

   C. Presidios

   D. Pueblos

Answer:

B. Ranchos

The answer is "Ranchos" (b). The goal of Spanish colonialism was to exploit, transform and include the native people of California. The Spanish empire sought to do this first by gathering the native people into communities where they could both be taught Spanish culture and be converted to Roman Catholicism and its value system. The social institutions by which this was accomplished was the encouragement of the Mission System, which established a number of Catholic missions a day's journey apart. Once the native people were brought to the missions, they were incorporated into a mission society and indoctrinated in the teachings of Catholicism. The Presidios were fortresses that were constructed to protect Spanish interests and the communities from invaders. The Pueblos were small civilian communities that attracted settlers with the gift of land, seed, and farming equipment. The function of the Pueblos was to produce food for the missions and for the presidios.

85. Potential customers for any product or service are not only called consumers but can also be called a:

   A. Resource

   B. Base

   C. Commodity

   D. Market

Answer:

D. Market

Potential customers for any product or service are not only customers but can also be called a market. A resource is a source of wealth; natural resources are the basis for manufacturing goods and services. A commodity is anything that is bought or sold, any product.

86. An early cultural group was so skillful in navigating on the sea that they were able to sail at night guided by starts. They were the:

   A. Greeks

   B. Persians

   C. Minoans

   D. Phoenicians

Answer:

D. Phoenicians

Although the Greeks were quite able sailors and developed a strong navy in their defeat of the Persians at sea in the Battle of Marathon, it was the Eastern Mediterranean culture of the Phoenicians that had first developed the astronomical skill of sailing at night with the starts as their guide. The Minoans were an advanced early civilization off the Greek coast on Crete more noted for their innovations in terms of sewage systems, toilets, and running water.

TEACHER CERTFICATION STUDY GUIDE

87. One method of trade restriction used by some nations is:

    A. Limited treaties

    B. Floating exchange rate

    C. Bill of exchange

    D. Import quotas

Answer:

D. Import quotas

One method of trade restriction used by some nations is import quotas. The amounts of goods imported are regulated in an effort to protect domestic enterprise and limit foreign competition. Both the United States and Japan, two of the world's most industrialized nations have import quotas to protect domestic industries.

88. A political system in which the laws and traditions put limits on the powers of government is:

    A. Federalism

    B. Constitutionalism

    C. Parliamentary system

    D. Presidential system

Answer:

B. Constitutionalism

Constitutionalism is a political system in which laws and traditions put limits on the powers of government. Federalism is the idea of a strong, centralized national government to hold together the nation. The parliamentary system, such as the governments of Great Britain and Israel, are systems in which a group of representatives are led by a prime minister contrasting with a presidential system which is run by a head of state, the elected (or sometimes self-appointed) president.

TEACHER CERTFICATION STUDY GUIDE

89. Which one of the following did not contribute to the early medieval European civilization?

   A. The heritage from the classical cultures

   B. The Christian religion

   C. The influence of the German Barbarians

   D. The spread of ideas through trade and commerce

Answer:

D. The spread of ideas through trade and commerce
The heritage of the classical cultures such as Greece, the Christian religion which became dominant, and the influence of the Germanic Barbarians (Visigoths, Saxons, Ostrogoths, Vandals and Franks) were all contributions to early medieval Europe and its plunge into feudalism. During this period, lives were often difficult and lived out on one single manor, with very little travel or spread of ideas through trade or commerce. Civilization seems to have halted progress during these years.

90. **The Roman Empire gave so much to the world, especially the Western world. Of the legacies below, the most influential, effective and lasting is:**

    A. The language of Latin

    B. Roman law, justice, and political system

    C. Engineering and building

    D. The writings of its poets and historians

Answer:

B. Roman law, justice, and political system

Of the lasting legacies of the Roman Empire, it is their law, justice, and political system that has been the most effective and influential on our Western world today. The idea of a Senate and different houses is still maintained by our United States government and their legal justice system is also the foundation of our own. We still use many Latin words in our justice system, terms such as *habeas corpus* and *voir dire*. English, Spanish, Italian, French, and others are all based on Latin. The Roman language, Latin itself has died out. The Roman engineering and building and their writings and poetry have also been influential but not nearly to the degree that their governmental and justice systems have been.

91. **Charlemagne's most important influence on Western civilization is seen today in:**

    A. Relationship of church and state

    B. Strong military for defense

    C. The criminal justice system

    D. Education of women

Answer:

A. Relationship of church and state

Charlemagne was the leader of the Germanic Franks responsible for the promotion of the Holy Roman Empire across Europe. Although he unified governments and aided the Pope, he re-crowned himself in 802 A.D. to demonstrate that his power and right to rule was not a grant from the Pope, but rather a secular achievement. Therefore, although he used much of the Church's power in his rise to power, the Pope in turn used Charlemagne to ascend the Church to new heights. Thus, Charlemagne had an influence on the issues between Church and state.

92. **Public administration, such as public officials in the areas of budgets, accounting, distribution of public funds, and personnel management, would be a part of the field of:**

    A. Anthropology

    B. Sociology

    C. Law and Taxation

    D. Political Science and Economics

Answer:

D. Political Science and Economics

Public administration, such as public officials in the areas of budgets, accounting, distribution of public funds, and personnel management, would be parts of the fields of Economics and Political Science. While political scientists would be concerned with public administration, economists would also be concerned with the distribution of public funds, budgets, and accounting and their effects on the economy.

93. "Marbury vs Madison (1803)" was an important Supreme Court case which set the precedent for:

    A. The elastic clause

    B. Judicial review

    C. The supreme law of the land

    D. Popular sovereignty in the territories

Answer:

B. Judicial review

Marbury vs Madison (1803) was an important case for the Supreme Court as it established judicial review. In that case, the Supreme Court set precedence to declare laws passed by Congress as unconstitutional. Popular sovereignty in the territories was a failed plan pushed by Stephen Davis to allow states to decide the slavery question for themselves. In his attempt to appeal to the masses in the pre-Civil War elections. The supreme law of the land is just that, the law that rules. The elastic clause is not a real term.

94. Which one of the following is not a use for a region's wetlands?

   A. Produces fresh clean water

   B. Provides habitat for wildlife

   C. Provides water for hydroelectric power

   D. Controls floods

Answer:

C. Provides water for hydroelectric power

A region's wetlands provide a number of uses and services not limited to but including production of fresh water, habitat and natural preserve of wildlife, and flood control. Wetlands are not used in the production of hydroelectric power the way dams or other power structures do.

95. The philosopher who coined the term "sociology" also stated that social behavior and events could be measured scientifically. He is identified as:

    A. Auguste Comte

    B. Herbert Spencer

    C. Rousseau

    D. Immanuel Kant

Answer:

A. Auguste Comte

Auguste Comte (1798-1857) was a French philosopher and social reformer who founded the school of positivism. Comte identified the uses of different scientific applications as dependent on the preceding science in the order of mathematics, astronomy, physics, chemistry, biology, and finally his coined term, sociology. Herbert Spencer (1820-1903) also helped spread sociology, although his evolutionary theory was more practical and popular than it was scientific. Rousseau (1712-1778) was a political philosopher who explored the idea of what has come to be known as liberalism. Immanuel Kant (1724-1804) was the German metaphysician and philosopher who was a founding proponent of the idea that world organization was the means for achieving universal peace.

96. The belief that the United States should control all of North America was called:

   A. Westward Expansion

   B. Pan Americanism

   C. Manifest Destiny

   D. Nationalism

Answer:

C. Manifest Destiny

The belief that the United States should control all of North America was called (B) Manifest Destiny. This idea fueled much of the violence and aggression towards those already occupying the lands such as the Native Americans. Manifest Destiny was certainly driven by sentiments of (D) nationalism and gave rise to (A) westward expansion.

97. A well known World War II figure who said that democracy was like a rotting corpse that had to be replaced by a superior way of life and more efficient government was:

    A. Hitler

    B. Stalin

    C. Tojo

    D. Mussolini

Answer:

D. Mussolini

(A) Adolf Hitler (1889-1945), the Nazi leader of Germany, and (C) Hideki Tojo (1884-1948), the Japanese General and Prime Minister, were well known World War II figures who led Axis forces into war on a quest of spreading fascism. (B) Joseph Stalin (1879-1953) was the Communist Russian head of state during World War II. Although all three were repressive in their actions, it was (D) Benito Mussolini (1883-1945), the Fascist and widely-considered incompetent leader of Italy during World War II, who once said "democracy was like a rotting corpse that had to be replaced by a superior way of life and more efficient government".

98. **The Radical Republicans who pushed the harsh Reconstruction measures through Congress after Lincoln's death lost public and moderate Republican support when they went too far:**

   A. In their efforts to impeach the President

   B. By dividing ten southern states into military-controlled districts

   C. By making the ten southern states give freed African-Americans the right to vote

   D. Sending carpetbaggers into the South to build up support for Congressional legislation

Answer:

A. In their efforts to impeach the President

The public support and the moderate Republicans were actually being drawn towards the more radical end of the Republican spectrum following Lincoln's death during Reconstruction. Because many felt as though Andrew Johnson's policies towards the South were too soft and were running the risk of rebuilding the old system of white power and slavery. Even moderate Republicans in the North felt as though it was essential to rebuild the South but with the understanding that they must be abide by the Fourteenth and Fifteenth Amendment assuring Blacks freedom and the right to vote. The radical Republicans were so frustrated that the President would make concessions to the old Southerners that they attempted to impeach him. This turned back the support that they had received from the public and from moderates.

TEACHER CERTFICATION STUDY GUIDE

99. The economic system promoting individual ownership of land, capital, and businesses with minimal governmental regulations is called:

    A. Macro-economy

    B. Micro-economy

    C. Laissez-faire

    D. Free enterprise

Answer:

D. Free Enterprise

(D) Free enterprise or capitalism is the economic system that promotes private ownership of land, capital, and business with minimal government interference. (C) Laissez-faire is the idea that an "invisible hand" will guide the free enterprise system to the maximum potential efficiency.

100. A political philosophy favoring or supporting rapid social changes in order to correct social and economic inequalities is called:

    A. Nationalism

    B. Liberalism

    C. Conservatism

    D. Federalism

Answer:

B. Liberalism

A political philosophy favoring rapid social changes in order to correct social and economic inequalities are called Liberalism. Liberalism was a theory that could be said to have started with the great French philosophers Montesquieu (1689-1755) and Rousseau (1712-1778). It is important to understand the difference between political, economic, and social liberalism, as they are different and how they sometimes contrast one another in the modern world.

TEACHER CERTFICATION STUDY GUIDE

101. China's last imperial ruling dynasty was one of its most stable and successful and under its rule, Chinese culture made an outstanding impression on Western nations. This dynasty was:

A. Ming

B. Manchu

C. Han

D. Chou

Answer:

B. Manchu

The (A) Ming Dynasty lasted from 1368-1644 and was among the more successful dynasties but focused attention towards foreign trade and encouraged growth in the arts. Therefore, it was the (B) Manchu Dynasty, the last imperial ruling dynasty, which came to power in the 1600s and expanded China's power in Asia greatly that was and still is considered to be among the most important, most stable, and most successful of the Chinese dynasties. The (C) Han and (D) Chou Dynasties were part of the "ancient" dynasties of China and while important in Chinese History, their influence did not hold impression on Western nations as the Manchu.

TEACHER CERTFICATION STUDY GUIDE

102. **Development of a solar calendar, invention of the decimal system, and contributions to the development of geometry and astronomy are all the legacy of:**

    A. The Babylonians

    B. The Persians

    C. The Sumerians

    D. The Egyptians

Answer:

D. The Egyptians

The (A) Babylonians of ancient Mesopotamia flourished for a time under their great contribution of organized law and code, called Hammurabi's Code (1750 B.C.), after the ruler Hammurabi. The fall of the Babylonians to the Persians in 539 B.C. made way for the warrior-driver Persian Empire that expanded from Pakistan to the Mediterranean Sea until the conquest of Alexander the Great in 331 B.C. The Sumerians of ancient Mesopotamia were most noted for their early advancements as one of the first civilizations and their contributions towards written language known as cuneiform. It was the (D) Egyptians who were the first true developers of a solar calendar, the decimal system, and made significant contributions to the development of geometry and astronomy.

TEACHER CERTFICATION STUDY GUIDE

103. The Study of "spatial relationships and interaction" would be done by people in the field of:

    A. Political Science

    B. Anthropology

    C. Geography

    D. Sociology

Answer:

C. Geography

Geography is the discipline within Social Science that most concerns itself with the study of "spatial relationships and interaction".

104. The circumference of the earth, which greatly contributed to geographic knowledge, was calculated by:

    A. Ptolemy

    B. Eratosthenes

    C. Galileo

    D. Strabo

Answer:

B. Eratosthenes

There is no doubt to Ptolemy and Galileo's influence as astronomers. (A) Ptolemy as an earlier theorist and (C) Galileo as a founder of modern scientific knowledge of astronomy and our place in the galaxy. However, it was (B) Eratosthenes (275 B.C. – 195 B.C.), the Greek writer, philosopher, and astronomer, who is credited with measuring the earth's circumference as well as the distances between Earth, sun, and moon. (D) Strabo was more concerned with geography and history than astronomy.

105. The first European to see Florida and sail along its coast was:

   A. Cabot

   B. Columbus

   C. Ponce de Leon

   D. Narvaez

Answer:

A. Cabot

(A) John Cabot (1450-1498) was the English explorer who gave England claim to North American and the first European to see Florida and sail along its coast. (B) Columbus (1451-1506) was sent by the Spanish to the New World and has received false credit for "discovering America" in 1492, although he did open up the New World to European expansion, exploitation, and Christianity. (C) Ponce de Leon (1460-1521), the Spanish explorer, was the first European to actually land on Florida. (D) Panfilo de Narvaez (1470-1528) was also a Spanish conquistador, but he was sent to Mexico to force Cortes into submission. He failed and was captured.

TEACHER CERTFICATION STUDY GUIDE

106. **Which one of the following events did not occur during the period known as the "Era of Good Feeling"?**

    A. President Monroe issued the Monroe Doctrine

    B. Spain ceded Florida to the United States

    C. The building of the National Road

    D. The charter of the second Bank of the United States

Answer:

A. President Monroe issued the Monroe Doctrine

The so-called "Era of Good Feeling" describes the period following the War of 1812. This was during the Presidency of James Madison and focused the nation on internal national improvements such as the building of the second national bank (Charter for Bank of United States), construction of new roads (National Road), and the Treaty of Ghent, which ended the War of 1812 by forcing Spain to cede Florida to the United States. Of the possible answers, only the Monroe Doctrine (1823), which called for an end to any European occupation and colonization in the Americas, was not a part of the "Era of Good Feeling", it came a bit after.

107. Native communities in early California are commonly divided into several cultural areas. How many cultural areas?

    A. 4

    B. 5

    C. 6

    D. 7

Answer:

C. 6

The answer is 6 (C). Due to the great diversity of the native communities, the state is generally divided into six "culture areas." The culture areas are: (1) the Southern Culture Area, (2) the Central Culture Area, (3) the Northwestern Culture Area, (4) the Northeastern Culture Area, (5) the Great Basin Culture Area, and (6) the Colorado River Culture Area. These areas are geographically distinct and supported different sorts of cultures depending upon the availability of an adequate water supply, the ability to cultivate the land, and the availability of game.

108. The world religion, which includes a caste system, is:

    A. Buddhism

    B. Hinduism

    C. Sikhism

    D. Jainism

Answer:

B. Hinduism

Buddhism, Sikhism, and Jainism all rose out of protest against Hinduism and its practices of sacrifice and the caste system. The caste system, in which people were born into castes, would determine their class for life including who they could marry, what jobs they could perform, and their overall quality of life.

109. The idea that continued population growth would, in future years, seriously affect a nation's productive capabilities was stated by:

    A. Keynes

    B. Mill

    C. Malthus

    D. Friedman

Answer:

C. Malthus

(C) John Maynard Keynes (1883-1946) advocated an economic system in which government regulations and spending on public works would stimulate the economy and lead to full employment. (C) Thomas Malthus (1766-1834) was the English economist who had the idea that population growth would seriously affect a nation's productive capabilities. Malthus' ideas also included predictions about running out of food and a natural selection-like process brought about by population that would maintain balance. His theory was proven wrong long ago. (B) Mill (1806 -1973), an English economist and (D) Friedman (1912-) an American economist contrasted one another greatly. Mill was almost a Socialist and wrote the early work in Political Economy while Friedman was a financial advisor in the arch conservative government of President Ronald Reagan.

110. After World War II, the United States:

A. Limited its involvement in European affairs

B. Shifted foreign policy emphasis from Europe to Asia

C. Passed significant legislation pertaining to aid to farmers and tariffs on imports

D. Entered the greatest period of economic growth in its history

Answer:

D. Entered the greatest period of economic growth in its history

After World War II, the United States did not limit or shift its involvement in European affairs. In fact, it escalated the Cold War with the Soviet Union at a swift pace and attempted to contain Communism to prevent its spread across Europe. There was no significant legislation pertaining to aid to farmers and tariffs on imports. In fact, since World War II, trade has become more liberal than ever. Free trade, no matter how risky or harmful to the people of the United States or other countries, has become the economic policy of the United States called neo-liberalism. Due to this, the United States after World War II entered the greatest period of economic growth in its history and remains a world superpower.

111. **France decided in 1777 to help the American colonies in their war against Britain. This decision was based on:**

    A. The naval victory of John Paul Jones over the British ship "Serapis"

    B. The survival of the terrible winter at Valley Forge

    C. The success of colonial guerilla fighters in the South

    D. The defeat of the British at Saratoga

Answer:

D. The defeat of the British at Saratoga

The defeat of the British at Saratoga was the overwhelming factor in the Franco-American alliance of 1777 that helped the American colonies defeat the British. Some historians believe that without the Franco-American alliance, the American Colonies would not have been able to defeat the British and American would have remained a British colony.

112. **What event sparked a great migration of people from all over the world to California?**

    A. The birth of Labor Unions

    B. California statehood

    C. The invention of the automobile

    D. The gold rush

The answer is "The Gold Rush" (D). The discovery of gold in California created a lust for gold that quickly brought immigrants from the eastern United States and many parts of the world. To be sure, there were struggles and conflicts, as well as the rise of nativism. Yet this vast migration of people from all parts of the world began the process that has created California's uniquely diverse culture.

TEACHER CERTFICATION STUDY GUIDE

113. Which of the following does not differentiate provisions of the California constitution from the U.S. Constitution?

    A. The governor of California has the pocket veto

    B. In California representation in both houses of the legislature is based on population

    C. The Governor and Lt. Governor are elected separately

    D. The equivalent of cabinet positions are elected rather than appointed.

Answer:

A. The governor of California has the pocket veto.

The answer is (A) "The governor of California has the pocket veto." One of the differences between the California constitution and the U.S. Constitution concerns the executive power to veto and nullify legislation enacted by the legislature. The pocket veto, a policy that permits the President of the United States to nullify an act of Congress by simply withholding signature on a bill, is not shared by the Governor of California. Although the Governor of California does not have this particular power, the Governor holds a power that has not been extended to the President of the United States. This is the "Line-Item Veto" which permits the Governor to veto individual items that are part of a piece of legislation without nullifying the entire piece of legislation.

114. A number of women worked hard in the first half of the 19th century for women's rights but decisive gains did not come until after 1850. The earliest accomplishments were in:

    A. Medicine

    B. Education

    C. Writing

    D. Temperance

Answer:

B. Education

Although women worked hard in the early 19th century to make gains in medicine, writing, and temperance movements, the most prestigious accomplishments of the early women's movement was in the field of education. Women such as Mary Wollstonecraft (1759-1797), Alice Palmer (1855-1902), and of course Elizabeth Blackwell (1821-1910), led the way for women, particularly in the area of higher education.

115. Nineteenth century German unification was the result of the hard work of:

    A. Otto von Bismarck

    B. Kaiser William II

    C. von Moltke

    D. Hindenburg

Answer:

A. Otto von Bismarck

(A) Otto von Bismarck is the man most often credited with the unification of Germany. Bismarck became the first Chancellor of a unified Germany. He ultimately lost power to his successor Kaiser William II, who ultimately led Germany into World War I, when nationalist sentiment proved too strong for the united Germany. Ultimately, Germany's concessions in the Treaty of Versailles to end World War I, and Adolf Hitler's Nazi regime's defeat at the hands of Allied forces in World War II had destroyed the unified Germany that Bismarck had achieved in the mid to late 1800s.

116. **The geographical drought-stricken region of Africa south of the Sahara and extending east and west from Senegal to Somalia is:**

   A. The Kalahari

   B. The Namib

   C. The Great Rift Valley

   D. The Sahel

Answer:

D. The Sahel

The (A) Kalahari is located between the Orange and Zambezi Rivers and has an annual rainfall of about 5 to 20 inches. The (B) Namib is a desert, rocky plateau along the coast of Namibia in Southwest Africa that receives less than .5 inches of rainfall annually. The (C) Great Rift Valley is a fault system that runs 3000 miles from Syria to Mozambique and has great variations in elevation. Therefore, it is the (D) Sahel, the region of Africa South of the Sahara and extending East and West from Senegal to Somalia. The Sahel experienced a serious drought in the 1960s and then again in the 1980s and 1990s. International relief efforts have been focused there in an effort to keep the region alive.

117. The idea or proposal for more equal division of profits among employers and workers was put forth by:

A. Karl Marx

B. Thomas Malthus

C. Adam Smith

D. John Stuart Mill

Answer:

D. John Stuart Mill

(A) Karl Marx (1818-1883) was the German social philosopher and economist who wrote *The Communist Manifesto* and numerous other landmark works in his goal to help the world understand the inability of capitalism to provide for the workers, the idea of class struggle, and the central role of economy. (B) Thomas Malthus (1766-1834) was a British economist who introduced the study of population and early on considered famine, war, and disease to be the primary checks on world population. He later modified his views and recognized his early theoretical shortcoming and shifted his focus to the causes of unemployment. (C) Adam Smith (1723-1790) is considered by many to be the "father" of modern capitalist economics. In the *Wealth of Nations*, Smith advocated for little or no government interference in the economy. Smith claimed that an individual's self-interest would bring about the public's welfare.

It is important to note that Smith was firmly against the free market systems of monopoly power and warned that the private sector, particularly large manufacturers, if left unregulated could potentially stand in opposition to the public welfare. (D) John Stuart Mill (1806-1873) was the progressive British philosopher and economist whose ideas came closer to socialism than to the classical capitalist ideas of Adam Smith. Mill constantly advocated for political and social reforms, including emancipation for women, labor organizations, farming cooperatives, and most importantly a more equal division of profits among employers and workers.

118. **The term that best describes how the Supreme Court can block laws that may be unconstitutional from being enacted is:**

   A. Jurisprudence

   B. Judicial Review

   C. Exclusionary Rule

   D. Right of Petition

Answer:

B. Judicial Review

(A) Jurisprudence is the study of the development and origin of law. (B) Judicial review is the term that best describes how the Supreme Court can block laws that they deem as unconstitutional as set forth in Marbury vs Madison. The (C) "exclusionary rule" is a reference to the Fourth Amendment of the Constitution and says that evidence gathered in an illegal manner or search must be thrown out and excluded from evidence. There is nothing called the (D) "Right of Petition", however the Petition of Right is a reference to a statement of civil liberties sent by the English Parliament to Charles I in 1628.

119. **On the spectrum of American politics the label that most accurately describes voters to the "right of center" is:**

   A. Moderates

   B. Liberals

   C. Conservatives

   D. Socialists

Answer:

C. Conservatives

(A) Moderates are considered voters who teeter on the line of political centrality or drift slightly to the left or right. (B) Liberals are voters who stand on the left of center. (C) Conservative voters are those who are "right of center". (D) Socialist would land far to the left on the political spectrum of America.

120. Marxism believes which two groups are in continual conflict:

    A. Farmers and landowners

    B. Kings and the nobility

    C. Workers and owners

    D. Structure and superstructure

Answer:

C. Workers and owners

Marxism believes that the workers and owners are in continual conflict. Marxists refer to these two groups as the proletariat and the bourgeoisie. The proletariat is exploited by the bourgeoisie and will, according to Marxism, rise up over the bourgeoisie in class warfare in an effort to end private control over the means of production.

121. The United States legislature is bi-cameral, this means:

    A. It consists of several houses

    B. It consists of two houses

    C. The Vice-President is in charge of the legislature when in session

    D. It has an upper house and a lower house

Answer:

B. It consists of two houses

The bi-cameral nature of the United States legislature means that it has two houses, the Senate and the House of Representatives that make up the Congress. The Vice-President is part of the Executive branch of government but presides over the Senate and may act as a tiebreaker. An upper and lower house would be parts of a Parliamentary system of government such as the governments of Great Britain and Israel.

122. What Supreme Court ruling established the principal of Judicial Review?

    A. Jefferson vs Madison

    B. Lincoln vs Douglas

    C. Marbury vs Madison

    D. Marbury vs Jefferson

Answer:

C. Marbury vs Madison

Marbury vs Madison established the principal of judicial review. The Supreme Court ruled that it held no authority in making the decision (regarding Marbury's commission as Justice of the Peace in District of Columbia) as the Supreme Court's jurisdiction (or lack thereof) in the case, was conflicted with Article III of the Constitution.

123. To be eligible to be elected President one must:

    A. Be a citizen for at least five years

    B. Be a citizen for seven years

    C. Have been born a citizen

    D. Be a naturalized citizen

Answer:

C. Have been born a citizen

Article II, Section 1 of the United States Constitution clearly states, "No person except a natural-born citizen, or citizen of the United States at the time of the adoption of this Constitution, shall be eligible to the office of President, neither shall any person be eligible to that office who shall not have attained to the age of thirty-five years, and been fourteen years a resident within the United States.

TEACHER CERTFICATION STUDY GUIDE

124. The international organization established to work for world peace at the end of the Second World War is the :

    A. League of Nations

    B. United Federation of Nations

    C. United Nations

    D. United World League

Answer:

C. United Nations

The international organization established to work for world peace at the end of the Second World War was the United Nations. From the ashes of the failed League of Nations, established following World War I, the United Nations continues to be a major player in world affairs today.

125. Which of the following is an example of a direct democracy?

    A. Elected representatives

    B. Greek city-states

    C. The Constitution

    D. The Confederate States

Answer:

B. Greek city-states

The Greek city-states are an example of a direct democracy as their leaders were elected directly by the citizens and the citizens themselves were given voice in government. (A) Elected representatives in the United States as in the case of the presidential elections are actually elected by an electoral college that is supposed to be representative of the citizens. As we have learned from the elections of 2000, this is a flawed system. The United States Congress, the Senate, and the House of Representatives are also examples of indirect democracy as they represent the citizens in the legislature as opposed to having citizens represent themselves.

www.ingramcontent.com/pod-product-compliance
Lightning Source LLC
Chambersburg PA
CBHW080535300426
44111CB00017B/2735